Weak Start Unapologetic Present

An Unlikely Journey from Jim Crow Through the Information Age to God

Lester Patrick

New Harbor Press

RAPID CITY, SD

Copyright © 2020 by Lester Patrick.

All rights reserved. No part of this publication may be reproduced, distributed or transmitted in any form or by any means, without prior written permission.

Patrick/New Harbor Press
1601 Mt. Rushmore Rd., Ste 3288
Rapid City, SD 57701
www.NewHarborPress.com

Weak Start Unapologetic Present / Lester Patrick. -- 1st ed.
ISBN 978-1-63357-378-9

This book is being dedicated to my children Nigel and Kenitra, two granddaughters, Kayla and Leilani, and my parents Winsler and Nellie Barrett. I certainly would not have been able to write this book without my parents' influence on my life. And to my loving wife, Linda, who has over the years given me extraordinary support in every project I have ever worked on in the community, including this one. I give my most grateful acknowledgments to her.

"Wow, I thought. When I was a young boy growing up, I can remember when the older adults would tell stories dating all the way back to my great, great grandparents being slaves."

Contents

PROLOGUE 1
PART I 5
  My Early Life 7
    Living between Three Households 9
    Uncle Charlie's House 11
    Uncle James' House 12
    Aunt Nellie's House 14
    My Other Aunts and Uncles 15
  Finally, a Permanent Home! 19
    Church and Sunday School 20
    Uncle Willie's House 23
    Who is Your Daddy? 28
    Separate and Unequal 31
    Hand-Me-Down Books 31
    Aunt Nellie's Spelling Lessons 32
    Miss Harris—Fifth Grade 34
    Miss Richardson—Sixth Grade 36
    Mr. Kennedy—Seventh Grade 37
    Miss Connie—Eight Grade 39
    Going to Greenville to the Nightclub 40
    A Taste of Freedom 42
    My First Girlfriend and my Future Wife 44
    W.H. Robinson High School 46
    Mr. Maye—Breaking the Trophy Cabinet 46
    Mr. Ward Created Competition 49

Miss Vines' Inspirational History Lectures 50
From Nigger to Colored to Negro to Black
to African American 51
Summers Working in the Tobacco Field 53
    Summer Slave Work for Black Youth 54
    May Farm Simon's Tobacco Fields 56
    The Tobacco Fields 59
    The Lightning Storms 61
    Slave Labor 62
    The Grimes Plantation—Slave Quarters 62
Hot Sun and Summer Fun 65
Living Under Jim Crow—Its Impact 69
    Reckless Eyeballing 74
    Jim Crow Etiquettes 75
    Modern Day Jim Crow Etiquette 77
    Living Out Jim Crow Practices -
    The Whites-Only Counter 79
    Coping with the Anger from Jim Crow 80
Graduating from High School 85
    Money for College 86
    Aunt Nellie's Determination 92

PART II 95
Off to College 97
    North Carolina A&T—Scott Hall 98
    Scott Hall 101
    Student Activism—SNCC 101
    Guest Lecturers 105
    Attitude Change 108
    On-Campus Entertainment 110
    Academics 112

- Thanksgiving Holiday 115
- Christmas 117
- Boss Webster's Grill 122
- Dudley High School in Unstable Condition 125
  - Response to the Disturbance by Local Officials 127
  - Greater Participation from AT&T Students 128
  - Willie Grimes Murdered 132
  - Situation Becomes More Intense 134
  - Guardsmen Bombard AT&T's Campus 138
- On the Way to Winterville 143
  - Building upon a Lesson Learned 144
  - Discussions with Willie Grimes' Father 148
  - Internalized Racism and Oppression 150
  - Educational Redlining 154
- Returning to North Carolina A&T 157

PART III 161

- Being Sworn into the Navy 163
  - Great Lakes Navy Base 163
  - Boot Camp 164
  - Introduction to Technology 172
  - Charleston Navy Base 178
  - Hitchhiking to Charleston 179
  - Jumping Off a Moving Amtrak Train 181
  - Selecting My Next Duty Station 183
  - Graduating from School–Orders to Morocco 185
- Getting Married 187
  - Briefing for Morocco about Spies 187
  - Returning Home Before Leaving for Morocco 188
- Arriving in Morocco 191
  - Sidi Bouknadel Morocco 192

Navy Radio Transmitting Facility, Morocco 193
A Secret Duty Station 195
Meeting with the U.S. Ambassador to Morocco 201
My Job at the Radio Transmitting Facility 203
Changing Encryption Keys 204
Russian Jamming Tactics 205
KamiKaze-Like Mission 206
Linda's Arrival to Morocco 207
Arabic Terrorist Captured in Front of Me 209
Purchasing Furniture in Rota, Spain 211
The Back Road to Rabat 214
Welcome to Algeria 216
Experiencing the Culture 219

Going Home 223
Back to the United States 223
Changes Had Taken Place 224

Off to the Philippines 229
Arriving in the Philippines 229
My Job at the Naval Communications
Station Cubi Point 230
A Typhoon Hits San Miguel 234
Moving to Subic Bay 237
Living and Working in the Jungle 238
The Story of the White Lady 240
Graduate School and Community Work 241
Dealing with International Jim Crow - Overseas 242
Eating Nontraditional Filipino Foods 246
Easter Crucifixion in the Philippines 248

Returning to the United States 253
Returning Home to Winterville 254

    Arriving in Stockton 256
    Jim Crow Behavior in Stockton 258
Working at Navy Communications Station Stockton (NAVCOMSTA Stockton) 263
    The Walker Spy Ring 265
    Settling in to Stockton 268
Fighting the Navy from Within 271
    Request for a Court-Martial 277
    Being Arraigned for Court-Martial 278
    Admiral Gravely Unannounced Visit 281
    Honorable Discharge or Not! 283

PART IV 285
Entering Civilian Life 287
    The Job Search 290
    Promoted to the Postal Data Center 297
Tragedy Strikes 303
Special Projects 307
    Jack and Jill of America 308
    A Second Tragedy–Is God Listening? 311
    Creating Parents and Citizens for
    Quality Education 315
    Making Math Fun 319
    The Algebra Project—Bob Moses
    Civil Rights Leader 321
Associate Professor of Telecommunications 325
Leaving the San Mateo Postal Data Center
for Another Position 329
Veteran Health Administration 331
    Renegotiation of Networking Contract 334
A Second Fire! 337

PART V 339

Going Back to Church 341
    Disagreement with a Senior Leader
    about Scripture 342
Veteran Information System Networks-
Telemedicine Networks 351
    Spiritual Awakening—My Wife's Carjacking 358
    Joining Bible Study Fellowship
    International (BSF) 366

PART VI 373
    Community Work and Advocacy 375
    Peer Mentoring Program 391
    The Urban Technology Vehicle 397
    Serving on Bond Oversight Committees 399
    Board of Directors for Family Resource and
    Referral Center 403
        The Center's staff reflects its belief system as it: 404

PART VII 409
    Retirement 411
    Commissioner of the Housing Authority of
    San Joaquin 413
        Internet Security Workshop 417
    The Hunger Task Force of San Joaquin 421
    Strong Communities Committee 423

Epilogue 429
Acknowledgements 441
Bibliography 443
Appendix 447

PROLOGUE

Several years ago when I was at home in Winterville, North Carolina, I was conversing with one of my older cousins. I asked her a question about a distant relative of ours. Her response was, "You know, Lester, all of the people who would know the answer to that question have passed away." Wow, I thought. When I was a young boy growing up, I can remember when the older adults would tell stories dating all the way back to my great, great grandparents being slaves. Or, at least, the stories that had been passed down from generation to generation. I remember, for example, my aunt telling me the story of her mother's grandparents, who sometimes worked such long hours that many times they left the fields and never got any further than the front porch before it was time for the master to gather them to go back into the fields. They were so tired that they fell asleep on the front porch and slept there all night.

There were many other similar stories, too. But the point being made here is that when I was younger, several older people in my family had stories like that to tell. Today, they have all passed away. And for the most part, my family didn't take the opportunity to document these rich experiences that we all could benefit from. I wish I had asked my older relatives more questions when I could and documented what I could. I will not allow that to happen to my offspring. This description of my life is being compiled to help my offsprings know about my life experiences, what kind of childhood I had, and make them aware of both my humorous and serious experiences. That is why I am taking the time to document parts of my life experiences. There is a lesson to be learned. I grew up in the segregated South during Jim Crow. That alone is a story within itself to be told.

I believe knowing some of these experiences will help them to become better individuals. Additionally, I believe that the time period in which I grew up, and many of my experiences, are pretty interesting. When you reach my age, you have heard lots of people's stories, and based upon what I generally hear from other people about their lives, I have had a pretty interesting life. For that reason, I am also sharing my story with anybody who wants to know it.

Not only did I survive Jim Crow, but like many others, I have overcome its effects. I will talk about that more later, but that is another reason I am writing this book.

I have had a long and enjoyable career in technology. I have been one of a handful of African Americans working with technology wherever I was in all of my career. In this book, I talk about my career and some accomplishments I also had. I hope that my description of the projects I have enjoyed working on might motivate some African American parents to encourage their children to pursue a technology career.

I believe very strongly in opposing racial injustice and exposing it when it is necessary. I think that is the only way we will ever meaningfully impact the degree of racial injustice in our society. When we identify or are made aware of negative circumstances, it becomes our responsibility to help in some way to resolve the problem. In this book, I cover some of the racial injustices I have spoken out against and include several of the solutions I have recommended and implemented to resolve the problem. I hope this book will inspire some who observe racial injustice to get involved and do everything possible to assist in resolving it.

I believe strongly in volunteering my time to help others. I have done that throughout my adult life. I highlight in this book some of the projects I have worked on to help others. I talk about how God has used me throughout my life to get involved and make a difference in the lives of those who can't help themselves. God was using me to do this even when I didn't know that it was God who was using me. I hope that part of my life will encourage some to seek God.

Lastly, I have lived a very private life and have only shared with my wife some of the stories I have recorded in this book. I would like this book to cause other family members to be energized to ask each other questions that can eventually motivate more family members to do the same. The overall aspiration is that we could end up with a very well documented version of our family history. That is what I would like to see. It would be a blessing to future generations.

PART I

My Early Life

My mother was born on May 28, 1934, in Winterville, N.C. Her maiden name was Christine Patrick. When she was about sixteen, she gave birth to me. The date was September 25, 1950. My mother and father were the children of two close families who lived in the rural area outside of an unincorporated area of Pitt County. Both families were farmworkers who lived very close to each other and were close friends. My mother and father were about the same age. I don't know the details, but my mother became pregnant at about fifteen. This caused a major conflict between the two families. Because of what happened, the friendship between families ended. This prevented me from having a relationship with my fraternal father and uncles, aunts, and grandparents. However, I had contact with a couple of my cousins on my father's side at school.

One of my paternal female cousins and I were in the same grade and homeroom class. Many times before class started, we would talk about the family that I didn't know. But I did get to know a little bit about them and the family we shared through conversations with her. Her name was Willie Pearl. I can't even begin to describe to you how weird this situation was growing up. By the time I was maybe eight or nine years old, both families lived in the tiny town of Winterville, North Carolina. Members from both families had built homes there. My uncles and aunts had all married, and most lived in a section of Winterville named Newtown.

A highway that hardly saw traffic separated the two sections of the Colored side of town. My relatives from my father's side of the family lived across town in the Colored section's unnamed part. They lived across the railroad from the Colored school. Most houses in the Colored part of Winterville were small by today's standards. Our house, for example, was about 1000 square feet. But my grandparents on my father's side had built a pretty large house for a Colored man. It was located across town in the unnamed section of the Colored side of town. Winterville was a segregated community. Whites lived on one side of town and Blacks on the other side. This, of course, was by design. It didn't just happen there any more so than it did in other parts of the country. I will address housing segregation later.

Winterville was a farming community. Its primary product was tobacco. The farms in the area also produced much corn, soybeans, sweet potatoes, and cotton. But tobacco was king. The city of Greenville was located about five miles away. It was and is the county seat. Greenville and Pitt County was considered the tobacco capital of the world. I am not sure who granted it that title, but we all grew up seemingly with this crazy sense of pride from living in the tobacco capital of the world. Now, there were no real benefits in it for most Colored people as we were at the time. You see, we did not see ourselves in those days as Black people but as Colored people. This was what White people called us for the most part, and who we saw ourselves as. Most Colored people either worked on the farm as laborers or, for the slightly more fortunate ones, as sharecroppers. But there were a few extremely blessed Colored people who owned their own farms. My grandfather was one of those. That is the reason he was able to build a much larger house than most other Colored people in Winterville.

The experience of knowing who my father's family was but not knowing them personally was a peculiar one. For example, I would see my grandmother being driven through town in her car on several occasions. I could be hanging out with friends or just walking and doing what kids did in those days. I remember seeing her sitting in the back seat of her car, but I don't ever remember making eye contact with her or her even looking at me to know who I was. This gave me a strange feeling. Because in some cases, the people I might have been with knew that I was related to her. I don't want to give the impression that it was a situation that left me with emotional problems or anything of the sort. That was not the case. You see, I had a strong family on my mother's side. I will talk about them later. But it was still bizarre, nevertheless. I never remember seeing my grandfather as well, except on a couple of occasions. Like my grandmother, he never knew who I was, either. Or at least I am not aware of it. I would occasionally see, though, one of my father's sisters, as I might have been walking to the store or the post office in the afternoon after school. She was a very nice lady, and she was young then. Her name was Nellie Gray. When she saw me, she would always attempt to make conversation with me. I realize now that I wasn't very receptive. But I was a teenager then, and that was my attitude.

Living between Three Households

I was born on September 25, 1950 at my uncle John's house. He was my mother's brother.

My uncle John was a Colored man way ahead of his time for Winterville. He had natural skills to design, build, wire, and finish houses. I remember all the conversations throughout the community about him when I was growing up. He was able to pull together a group of Colored men from Winterville and teach some of them necessary house-building skills.

He developed, operated, and managed a construction crew.  Consequently, he built several of the houses for Colored people in Winterville and other surrounding areas. He made a major impact on the community. He also provided a source of nonfarm employment for some Colored men in the community. That was very uncommon for that local area. Can you imagine a Colored man with no formal education who could read blueprints, provide electrical wiring, plastering, and other carpenter related activities well enough to operate a successful house building business? Unfortunately, he died at a very early age from kidney failure. He had ten children. These were my first cousins Jessy Ray, Annie Mae, John Junior, Bet, Jean, Evelyn, Alice, Doug, Jason, and Beverly.

My uncle John also built a barbershop that was attached to the back of the house. Men and young boys came there primarily on weekends for their haircuts. Like any other black barbershop, it was the place where men discussed everybody's business, whether it was personal or not. It was also a place where the older men interacted in discussions with teenagers and younger boys. It was the typical Black barbershop, just, for the most part, it was only opened on weekends starting on Friday evenings.

After Uncle John passed away, my cousin Jesse Ray continued to operate the barbershop. When John Junior became a teenager, he started to cut hair also. And when he graduated from high school, he went on to barber school to complete his training. He managed the barbershop for a while until he decided, one day, he would go into another career.

Uncle Charlie's House

Uncle John had built a house next door to Uncle Charlie's house. Shortly after I was born, I lived with my mother in Uncle Charlie's house. Because of her pregnancy, my mother had to drop out of high school in the tenth grade. In those days, young women who gave birth could not return to the same school they attended before their pregnancies. So, after giving birth to me, my mother attended high school at a Colored high school in Ayden, about four miles away from home. Ayden was still in Pitt County. She commuted to Ayden and, in due time, graduated with her high school diploma.

About four years later, my brother Cleo was born. Like so many other Colored people of that time, shortly after his birth, my mother migrated to the North, seeking a better life. She moved to New York, while Cleo and I were left behind. Cleo lived with Uncle Buck and Aunt Sis in the country, but I lived between three households. I am not sure if there were ever any actual plans for her to bring us to New York. But I will address that later.

Uncle Charlie was married when I was about three or four years old. I vaguely remember the wedding, but I was told I was the ring bearer. Aunt Georgianna was a school teacher, so naturally, she was at school during the day and Uncle Charlie was at work.

Next door was Uncle John's house, and as I pointed out earlier, he had ten children. So, I had plenty of playmates during the day because several of the children were about my age. I was sort of just left there with them for the most part during the day. At night, there was always a decision that had to be made. Where will "NEP" stay tonight? Please don't ask me why I was called "NEP." I have never been able to figure that out. It didn't matter until I started school because it was then that I learned my name was Lester Earl Patrick. This was when it really became confusing since my initials were LEP and not NEP. To this day, I have not been able to figure that out, but at an early age, people ceased to refer to me as "NEP," so it all worked out OK.

Uncle James' House

Every night, a decision had to be made as to where "NEP" would stay that night. There were three options. I would either stay next door at Uncle Charlie's, down the street with my Uncle James and Aunt Mable Ruth, or with Aunt Nellie and Uncle Winser. We all called him Uncle Winser. For whatever reason, we just dropped the "l' in his name. So for us, it was not "Winsler" but "Win-ser."

Now, Uncle James was a lot of fun. He worked on the railroad. He and Aunt Mable Ruth had no children, so they were usually delighted to have me stay with them. It was never more than a week or two. Uncle James also always had a brand new Pontiac that I used to love to ride in. He would sometimes put me in his lap as if I was driving. I used to like that as a young boy. They would buy me new Sunday outfits to wear to church and a lot of toys, but they didn't go to church. They lived a fun life for that time and place.

North Carolina was at the time a dry state, and Pitt County was a dry county. There was no legal sale of alcohol except in the ABC store. There were no bars, nor was it legal to sell liquor by the drink. But some people did sell liquor by the drink in their homes. They were all bootleggers. My uncle James sold liquor at his house and was a bootlegger and a railroad employee. After work and during the weekend, there were always lots of people at Uncle James' house drinking liquor and gambling.

He also sold the "numbers." This was an illegal numbers gambling game whereby people purchased a number from a book of tickets that he usually sold for five cents, twenty-five cents, or fifty cents. The winning number was published daily in the newspaper. The numbers published in the newspaper supposedly were not published for gambling. But that is the way it was used. So, at the top of the paper, every day, there was a number published. If your ticket matched the number printed in the newspaper, then you were a winner. Even church people played the numbers. Nobody made any real money, but winning twenty-five or fifty dollars was not bad. Winners would say, "I hit the numbers." Uncle James was one of the runners. He made some money every week from the sale of the tickets.

On several occasions, his house was raided by the local police for the illegal sale of alcohol, but he always had an excellent plan of disposing of the liquor and was never caught. I knew where Uncle James hid his liquor because I would sometimes accompany him when he either placed it in its hiding place or when he retrieved it. He never kept more liquor in the house than what he could sell at any given time. That was his basic rule, so he never got caught. If the police showed up and many people were drinking, he was just having a party.

One day when he was away at work, a White man and woman knocked on his door. Aunt Mable Ruth answered the door.

They asked her if Jimbo was at home. Jimbo was Uncle James' nickname. She said no and asked what they wanted and why they needed him. They told her they were driving through town and had heard they could get a drink of liquor at Jimbo's house. And they liked to have a drink. She told them they were mistaken, and she didn't know anything about liquor. They left but continued to monitor the house. Later they saw some people go to the house, and they observed Aunt Mable Ruth go outside to the liquor hiding place. They were undercover cops and rushed in and arrested Aunt Mable Ruth. She was sent to jail for several months. When she was released, Uncle James changed his life and became an upright citizen. He joined the church and eventually became a deacon and a respectable community person for the rest of his life. Most of my relatives younger than I don't even know that he had lived that type of life.

So that was one of my options. Sometimes, I did go to live at Uncle James' house. That is how I know about his involvement with the liquor and numbers game. His house was a lot of fun, but, clearly, it was not a good place for a child to live. At the time, I was only about five years old.

Aunt Nellie's House

My other option was to spend time with Aunt Nellie and Uncle Winser. All children loved Aunt Nellie. She was exactly twenty years older than I was because we shared the same birth month of September. When I was five years old, she was twenty-five and full of energy. I loved being at her house. She didn't have any children of her own. But my cousin Betty, who we called "Bet," lived with her. Bet was Uncle John's daughter, who had fallen in love with her and had lived with her, I think since she was around two years old. Bet was two years older than I was.

Uncle Winser was a tall, very broad, Black man. His arms and upper body looked like he worked out every day. And he was very strong. His nickname was "Big Six." Just being around him made me feel like a man, even though I was only five years old. Uncle Winser was a very calm person. He never raised his voice, and nothing ever really seemed to make him lose his temper. But from what I heard, you didn't want to make him mad because he had been a tough guy when he was younger and single.

In addition to being very playful, Aunt Nellie was an excellent cook. I loved her cooking. She cooked puddings, like molasses puddings, chocolate puddings, banana puddings, sweet potato puddings, and cakes. I loved them all! I didn't mention it earlier, but Aunt Georgianna was a new bride and had not mastered the art of cooking. I don't believe she ever did. I do remember that she cooked fish a lot. That was for breakfast and all other meals. Aunt Mable Ruth didn't do much serious cooking then either. She was more or less a sandwich type of cook. As a child, sandwiches were good at times, but that got old.

My Other Aunts and Uncles

Aunt Mae, Bell, Nellie, Uncle Charlie

I had several aunts and uncles. Two of my uncles I have already talked about, Uncle James and Uncle Charlie. I have also talked a little about Aunt Nellie and Uncle Winser. But I had two other uncles. One was my mother's brother Arthur, who we called Uncle Buck. And the other was Uncle Rufus, who was married to my mother's sister, Aunt Bell.

Uncle Buck was married to Aunt Sis and had several children. Of course, they were my first cousins. They were mostly all older than me by a significant number of years. A couple of them were actually the same age as my maternal mother. Their names were: Linwood, Junior, Goldie, Rosa, Jimmy, and James. Today the only one living is my cousin Rosa. I especially like seeing her because she looks identical to my aunt Nellie when she was younger. Cleo lived with Uncle Buck and Aunt Sis until he moved to New York to live with my mother.

There was also Uncle Charlie and Aunt Georgianna who I talked about earlier. Aunt Nellie cooked all the time, and both Uncle Charlie and Aunt Georgianna were regular guests for dinner. They had a son by the name of David. Unfortunately, they have all passed away.

Aunt Fannie was Jackie's biological mother, who lived most of her life in New York. She had three children by the name of Junnie, Kevin, and, of course, Jackie.

Lastly, there was my Aunt Bell and Uncle Rufus. Aunt Bell was my mother's sister. Throughout my whole childhood, I always spent time at their house. Aunt Bell and I shared the same birthday of September 25th. She was a very calm individual about everything. She had the calmest demeanor of anybody I have ever known in my life. She had a way through her smile of giving you silent encouragement. When I was very young, she used to call me "Buster," and other times, "NEP." I don't know the origin of either nickname, but I answered to whichever I was addressed.

Uncle Rufus was full of encouragement. On his off time, he coached a baseball team. He was able to bring together young men from the local Winterville community and surrounding areas for that purpose. They played every Saturday and Sunday against local teams. I used to attend some of the games that were played at the baseball stadium in Greenville. Through that baseball team, he kept many high school-age boys from getting into trouble. That was true also for some of the young married adult men involved with the team. It also provided entertainment for older baseball fans. I guess the bottom line is that he made a difference in the lives of a lot of African American males in the community. I take my hat off to Uncle Rufus.

Aunt Bell and Uncle Rufus had several children. Their names were; Jimmy, Joyce, Gen, Della, Jeanne, and Louise. They are my first cousin. All are still living except Jimmy. And of course, Rander, is adopted through marriage to Gen.

Finally, a Permanent Home!

There came a time when it became apparent to all involved that I needed a more stable life. I was confronted with the question of who I wanted to live with. For the average five-year-old that was probably a huge decision. But for me, it was a straightforward one. I immediately responded by saying I want to live with Aunt Nellie. It was easy for me to see as a child that she didn't just think I was cute and wanted to see me dressed up on Sunday morning. She wanted what was best for me, and even at that age, I could see that. I could also observe and compare the three lifestyles.

At Aunt Nellie's house, she cooked dinner, we waited for Uncle Winser to come from work, and then we sat down, said grace or prayer, and had dinner. That was a major difference between the two other households. Whatever we had to eat at the other two households, it was eaten when any person decided to eat. That meant you might have had another person sitting at the table with you, or you may have sat alone. That was very important to me at five years old.

Another thing that was so different from the other households was that I had a bedtime at Aunt Nellie's. Before bedtime, I was reminded to prepare for bed and put up the toys. And then we said a bedtime prayer before getting into bed. That simply didn't happen at the other households. There I played until I fell asleep. Then I would wake up the next morning having been put to bed by somebody. Only the Lord knows who.

To make a long story short, I considered all these things and that Uncle Winser bought a television—and remember, television was a relatively new invention. Not everybody had one. There was no choice to make but to live with them. If faced with making a similar decision, I do not suggest that all five-year-olds can decide what is best for them. I can only speak for myself. But I did know at the time that I was making the right decision. And I never regretted it!

Church and Sunday School

Aunt Nellie was a member of Good Hope Freewill Baptist Church. She joined the church in 1944 when she was fourteen years old and was a very active member for seventy-one years. She was the superintendent of Sunday school and taught Sunday school for forty-three years.

I remember as a little boy getting dressed up on Sunday morning to attend Sunday school. The Colored Citizens of Winterville at the time were very young. Like many communities where lots of young people live, they didn't like to get up on Sunday morning to go to Sunday school. But many of them did see to it that their children were ready for Sunday school.

This was where Aunt Nellie came in. Because starting at our house with Bet and me, Aunt Nellie would march us from house to house to pick up children who wanted to go to Sunday school. She would march us down the dusty dirt road a few houses picking up children along the way. Then she would make a right and pass through some of our neighbor's yards where we would reach the ditch behind their houses. The ditch separated Newtown into two parts. Why the dusty, dirty road, the ditch, and the cornfield? Well, you see, this was during the Jim Crow period of our country's history. And even though our parents paid taxes just like the White people did, they didn't benefit from their tax dollars. So in the Colored part of town, there were dusty dirt roads and open ditches with no proper piping for drainage when it rained. This was taxation without representation. Today, Black parents pay taxes that support schools that give their kids an inferior education. No difference.

To make things worse, a White farmer owned several land plots in the middle of Newtown. During spring and summer, he would plant corn on the land. The impact was that the cornfield cut off the Colored people in Newtown from the Colored people who lived on the side of town across business highway 11. That was one impact of the cornfield. The other impact was that the Colored people ate the corn freely whenever they had a taste for fresh corn. You can make a lot of meals from corn. Since he chose to plant it there every year, they felt entitled to eat it every year. So they did—kind of like a form of reparation. Later on, when I became a teenager, the farmer sold the land to some Colored people, and they built new houses on the land and still live there today. Some of my relatives still live there.

There is another thing about the taxation without representation we experienced living during the Jim Crow era. Most of the houses in the Colored part of Winterville did not have indoor running water. This had nothing to do with the age of the house. Many of the homes in the Colored part of town had been recently built and had bathroom facilities, but the city government would not agree to extend running water and sewer to that part of town. This was true, even though the Colored people of Winterville paid the same taxes as their White counterparts. To have indoor bathrooms, Colored people had to dig a well and a separate tank for sewage. I think you get the picture.

There was a plank across the ditch put there by somebody to transition to the next street, an easy one. So on our way to Sunday school, we would cross the plank, pick up more kids, and shortly be on our way back across the plank. At this point, we had to travel through a path that took us through the cornfield. Once we were through the cornfield, we were only a few steps from Good Hope Freewill Baptist Church, where we attended Sunday school. This was a gratifying experience for us all as children.

In Sunday school, we would sing, "Yes, Jesus loves me, yes, Jesus loves me. Yes. Jesus loves me. Because the bible tells me so." Aunt Nellie taught children's class, toddlers, through about the fourth grade. Each Sunday, we discussed the lessons in separate groups. But then we would all reassemble into one big group. At that point, each person would rise and comment on what they learned that day from the lesson. For those children who could not remember what they had learned, it was permissible for them just to say, "Jesus wept." For some reason, this always got robust applause from the adults when a very young child stood and said, "Jesus wept." I did not understand then why this drew such loud applause. But now I realize that the adults were actually giving the child a special dose of encouragement for next Sunday when they would have another opportunity to state what they learned from the Sunday school lesson.

Learning about Jesus in Sunday school was a crucial thing. But another significant benefit for us all was that we were required to stand and address an audience. That helped us to overcome our fear of speaking in front of a group of people. Some research shows that most people would rather jump off a building than to speak in front of a group of people. The bottom line is that most people are not comfortable speaking in front of a group of people. But we were getting the experience in Sunday school to overcome that fear at a very young age.

Uncle Charlie was also a member of Good Hope Freewill Baptist Church and one of its leaders. I can remember several occasions as I got older whereby he would ask me to learn and recite either a poem or scripture on Sunday morning at church. His request was always directed through Aunt Nellie. So usually, on Saturday, she would say to me, "your Uncle Charlie would like for you to memorize and recite this poem or scripture tomorrow morning." There was never any real time to prepare. But this also was not a situation where I had a choice. Having an attitude would only have made it worse, so my response was always to ask the question, "Why didn't he ask me earlier?" I was never excited about doing it. But then I would proceed to get prepared to memorize the material and recite whatever it was I was expected to recite. I didn't realize at the time, but this was also an excellent experience for me that paid off for me in school, work, and other situations. That is just one situation of how the church helped to prepare me for life. In many churches today, that is almost a foreign concept.

Uncle Willie's House

After Sunday school, we would stay for church most of the time, but there were those Sundays, like the fifth Sunday when after Sunday school, our family and other family members would meet out in the country at Uncle Willie's house. That was a lot of fun because everybody would play games most of the day, and then we would all eat way too much. The children would then play more games until the end of the day when we would return to our homes and get ready for school the next day. I can still remember our Sundays at Uncle Willie's. Uncle Willie lived outside of the city limits in the country. We would drive about a mile down a long dusty road before taking a right onto another shorter dusty road that led up to Uncle Willie's house. When we made the right turn at the end of the road, my cousin Tit and his wife lived just on the left side on the corner. Tit was Uncle Willie's only son. Tit and Mary didn't have any children then. Naturally, we wouldn't stop there because this was when cousins got together and played all day long and overate.

My uncle Willie was a sharecropper. Like most other Colored farmers in the area, he did not own the land. He only worked on the farm, along with his children, who were old enough to work. He did get to live on the farm in the farmhouse. He grew tobacco, corn, soybeans, cotton, etc. Like most other sharecroppers, he also had some livestock like chickens and hogs. It would take a lot of time to describe sharecropping fully. But in a nutshell, it provided an opportunity, if you could call it that, for a Colored man with children to live on a farm owned by a White man, live in the farmhouse, and maintain employment for him and his family by working on the farm.

If you notice, this relationship was referred to as sharecropping. So the owner and the Colored family were supposed to equally share in the expenses, labor, profit, etc. In almost all cases, the Colored sharecropper did not have any capital nor cash to go towards the partnership. So usually, their contribution came about strictly through labor from their family members and themselves.

This is a critical point to make. Because in many cases, school-age children of Colored sharecroppers did not attend school when there was work to be done on the farm. Many children of Colored farmers were prevented from ever finishing high school because there was work to be done on the farm almost all year. So at a certain age, many of them just gave it up, and when they came of age, they left the South and moved to the North where they could find a job working in a factory that didn't require any education.

It wasn't that children of sharecroppers didn't want to get an education or didn't want to go to school. Still, by the time the harvesting times for tobacco, cotton, potatoes, corn, and all the other crops grown was over, they could only attend school a few consecutive days at a time. This situation prevented them from keeping pace with what was going on in school. It also caused many of them to have an inferiority complex about even attending school. The other students knew why they were not present. So as soon as they were old enough they migrated to the North seeking a better life. Needless to say, many of them experienced working conditions equal to or worse than what they had on the farm.

Few Colored sharecroppers ever received their share of the profit at the end of the harvesting season. Even though they did not have cash or capital to contribute to the partnership, they always provided all the farm labor and management. Their contributions were great. They were uneducated, so they usually only received what their so-called White partners gave them. And that was not a lot. Of course, they did get to live on the farm. But there were some exceptions to these sharecropping situations. I will comment on one of them later. Now in most cases, the White farm owner would tell them that it had not been a good year, and they simply didn't make any real profit that year. That was the annual report to the Colored sharecropper no matter what the situation was. But the Colored sharecroppers had few options available to them. And one of them was not to leave the farm because they simply had nowhere else to go.

Lester Patrick

That was not so for their children. Because as soon as they got old enough to leave, they fled to the North for a better life. One after the other, they left the South and went to the North to work in factories. I even know of situations whereby some children of Colored farmers left the South for a better life and continued their education and got professional jobs. This was not the norm, but it did happen. One by one, they would leave the farm as they became old enough. Eventually, when all the children were gone, the White farm owner would require the parents to move. After all, they had nothing to contribute once their children had left. And local employers usually would not give them employment. They could not go to work in most cases in the factory. Because in most cases, knowing that they had been sharecroppers whose children had exited the farm and migrated to the North, the factory would not hire them. That would have been like harboring a runaway slave. I will talk more about that practice later.

Think about this for a moment. Many of these Colored sharecroppers had spent their entire lives working for the White farmer, unwillingly sacrificed their children's future by robbing them of the opportunity to receive an education, and had done this while living in poverty their entire life.

Meanwhile, the White farmer, with few exceptions, had become rich. Becoming rich is a significant point to be made here because not all White farmers started rich. But many White farmers became rich while sharecropping with Colored men. Now, this didn't stop White farmers who were already rich from becoming richer off the backs of Colored sharecroppers. But to make things even worse, it was almost an insult for a Colored sharecropper to sharecrop with a poor White farmer. If they were going to sharecrop, they at least wanted to sharecrop with a wealthy White farmer. He had standing in the community, and many Colored sharecroppers derived some sense of worth from their relationship with the rich White sharecropper. That was very sad, but it was true. Remember we were Colored at the time and not Black yet!

After passing Tit's house, we moved further down the dusty dirt road to where Uncle Willie's house was in sight. One of the things that I remember about Uncle Willie's house was that it had a tin rooftop. It could get hot in there. He had a porch on the front that the grownups sat on and watched us children run, play, and do crazy children things all day long. Uncle Willie had several daughters. Their names were Geneva, Dess, Duck, Jean, Sis, Dee, and Louise. And there was also Shirley, who was Geneva's daughter. Aunt Ella was my great aunt. She was my grandmother Rosa's sister. As we would approach Uncle Willie's house, he had a huge dirt farmyard covered with chickens. When we approached, it was as if the chickens knew it was the fifth Sunday and that they had better be on their toes. When we would get out of the car, the chickens would start running everywhere as if they were hiding. When we were much younger, some of us would cry because we wanted to play with the chickens. But the chickens knew that, after we finished playing with them, two or three of them would be slaughtered for an early Sunday dinner.

Later in the afternoon, we would follow Uncle Willie across the yard as he selected the chickens that we would eat that day. He would randomly grab one by the neck and wring its neck until it was about dead, and then he would toss it to the ground and grab another one. Meanwhile, the first chicken would still be moving all over the yard, trying its best to live. Eventually, three or four chickens moved around the yard on their sides with broken necks until they passed out. That was a tough one to watch, but it didn't seem to curb anybody's appetite.

Lester Patrick

Who is Your Daddy?

Now I had a mother, a daddy, and a permanent home. Things were about to get very complicated because I started school at age six, just a few months from when I began to live with Uncle Winser and Aunt Nellie. By the way, I never called them mom and dad or anything similar. For no particular reason, I always called them aunt and uncle. But I always referred to them as my mother and father to everybody, if that makes any sense. I started school at age five in 1955 at Robinson Union School, short of a few months before I'd turn six in September. Robinson offered classes from grade 1 through 12 with all grades located on the same campus. It was also a segregated school, with no students or teachers of any race other than Colored.

The start of the first grade was relatively uneventful because Aunt Nellie took me to school and enrolled me, and made sure I was settled in. She answered all the personal questions that needed answering. Questions that I would not have known the answer to. But the following year was a bit different. For some reason, the teachers had a routine whereby they started the school year by updating their records with additional information about students. That alone was not a problem because I suppose some things in the life of a six-year-old could have changed since the previous year—things like whether you moved, any new family members, and so forth. But even if I had moved, I wouldn't have known my address at that age. This line of questioning by my new teacher at the beginning of each school year started a very uncomfortable and embarrassing trend for me that would last for several years.

At the beginning of each school year, my new teacher would document my parents' names starting in the second grade. Think about that. What could have changed about your parents' names? Nevertheless, I was faced with that situation. The first time I had to respond to that question, I had been called up in front of the class facing my teacher, while she thumbed through a milk carton crate of folders to locate my records. She then proceeded to ask me the names of my parents.

That was already in my record, but I responded the best I knew how. I was now six years old and, since I was five, I had lived with my Aunt Nellie and Uncle Winser. They were my parents. But I also knew that Christine, was my mother, too. So when I was asked who my mother was, I said, "Christine Patrick." When asked who my father was, I said, "Winser Barrett." That didn't sound quite right to the teacher, so she asked more questions. She asked who I lived with. My response was I live with my Aunt Nellie and Uncle Winser.

"Who is Aunt Nellie?" she asked.

"She is my mother's sister," I said, re-emphasizing that my mother's name was Christine Patrick. Just to clarify, she asked again, "Who is your daddy?"

"Uncle Winser is my daddy, and Christine Patrick is my mother," I answered.

"So, Christine Patrick and Nellie Barrett are sisters?"

"Yes, Mam."

She got up from her desk and left the room. Meanwhile, I was standing trembling in front of the class facing the teacher's desk. My back was to the classroom and the other students. I didn't know what I had done wrong, but I knew what I had said had something to do with the teacher leaving the classroom. She returned shortly with another teacher, and they continued the questioning. I was embarrassed and terrified but continued to respond to their questioning as I had already done.

Luckily, the second teacher knew my family name and went to get my older cousin Annie Mae. She came in and explained the situation in a way that they could understand. But she knew my daddy's name was Charlie Edwards. I knew that also, but it seemed right to me at the time that Uncle Winser was my daddy. So that was what I said. To make a long story short, the grownups got a big laugh out of that when Annie Mae told them about what had happened. But for me, it was a tremendously embarrassing situation. I can still remember turning around, walking back to my seat, and the students looking at me as if I had done something wrong.

Unfortunately, this was not the last time this would happen. It repeated itself every year until I explained it in a way that was acceptable to my new teacher. Now I don't know why it was important for each teacher to verify your daddy's name as if it would change from year to year. But they did. I finally got over it. I gave several responses over the years ranging from: "I don't live with my daddy" to "I don't know who my daddy is." Whatever the case is, it seems that the older I got, the less often the question would come up.

A few things stand out to me from the third grade. First of all, my teacher in the third grade was Miss Lang. I remember several of us boys competing every morning to carry Miss Lang's bag. She wasn't the only teacher whose bag we competed for to carry. But the thing that stands out to me about her is that if several of us reached her car at the same time, for some reason, she would always give me her purse to carry. Women then carried huge purses. Looking back, I assume she either trusted me with carrying her purse or by giving it to the same person she could always keep up with who had it. Whatever the case is, the third grade was an exciting year not only for what was happening at school but also for what was going on at home.

I was nine years old when I was in the third grade. One winter morning in 1959, I woke up, and there was a little girl named Jackie there. Jackie was Aunt Fannie's three-year old daughter.

Aunt Fannie was Aunt Nellie's sister. She lived in New York, had become ill, and sent her two children to Winterville to live while she recovered. It was meant to be for a short period, but it ended up being permanent. Jackie was three years old and talked continuously. I now had a little sister. Now there was Bet, Jackie and I.

Aunt Nellie and Uncle Winser had become parents to three family children.

Separate and Unequal

In 1954, just one year before I started school, the U.S. Supreme Court ruled unanimously that separate but equal schools were unconstitutional. They ruled that even if schools were physically equal, to separate students based on race created a feeling of inferiority for Colored children that could have a permanent negative effect on them.

At my age, I had no idea what that meant. I had no idea what the U.S. Supreme Court was nor how I would be impacted by its ruling. But what I do remember throughout my school years was our teachers drilling into our heads that we would soon sit in the classroom with White children and would have to compete against them one day. Although Brown vs. the Department of Education was passed in 1954, when I graduated in 1968, the schools still had not been desegregated. That didn't happen until about two years after I had graduated.

Hand-Me-Down Books

A couple of things stand out to me about my experience attending a segregated school and the impact of separate and unequal. First of all, my teachers were very interested in my success. Secondly, to the best of my recollection, the graduation rate was good for a rural area. I only remember throughout my entire school years a couple of people being suspended from school. We did not have a suspension and expulsion problem.

Another thing, in particular, stands out for me about my experience attending a segregated school. A couple of summers, I got to work for a short while for the County Department of Education. One of our primary duties was to pack up and deliver books from the White schools and deliver them to the Colored schools. But the interesting thing about this was not that we were receiving second-hand books from the White schools, but how the teachers and our parents responded to it.

I remember taking my second-hand books home with a list of White students' names in them. These were the names of the previous owners of the books. Aunt Nellie would take a brown paper bag and cut it open so that it would just become a flat and open piece of paper. She would then lay the book open on the paper and cut out enough paper to wrap the book. Lastly, she would cover the book and secure the covering with tape.

The bottom line is that she was grateful that we had books and expected us to take good care of them. She knew it wouldn't be that way forever. Our teachers would acknowledge that the books were hand-me-down books but would remind us that we would be OK if we learned the book's material. Some of us believed them and did just that. They were right!

Aunt Nellie's Spelling Lessons

One of my most important lessons about preparing for school was taught to me by Aunt Nellie through the spelling lessons she gave me when I was very young. She was not much on math, but she put a lot of emphasis on spelling.

Every afternoon after I had played outside for a while, Aunt Nellie would call me into the house and start my spelling lessons. She would give me words to learn, send me into my bedroom, and then call me back later for a test. Most of the time, the tests were oral. If I didn't do well, then I was sent back for more study of the words. Once or twice, due to a noncooperative attitude, she had to pull out a switch. These lessons proved to be invaluable to me later on in life. It taught me confidence, and it showed me that my memorization could be above average when I applied myself and put my mind to it.

When I was working on my master's at Pepperdine University, I had completed all of my graduate work for my degree except for taking a comprehensive written exam. The requirement was that I had to answer two questions from a list of multiple questions for each of the six courses. We were given booklets of the sample answered questions and the expectations of how they should be answered months before taking the test. If the questions had been answered properly, then the answer to two questions would fill up two booklets. We were encouraged to split the exam into two parts, focus on three courses in one setting, study for a few months for the second part, and come back to take part two of the test.

If you were not successful in any given part, you could retake the exam for either part a maximum of two times. Everybody in my class split the exam into two parts.

This is one of those times when Aunt Nellie's spelling tests paid off for me, because I studied for the entire exam and went in and passed it in one sitting. The exam started at eight o'clock sharp. I took my booklets up to my instructor at noon, as all other students did. I asked how much time I had for a lunch break. The instructor, along with the other students, looked at me as if I was crazy. He asked, "Are you saying that you are going to take the second part of the exam this afternoon?"

"Yes, I am," I said.

"OK, I will see you at one o'clock."

I returned at one o'clock and took the second part of the exam. I remember turning in my booklets just in time at five o'clock. I was exhausted, and the instructor was ready to leave. I got a letter of congratulations a few weeks later informing me that I had successfully completed the exam. I was able to have the confidence and success to memorize all of this material because of the lessons Aunt Nellie taught me through those spelling tests when I was young. There are more incidents like this, but I will not share them here.

Miss Harris—Fifth Grade

I was a poor student from the first grade to the fourth grade. Apparently, the school administrators had determined that I would continue to be a poor student because they placed me in the "slow section" in the fifth grade. This was not the official name for this class section, but there were usually two classes for each grade. It was pretty clear that most of the smart students were all in the other class. This section primarily consisted of students who had poor school attendance and had not been consistent in performing in the classroom. I was in Miss Harris' room. It was in her class that I became a good student.

Miss Harris was what you would call by today's standards a very, very full-figured woman. She had the propensity to fall asleep in the classroom. And when Miss Harris woke up, she would beat whoever she thought was talking while she was sleeping. And I do mean beat! You see, it was legal in those days to beat a child to death. The school district did not care, the principal was OK with it, and parents gave their consent. There was no appealing against a beating. Because if you went home and complained to your parents about a beating you got at school, then you got another beating at home. Their rationale was, they were sending you to school to become educated, and you were going out there acting like a fool and embarrassing them. So you got another beating!

Miss Harris could swing that paddle, so you did not want your butt to be at the receiving end of her paddle. One day Miss Harris fell asleep and woke up and asked us to take out our homework. We all looked at each other. What homework was she referring to? Was she dreaming? She called one student up and asked him where his assignment was?

"I don't know, Miss Harris," he replied.

"You didn't do it, did you?" she said.

"No, Miss Harris."

She called the next person who sat behind him to bring his homework up for her to see it. He came up but he, too, had no homework to show.

"You didn't do your homework either, did you?" she said.

"No, Miss Harris."

Miss Harris then took out her paddle and used them to illustrate what happens when you don't complete your homework.

I watched in complete horror that day while Miss Harris beat two students half to death. It was at that moment that the light came on for me! I suddenly realized that I had not been working up to my full potential. I could do better. I vowed right then that from that moment on, I would be a good student and always do my homework, even if I didn't have any.

Because of the separate and unequal result of segregation, we did not have a cafeteria to have hot food. We had a snack bar that Miss Harris operated. She would leave class early before lunch to get set up and return late after lunch after taking care of her responsibilities in the snack bar. In the snack bar, you could buy: a rocky road, Baby Ruth, black cow, Sugar Daddy, a wide assortment of potato chips, and Pepsi Colas. Now that was a good lunch!

When Miss Harris returned, somebody would get beat because we all would talk extremely loud, and the teacher next door would come over to quiet us down. One day after lunch, we were in language class, and Miss Harris was teaching us to diagram sentences. In the middle of a sentence, she fell asleep. Students started to talk, but I got up, went to the board, wrote the sentence on the board, diagramed it, and explained it. I had completed all of the exercises at the end of each chapter already in preparation for whatever Miss Harris would ask us for.

She woke up momentarily and slightly opened her eyes and saw me explaining the diagramed sentence. She said, "Excellent, Patrick," and she went back to sleep. I completed the entire exercise and took my seat. By that time, she had awakened and was ready to teach. She complimented me in front of the class and assigned me to be the "class monitor." So from that day on, when Miss Harris left to go to the snack bar, and until she returned, I was to take the names of anybody talking and not doing their assigned work. So when she came in, she would ask me if I had any names for her. And if I did, unfortunately, they got a good beating! Miss Harris also used me and another person named Carol to do the oral reading in classes such as science, geography, and any other class that required a lot of reading. She would always call one of us to read aloud to the class. We were tired at the end of the day, but it was excellent training for us both.

Miss Richardson—Sixth Grade

I moved on to Miss Richardson's room. I was still in the "slow section," but I was a good student and on the honor roll. My reputation for being a reliable "name-taker" also went along with me. So if there was ever a time when that skill was required, I was called upon to provide the service.

Miss Richardson was a very new and young teacher. She was fresh out of college and had a lot of new ideas. She did a lot of teaching. We were given many reports, and we were required to present some of them before the class. This was all good. Additionally, she didn't ask me, who my daddy was. She already knew my situation because she was related to some of the same people I was related to. Whatever the case was, it was a good year, and I became an even better student.

Mr. Kennedy—Seventh Grade

By now, I was thirteen years old, a well-established "name-taker," and a good student. But I was still in the "slow section." Now I had come to realize that the primary difference between the "slow section" and the "regular section," —I guess you might call it—was that there were only two or three kids in the "slow section" who cared about doing their work. Several students in that section were smart, but they didn't come to school regularly enough to make any progress. Many of them lived on farms and had to work during the harvesting season. So when they had the opportunity to come to school, it just didn't mean the same thing to them. But Mr. Kennedy, by my assessment, was an outstanding teacher. He understood how to reach those students who may not have had all of the backgrounds they needed to comprehend the material he may have been covering at the time.

I loved the way Mr. Kennedy taught math. He loved math, and when we started to cover a new concept, it didn't matter to him how quickly the general class got it. He would stay on the same concept for two or three days if he needed to. He would just keep finding different ways to present until everybody got it.

For example, he knew how to reach the students whose interests were primarily with cars. He might say to them. I need to change the spark plugs in my vehicles. I have three six cylinders and four eight cylinders. How many spark plugs do I need? They would take out paper and pencils, make some lines representing the spark plugs for each type of car, add them up and give him the answer. It wasn't exactly rocket science, but it did allow them to work through a word problem. In most classes, they would never have arrived at an answer. I won't talk about Mr. Kennedy's teaching techniques other than to say he worked very hard at trying to reach everybody. He was huge on softball. Every day, we played a game of softball in the afternoon. This kept the boys who were behind and older than the rest of us engaged in school.

Once when I was in Mr. Kennedy's class, I was asked by Miss Richardson, who was my teacher from the previous year, to participate in a talent show she had organized. She created a dance routine for two couples. I was the male partner for one of the pairs. All four of us were in Mr. Kennedy's class. We practiced for weeks, but on Sunday afternoon, when I was to get up on the stage and dance in front of many people, I suddenly got a terrible stomach ache and could not make it to the show. In other words, I got cold feet. This is worth mentioning because it is the only time I ever dealt with a problem by simply not showing up or running away from it as I did then. I felt terrible about not showing up. It was an excellent lesson for me.

It was about this time also that my cousin Butch was born. A lot of changes took place that year at home. Up to this point, there was only Bet, Jackie, and me. But during the time I was in Mr. Kennedy's room, Aunt Nellie and Uncle Winser had a son. His nickname was Butch. Bet was already in high school, and shortly after then, she went to live with her biological mother and family. About three years before then, my cousin Jackie started to live with us. Jackie is my Aunt Fannie's daughter.

They lived in New York, but my Aunt Fannie got sick, and she had to come to live with us. It was intended to be temporary, but it ended up being permanent. Once every year, Aunt Fannie who lived in New York, would come home with a plan to take Jackie back with her. Then, at about the time for her to return, something would come up, and then she would change her mind. One year, she came home to pick her up, and at the last minute again, something came up, and she was in the process of changing her plans to do so. Uncle Winser interrupted and told her that if she left this time without Jackie, then don't return, expecting to take her back to New York. She did go without her. So then I had both a little brother and a little sister in just a short time frame, just as I was turning thirteen when I was also promoted from Mr. Kennedy's class to Miss Connie's class.

Miss Connie—Eight Grade

Leaving Mr. Kennedy's class, I was promoted to Miss Connie's class. I still kept my reputation as a good "name-taker." I was also still a good student and on the honor roll. In Miss Connie's class, I was no longer in the "slow section." Miss Connie was a strict disciplinarian. You didn't get to make a lot of mistakes. She loved to swing her paddle. She was not a very large lady, but she could still use her paddle very effectively. Something that stands out about Miss Connie is that she visited everybody's home to make sure she knew their parents at the beginning of the year. So when she came to my house, I made sure I was not there because I had no idea what she and Aunt Nellie would talk about.

As stated earlier, I continued my duties as the class "name-taker." One day, we took a break to the bathroom from Miss Connie's room to the school's central section, where the bathrooms were located. In keeping with the routine, we walked single file boys in one line and girls in another to the bathroom. Once we got inside the toilet, everything was going well until something funny happened, and everybody started laughing. Just about that same time, Mr. Kennedy opened the door and came into the bathroom. There was no talking, but some boys were still snickering.

When we returned to Miss Connie's classroom, she called me up before the class and asked if I had a report for her. I said, "No, I didn't."

"Are you sure?" she pressed on.

"Yes, I am sure."

She then informed me that Mr. Kennedy had already reported that we were making a lot of noise in the bathroom. I explained that there was no talking, but somebody had made a funny noise, and everybody started to laugh, but nobody talked. To make a long story short, she didn't believe me. So she took out her paddle and asked me to bend over. I bent over, and she blasted me with about five strong licks on my behind. She then reprimanded me and told me to make sure I reported any talking in the future. So from then on, I did. I learned that day to always tell the whole truth.

There was not a lot happening in Miss Connie's room out of the ordinary. She was a good teacher and gave a lot of homework.

Going to Greenville to the Nightclub

For me, the eighth grade ended with me being promoted to the ninth grade and remaining on the honor roll. Not directly related to the eighth grade, something did start to happen for several boys my age during the summer as they moved on to high school. When I completed the eighth grade, I was thirteen. But I would be fourteen shortly after starting the ninth grade in

September. We lived about five or six miles from Greenville. The Colored movie theater was located there. Everybody my age on the weekend, it seemed, was at the movies in Greenville, then after the movies, at the local club. It really was not a "nightclub" but more like a "juke joint." They did have on the weekend live music at one of the clubs.

There was a cover charge, but practically everybody who showed up could get in. I guess they figured that you must have been old enough to get in if you were out that late. So there was no such thing as checking ID. But, and the big but, is that Aunt Nellie disapproved of this arrangement. So at that age, I could not go to the movies in Greenville and then the club on the weekend like some other boys from school who I knew.

I was not pleased with her position on this at all. Uncle Winser would say to me, "Boy, there is nothing out there that late at night but trouble." That made me want to be out there even more. Because it sure seemed like everybody else was having fun and not getting into trouble. When I got a little older and had more freedom to go and return as I pleased, I did see what he meant. Although I never got into trouble while out at night, it sure wasn't because of a lack of opportunity.

It is a scary thought today when I think about what kids did to have fun. First of all, none of the kids I am referring to were old enough to drive or even had a car to drive, so they had to hitchhike to Greenville. Then when they wanted to return home, they had to hitchhike back home again. This was a dangerous situation. The bottom line is that my parents knew the potential danger involved. They were right, and I was wrong. Today, I am very grateful that they didn't give in to my complaining about not having the freedom to go and come as I pleased at that age.

A Taste of Freedom

Now I am in high school. All kinds of stuff were happening for a country town. We were listening to soul music on the radio. We would sometimes get together as friends at somebody's house and call into the radio station for requests. We would request James Brown, Aretha Franklin, the Four Tops, the Temptations, Al Greene, and others. That was a magical time for music. But music wasn't the only thing that was happening.

We were also in the middle of the civil rights movement. There seemed to have been freedom in the air. You could feel it, sense it, and even taste it. We experienced it through the way we dressed, lived, and the music we listened to. The music helped shape our attitudes and reaffirmed that what we were feeling was good and right.

"Keep on pushing. I can't stop now. Move up a little higher, someway, somehow, cause I've got my strength, it don't make sense, not to keep on pushing."

Those were very encouraging words by Curtis Mayfield that got everybody's attention. It filled African Americans with hope and White people with fear. White America feared this song so much that many radio stations across the country banned it from being played over the air. But there were ways to hear it, like at the juke joint on the jukebox. This was amazing. Here was a song that uplifted African Americans, gave us a can-do attitude, gave us hope, and White people had it banned!

Weak Start Unapologetic Present

This song was released in 1964, but another song that White America saw as being even more radical was released in 1968 by James Brown, "Say It Loud, I'm Black and I'm Proud." The attitude that Curtis Mayfield helped to foster in 1964 through music was greatly strengthened in 1968 by James Brown.

I still remember the first time I heard that song. I couldn't believe it! He acknowledged that the conditions we lived in were not good and that we would not have to continue living that way. I remember one line of the song in particular that stood out for me.

It went, "I would rather die on my feet than to keep living on my knees. Say it loud, I'm Black, and I am proud."

In one song, he had expressed for me so clearly what I felt but could not articulate. That was a powerful song. It just made me feel good about being Black. It quickly moved me from being Colored to being Black.

Another verse of the song said, "Some people say we got a lot of malice, some say it's a lot of nerve. But I say we won't quit moving until we get what we deserve."

The words to these songs infuriated White Americans.

They interpreted these words as a call for a revolution. The owners of radio stations banned this song from being played on the radio also. It was especially true in the South. White people could no longer call us Black, and it would hurt us. We loved being called Black. They were so confused and scared at the same time.

Just to put things into perspective, I was in high school from 1964 through 1968. It was the middle of the civil rights movement and the beginning of us fully accepting becoming Black and African American.

In 1960 four students at North Carolina A&T had organized a successful sit-in of the Woolworth's lunch counter that had spread across the South and resulted in the full integration of dining facilities throughout the South.

Additionally, this movement led to the eventual passage of the Civil Rights Act of 1964. There were also demonstrations taking place all across the country in protest of racism. Seeing African Americans change the way they looked, dressed, behaved, and hearing the protest music that we listened to, caused great fear among White people. But this was an exciting time for me, my friends, and most African Americans.

My First Girlfriend and my Future Wife

When I was in the ninth grade, I had the opportunity to attend a ball at another high school in the county. My Aunt Georgianna had a friend at her church who had a daughter that wanted to attend her high school's sweetheart ball during her freshman year. Her parents didn't know any boys who they trusted to escort their daughter to the ball.

Aunt Georgianna informed them that she had a nephew about the same age that they would love. That was me, of course. She arranged for us to meet and for me to escort the girl to the ball. Aunt Georgianna took care of all of the expenses such as renting me a white dinner jacket, a corsage, and driving me to pick her up, etc. It was a very nice event, and the girl was a very nice church girl. We both enjoyed the event and continued communicating by phone and through letters. A few times, I visited her at her house on Sunday afternoons.

I was at the stage now of being very interested in girls. Because at the same time, somehow, I started a dating relationship with another girl in Winterville. That relationship didn't last very long. But I continued the long-distance relationship with the out-of-town girl until I met and started to date another girl who would become my wife.

I was a junior, and Linda Jones was a sophomore. We met at the county fair, but I had known who she was already from school. We spent the evening riding the fair rides together and enjoying each other. That weekend I visited her at her house, and we dated throughout high school.

Linda attracted me for several reasons. We both knew and understood that we had to attend and finish college. That was a big thing for both of us. So we were both focused on doing the things we needed to do to go to college. That meant doing our best in school and staying out of trouble. I was one year ahead of Linda, but we had a lot in common. And we also had some common friends. Linda's meticulous style of dressing also captured my attention. She was always very neat, and I liked that about her. She was small, attractive, very active. She was a cheerleader. She was on the honor roll and showed a lot of enthusiasm about learning. I liked that we could have a very in-depth conversation about the things that were going on and impacting Black people. She was always interested in listening to what I had to say about things that were of great interest to me, even if she didn't have an interest herself. So we hit it off right away.

When I graduated from high school and went to college, we continued the relationship. I guess that is when we both realized that we had a serious relationship. You might say we were young and in love.

The tenth grade was traditionally when a couple of students were selected to attend the junior/senior prom—I believe it was called. Whatever it was called, the two of us selected to attend, worked in the coatroom. I was one of those chosen for the honor, and Carol Knox, I believe, was also selected. So I got the opportunity to attend this event while I was in the tenth grade. Because you usually had to be a junior or senior.

W.H. Robinson High School

Robinson Union was a pretty good school and had some outstanding teachers. I hung out with Rander, Monia, Earl, Clint, Lyman, and Jeffrey. Except for Clint and Jeffrey, we were all classmates. And we were all good students except Clint.

Several of us were in the school marching band together. That was a real experience. Rander, Jeffrey, and I played the coronet, Monia, the tuba, and Earl played the saxophone. Mr. Wooten was the band music teacher. When Mr. Wooten organized the band, it brought a real sense of pride to the community. After we were able to play some songs, we would march around the street next to the school and back to the band room. While we were marching and playing, adults would come out of their houses and march in place as we marched through the community. That was a great experience, and it made us all feel very proud every time we marched through the streets. We also played at parades. In general, we could not play many songs, but we played well the ones we could play.

But due to the separate and unequal distribution of resources, we had second-hand uniforms from the White school. But at least we did have uniforms. And while we owned them, we took outstanding care of them. We also looked excellent in them. No book covering my experience as a youth would be complete without mentioning Mr. Ward, Mr. Maye, and Mrs. Vines. Mr. Maye was the principal of Robinson Union High School. Mrs. Vines was my history teacher in high school, and Mr. Ward was my math and science teacher.

Mr. Maye—Breaking the Trophy Cabinet

Anybody who attended Robinson Union High School has a favorite story about Mr. Maye our principal. He was a powerful personality and an outstanding role model.

Weak Start Unapologetic Present

One class I took while in high school was industrial arts. In industrial arts, we learned how to draw house blueprints and build wood products like coffee tables, end tables, bookstands, bookshelves, etc. Some people like my cousin John Junior were very good at it. When I say built, I am saying that we learned how to draw the design for whatever we were building—sand, finish, and varnish the product. Some students could make furniture items well enough to be sold. And some did sell some of their things.

One semester I had purchased a board about eight-foot-long and about a foot wide for a project I was doing in industrial arts. For some reason, I was taking the board home because I needed to have Uncle Winser help me do something with it. I don't recall precisely what. It was the end of the school day, and we were in the process of changing classes. I was on my way to my next and final class for the day.

Just to reemphasize, we attended a segregated school. The Pitt County School Board members were all White except one Black man. On occasions, the school board members would make site visits to our school while being accompanied by the one African American board member and Mr. Maye, our principal. They would tour the campus and sometimes visit the classrooms to observe what we were being taught.

We had a very competitive basketball team. The school had won several county championships going back to when the founders established it. In the center of the school's main section in the hallway was a large glass trophy case that was home to all the trophies the school had won either through athletics or academics since its founding.

On this particular day, while we were changing classes and the White school board, Mr. Maye, and the Black member of the school board were making their way through the hallway, I was coming through the hallway at the same time. We were going in the same direction, and they were just a few feet behind me. So I was in their direct sight. I was on my way from my industrial arts class carrying the eight-foot long board on one side and my books on the other side. Mr. Maye had warned me in the past not to bring any item from industrial arts through the hallway in the crowded hallway while students were changing classes because it could be dangerous.

As I made my way through the hallway, somebody from behind called my name. As I turned to see who it was, the board I was carrying turned with me naturally. I turned, and I instantly heard the trophy case shatter with glass and trophies falling everywhere in the hallway.

I looked back, and Mr. Maye and the school board members were staring at me as I froze in my tracks. I could see the veins in Mr. Maye's head popping, his neck stiffened, and his eyes homed in on me like a laser beam. The hallway was full of students, but it became quiet enough that you could have heard a pin drop. Everybody was holding their breaths in anticipation of what method Mr. Maye would use to kill me. All I remember saying was, "I'm sorry! I didn't mean to do it!"

More significant than the fear I had of what he was going to do to me was the surprise of Mr. Maye's response. After he had calmed the veins in his head down, relaxed his laser beam eyes off my body, loosened his neck, and removed the hardened expression on his face, he said in a very stern voice, "Go get Mr. Ed quickly to help you clean it up." I said, "Yes, sir!"

I quickly proceeded to find Mr. Ed, the janitor, to help me with the mess I had made. I learned that day that Mr. Maye was alright after all. But I never brought another item such as that board through the hallway ever again. Nor did I ever do anything else that would cause Mr. Maye not to view me in a positive light.

Mr. Ward Created Competition

Mr. Ward was my math and science teacher for several classes. I loved the way he taught math in particular. The way he taught naturally created competition among us who were looking to excel academically. For example, in algebra class, he would introduce a concept and then work problems on the board to further explain it. We had a chance at that point to ask questions. That night he would assign the homework assignment at the end of the chapter covering the concept he had covered that day.

During class, Mr. Ward would call about four people at a time to the board to resolve a problem he would assign to each individual. Each student solved the problem and then explained it as expected. After completion of the problem, Mr. Ward would grade each student's work. He would then correct any errors and explain them. Lastly, he would go from problem to problem on the board and place a score of either 65 or a 95. A person who understood the problem well enough to set it up and attempt to solve it got some credit. That being a score of 65. But the person who solved the problem correctly and explained it to the class correctly got a score of 95. He would then record the scores in the grade book that he kept with him all the time.

This activity created a competition in my class between Rander, Lyman, Monia, Earl, me, and some of the girls, Emma, Barbara, Lillian, Carol, Mavis, and Margee. But mostly among the boys. We would find ourselves working problems after school, even on the ground in the dirt that one of us might have missed in class. Whenever one of us didn't get the full credit of 95, we teased each other very strongly until the next time we got the opportunity to go to the board and work another problem to redeem ourselves.

Of the people I named, mostly we solved the problem and got a 95. That is why we were teased so much if we messed up and missed solving a problem for some reason. That was a lot of fun and helped us all in our development.

Miss Vines' Inspirational History Lectures

Miss Vines was my history teacher. I don't think there was anything about historical events she didn't know. She had a very clear, lecturing style. But you had to take notes to be prepared for her tests. She would lecture us about Plessy vs. Ferguson, for example. This case was so important because the Supreme Court decided that maintaining separate facilities for Blacks and Whites did not violate the Fourteenth Amendment, which guaranteed Blacks equal protection under the law. After all, separate facilities did not automatically mean that the facilities were inferior just because they were separate. We were living in segregation right then.

Miss Vines had a lot to say about that. And she challenged us to assess that situation to the best of our abilities. Remember, separate facilities and segregation were all we knew then. She tried to help us understand that it would not remain that way because Brown vs. the Board of Education had already started eliminating segregation. She emphasized the importance of us working hard to prepare ourselves because we would have to compete against White children one day, and we needed to be ready.

One of my favorite lectures of hers was on the Dred Scott Case. She went into all the details of how Dred Scott was transferred from owner to owner, how he had lived in several slaves and non-slave states, and the several court filings. And as you know, the Dred Scott Case eventually led to the Civil War. We had excellent class discussions about this case.

The thing I remember most about Miss Vines is how she continued to remind us that we would experience desegregation and how we needed to be prepared to take advantage of it. I don't know if this has had any long-term impact on other students of her history classes, but it has significantly influenced me.

One of the things I loved the most about junior high and high school was the Boy Scouts. Shown here is Troop 88 from Robinson Union High School. From top left to right: James Lacy, Samuel Holloway, Willie Grimes, Danny Smith, Dalton Knox, Earl Daniels, and me— Lester Patrick. Bottom left to right: Douglas McKensie, Milton Knox, Kenneth Hammond, Willie Flemming, and Lloyd Hooks.

This picture was taken at a weekend camporee in Greenville, North Carolina.

From Nigger to Colored to Negro to Black to African American

All kinds of things were going on in the United States when I entered high school. The most important events for me were the passage of the Civil Rights Act of 1964, Rev. Martin Luther King's assassination, and becoming more aware of my identity. Up until that point, we were called Colored by White people. And we even thought of ourselves as being Colored people. But around 1964, we started to refer to ourselves as Black, and not Colored as White people had named us.

Lester Patrick

The reality is that even though we were thought of as Colored, most White people still wanted to call us "Nigger" or some version of it. Some never entirely made the transition from Nigger to Colored. They had an in-between word like "Niggg-gra."

Calling ourselves Black was significant because, for the first time, we as a race of people determined who we were and what others would call us. And at that time, it was Black. Shortly after, we renamed ourselves African Americans. It took a while before we could agree whether we preferred to be called African American or Black. To make it more complicated, some of us still chose to be called Negro. The final consensus was that either Black or African American, or both, were OK. But there were no more Negroes in America!

Also, at that same time, I watched athletes like then basketball player Lou Alcindor let his hair grow long into an Afro. It had a significant impact on us in the South. We stopped getting haircuts. We didn't know anything at first about Afro sheen, Afro picks, and the other things that we needed to keep an Afro's groomed. We just stopped getting haircuts. That might explain why our Afro's didn't look like the ones we saw in the Ebony magazine, Jet, on Soul Train, etc. And could also explain why Mr. Maye disapproved of us growing Afro's. But after a while, those products became available to us, and we were able to take advantage of them.

There was a vernacular that went along with wearing an Afro and a pick in your hair. Now everybody became either your brother or your sister. Right on!

Summers Working in the Tobacco Field

Every summer, from the time I was about eleven or twelve years old until I graduated from college, I worked on the farm doing what was called "putting in tobacco." This activity continued until I graduated from college. As I pointed out earlier, North Carolina was the world's tobacco capital when I grew up. And Pitt County was the county with the most tobacco activity in the state. Other crops were grown in the state like corn, soy beans, sweet potatoes, etc. But nothing came close to matching the tobacco crop in volume and revenue generated for the state, nor the level of difficulty involved with the harvesting process.

Tobacco was first introduced to eastern North Carolina by slaves brought over from Africa beginning in the early 1600s. Slave traders took them from the western part of the continent of Africa. Most of them came from what are now the African countries of The Congo, Nigeria, Togo, Mali, and Cameroon. They took them to the Atlantic coastal areas of Virginia and eastern North Carolina. My ancestors were from Nigeria, Togo, and Mali. The humid climate and rich black soil made conditions exceptionally suited for growing tobacco in eastern North Carolina. So tobacco became king in that area.

The first group of slaves brought to these areas were indentured slaves. Meaning like other indentured slaves, they could work and pay for their freedom over time. But this did not last very long after the white farmers realized the value of tobacco and the economic benefit of using the African slaves to provide free labor.

In 1669, Article 10 of the Fundamental Constitution of Carolina stated, "Every freeman of Carolina shall have absolute power and authority over his negro slaves, of what opinion or religion soever." Slave owners were granted complete control over the lives of their Negro slaves. This meant the power of life and death of their slaves. Even being Christian didn't change the civil dominance over their slaves. Meaning they couldn't even take refuge in God as it related to their master's legal control over them, as far as the state government was concerned.

Summer Slave Work for Black Youth

Working in the tobacco fields was practically the only means that African American teenagers had of making money during the summer in this part of the South. If you were a Black youth and a non-farm employer hired you for any other job, then you were released or laid off at a particular time, so you could be available for employment by farmers when the time came to harvest tobacco.

There was an unwritten agreement in Winterville and surrounding rural areas that employers would not interfere with the farmer's ability to harvest tobacco when it was time. There are several examples I can personally cite whereby a business hired me for a summer job, but when it came time to harvest tobacco, they laid me off. On several occasions, the county department of education hired me directly after school closing for the summer, but as soon as it was time to harvest tobacco, released me. I was not the only one impacted in this way. There was never anything specific to point to other than to watch it happen. After all, nobody said I am laying you off because they need you in the fields. But we knew the reason even though we

Weak Start Unapologetic Present

didn't want to believe it. It happened every summer, just like clockwork.

It was not until I was in college, and was home during the summer working for a construction company, that it became so clear to me. A construction company from South Carolina hired two or three of us to work on a contract with East Carolina University to build a campus dormitory. The university was about five miles from my home, so it was ideal. The wages were excellent.

We worked for about six or seven weeks from May until around the middle of June. Every Friday at around lunchtime, we would get our checks. We usually didn't work a full day on Friday because most of the people were from South Carolina, and they always wanted to get an early start on their way back to South Carolina for the weekend.

On this particular Friday, we got our checks, and there was a letter attached thanking us for our service. The letter also informed us that we were being laid off. I was so disappointed. I remember Rander and I engaging in conversation as to why. Another young African American male about the same age was from South Carolina and was not affected. He was standing there with us, listening to our conversation. But another person our age, a White student from East Carolina University, was also listening to the discussion.

He said, "Brothers, they need you guys to work in the tobacco fields." I was so angry that he was bold enough to make that comment but even more furious that I knew what he had said was true. He didn't make the comment to be disrespectful. He was simply answering our question. Why were we being laid off?

The worst thing about his comment was it was true. But equally disturbing was the realization of not hiring young African

Americans to work who were needed for harvesting tobacco was not just a practice that was upheld by local employers. This company was from another state, and had nothing to gain by supporting it. Additionally, to that point in my life, that was the most money I had ever made. I made almost as much in one week as I would make in six or seven weeks during the summer working in the tobacco fields. Not to even mention the working conditions between the two jobs. Being laid off was a significant disappointment.

May Farm Simon's Tobacco Fields

After being laid off, I started to work in the tobacco fields in a few days. Working in the tobacco fields was about as bad of a job as any person could have. First of all, I was required to get up about 4:30 in the morning to get dressed, to have breakfast, and ride out to the farm with the others. My older cousins and I had to be on the farm early, catch the mules, harness them with their reins, etc. and then get in a position to be ready to go into the tobacco field at daylight. The objective of getting in the field at daybreak for farmers was so that you could finish your day early in the afternoon before it was sweltering hot. And most tobacco crews were able to do that.

Uncle Simon was a sharecropper. I worked for him in the tobacco fields. He was my uncle by marriage because he had married Aunt May. Aunt May and Aunt Nellie were sisters, and Uncle Winser and Uncle Simon were brothers. So he was my double uncle. There indeed were advantages to working for your uncle, but ending the day early was not one of them. Uncle Simon had his way of doing things. And they generally didn't agree with the way others did them. He was a Black sharecropper and did his sharecropping on the May Farm. The May brothers had owned the May Farm. As I understand it, before they died, it covered almost the entire county. After they died, it was broken up and sold into chunks of smaller farms, with the May Farm being one of them. At one time, it had been a plantation. I will talk more about that later.

Typically, a tobacco crew started work very early, didn't take official breaks, no official lunch, and ended the day by midday. In the case of Uncle Simon, he took breaks, had a hot breakfast, stopped for lunch, and went home so everybody could wash up and eat in the comfort of their homes. Then after about an hour, he would pick the individual crew members up, drive back to the farm, suit the mules up again, and go back into the blistering hot afternoon hot and humid weather. He had also been known to take his time after lunch to finish up watching a good baseball game. Usually, when we returned to work after lunch, other crews returned home from completing their day.

Uncle Simon had such a reputation for working long hours and some other things that people in the community called him "May Farm Simon." He was a tobacco farmer but was also known for his sweet potatoes. They were delicious! You could comfortably eat them raw without any cooking if you needed to, or you could bake them. Either way, they were the best sweet potatoes in the country. I know because I love sweet potatoes. He also grew corn, soybeans, and some other minor crops. He did not grow cotton. Thank God! He was a Black sharecropper, but one of those sharecroppers who got something out of sharecropping. He had four children, Rosa Lee, Hellen Ruth, Dick, and Skip. They lived next door and were my first cousins. They were older than me by several years, but they significantly influenced me and my life.

May Farm Simon suffered some of the same disappointments that other Black sharecroppers faced, but he sent all of his children to college by sharecropping. And after they graduated and had professional jobs, they bought him his farm so he wouldn't have to sharecrop with anybody, but only work for himself. So I had four cousins living next door to me who had a major impact on me and my decisions, like going to college, etc. There was not an abundance of professional Black people living in Winterville, the small town that I grew up in, but I had four first cousins living next door who became professionals. Dick was an architectural engineer, Skip, an agricultural economist, and Rosa Lee and Helen Ruth were school teachers.

My two male cousins significantly influenced me to the point that one of them, when he came home from North Carolina A&T, would ask me what I knew about a given math principle. If my response were not what he wanted to hear, he would take me into the kitchen and, on the kitchen table, proceed to teach me the concept he thought I should know. There was no rejecting this kind of teaching because Aunt Nellie was thrilled to death. She knew he was doing that to make me aware of the things I needed to know to be academically successful. His tutoring would continue during the summer and at times when we were working in the tobacco fields.

When it became time for me to select a college, my cousin told me to go to North Carolina A&T State University. I did what he said precisely, for that and many other things he advised me to do. You see, they were living examples of what they were telling me to do. Because I could look at them and see the success they were experiencing.

May Farm Simon's tobacco crew primarily consisted of family members for the most part. Consequently, he managed the farm and us, as you would expect one to manage his relatives.

The Tobacco Fields

Tobacco grows on what are called tobacco stalks. The stalks grow to a height of about seven feet. Tobacco leaves grow from the bottom, touching the ground, to the very top of the stalk. Stalks grow in rows of twos and can reach about a quarter of a mile long. Removing the leaves from the stalks is called "priming tobacco." The people who pull the leaves from the stalks are called "tobacco primers."

There are usually three or four tobacco primers in a tobacco crew. I was a tobacco primer. There are also several other steps and positions involved "with putting in tobacco," but there isn't time to explain all of them here. This brief description should give some idea as to what the conditions are like in a tobacco field.

When priming tobacco, each primer primes two rows at a time in unison with the other primers. In the first week, you start at the very bottom of the stalk, removing the bottom-most leaves. Generally, a primer removes three or four leaves per stalk from the stalk's bottom each week. Once all the bottom-most leaves are removed throughout the entire field, the primers go back to the original starting point in the field, and remove the next three or four leaves. The leaves being removed from the stalk is a process that continues week after week until completed. It usually takes around six weeks to remove all the leaves.

The rows are grown very close to each other. A primer standing at the entrance to a tobacco row cannot see down and between the rows. The leaves entirely cover the primmer's body from head to foot as he steps between the rows. Early in the morning, the morning dew completely covers the whole stalk and its leaves. As the primer steps between the two rows, he emerges in the morning dew from the leaves that wraps around his body as he primes the tobacco. Sticky tobacco dew soaks his body most of the morning.

Then the hot blistering sun dries up the hot sticky dew on the  primer's body. The hot sun strikes and scorches the primer's back because, for the first few weeks of priming tobacco, the primer's back is bent over at about a ninety-degree angle with his legs bent at about a forty-five-degree angle all day long as he moves down the row. This work is excruciating, and by the end of the day, the most the primer can do to relieve the pain is to lay flat on his back for temporary relief. There is nothing he can do for the leg pain but endure it. This condition of constant pain lasts for the duration of the tobacco harvesting season.

At all times, primers have to be cautious not to pick up a snake as he primed tobacco.

In my case, everybody from the community knew that the May Farm had an infestation of "rattlesnakes." Other teenagers in the community always asked how I could put up with those working conditions. I saw my share of snakes, but I never saw anybody in our crew get bitten by one. I saw people accidentally pick up snakes along with the tobacco leaves, but never anybody bitten. Now I know that was the protection of God.

Some days it rained all day long. Some weeks it rained all week long for a couple of weeks. When this happened, we continued to work in the tobacco fields. That simply meant that we were soaking wet and dirty with sticky tobacco gum all day long for a couple of weeks.

The Lightning Storms

To the best of my knowledge, the only thing that could delay tobacco harvesting was a thunder and lightning storm. The thunder and lightning storms were unlike anything I have ever seen anywhere. The lightning could be so bright and thunder so loud that it seemed like it was right next to you. Sometimes you could actually feel the heat from the lightning. We would have to rush out of the fields and take shelter. But we were still in danger because we usually took refuge under a tin metal structure, which would serve as a conductor of electricity if lightning was to strike it.

Aunt May was terrified of lightning. So whenever a thunder and lightning storm came up, she would have to find a place where she could cover her eyes entirely so as not to see the flashes of lightning. The storms could be terrifying, but most of all, they delayed the harvest for that day. Consequently, after the storm was over, we had to go back into the wet and muddy field and prime the wet and sticky tobacco while we were soaking wet for the remainder of the day.

Tobacco is sticky with a substance called tobacco gum. The tobacco gum is green and looks almost like chewing gum. It cakes up on your hands, your face, your clothes, and your entire body. When you take a bath, it is impossible to get it all off. You never completely rid yourself of tobacco gum until weeks after the tobacco season is over.

Think about it for a second. All these terrible working conditions and we only received $10 per day and about $60.00 per week if we worked all six days. Generally, we made about $400.00 the entire summer. With the money, I bought some of my school clothes, but it wasn't always enough.

Slave Labor

This was slave labor, and no question about it. The working conditions had not improved much since slavery. Now there was a small difference. They didn't get paid at all. But the thing that I couldn't help thinking about was that I was probably working in the same fields that my enslaved forefathers worked. The experience of working in the tobacco fields made a very long and lasting impression on me as a teenager. It made me know for sure, without a doubt whatsoever, that I would become an educated African American man! That work motivated me as nothing else could, or has since then! And I could look at my cousins and see it was possible because they had successfully done it!

The Grimes Plantation—Slave Quarters

A vacant tobacco barn was needed on the May Farm for the tobacco to be placed in. Sometimes there were no empty barns. In those situations, we had to pack the tobacco up on a truck and transport it about fifteen miles away to the Grimes Plantation in Grimesland. The farm owner was the same White man who owned the May Farm and sharecropped with my uncle Simon.

The trip added hours to what was already a very long day. But there was something about the Grimes Plantation that was very interesting and upsetting at the same time. The Grimes Plantation during slavery had been a slave plantation. There were remnants from slavery all over the farm. There was a small jailhouse in the middle of the farmyard just in front of the master's house or the big house where slaves who misbehaved were locked up.

It had been owned and operated by a man by the name of General Brian Grimes, who was a confederate general. In front of the slave quarters was a monument to the general. A slave assassinated General Grimes, according to the overseer and historian of the plantation. The General was sitting on his horse in front of the slave quarters, according to him. The slave jumped from the second floor of the slave quarters and stabbed the general to death while he sat on his horse with his back to the slave quarters.

In the slave quarters, the beds that the slaves slept on were still there. Their straw mattresses were very close together, with not even space for a person to squeeze through. It looked as if they never left. This visual image of the slave quarters was very depressing. I usually had this experience at least one time each summer. There I was as a teenager working, for the most part, doing the same work the slaves had done. But going to that plantation brought me face to face with the reality of it!!

They had been brought there during the late 1600s and were slaves there until slavery ended in 1863. That was not a good feeling. Other things also added to the depression I experienced when I worked there. One thing was that the overseer and historian were from the same line who had served as the plantation overseer since the slave days. The stories he told us had been passed down through his family since that time. He still lived in the master's house or the big house. This was not an experience I was excited about having each summer.

Hot Sun and Summer Fun

With all the hard work, aching backs and legs, there was still time during the summer for some summer fun. Winterville was a small town. And Black people didn't have a community center or recreational facility. One was downtown that our parent's tax dollars helped support, but we couldn't use it. And by now, you probably know why. I'm not even aware of any of us even trying to use the facility downtown.

But during the summer, the high school gym was open in the afternoon at around lunchtime. Those who didn't work hung out there. But those who did work in tobacco attended after they finished with their day in the tobacco field.

We played basketball, table tennis, shuffleboard, dominoes, card games, and other games. On late Friday afternoons, there was usually music and dancing. Now you would think that we wouldn't feel like dancing with all the young aching backs and legs from working in tobacco. Not so. I guess young is the key concept here. Because on Friday afternoon when we heard the beat of James Brown, and the sound of Junior Walker and the All-stars, the pain just sort of went away. And nothing could stop us from dancing and having fun. At least in my case, from trying to dance.

Linda and I would see each other every day in the late afternoon and spend time together. Every Saturday night, there was a party in somebody's backyard. We called it a "weenie roast." The hosts always served hot dogs and birthday cake, whether it was anybody's birthday or not. These times were just another reason for teenagers to get together and have fun.

There was no pain in our young legs or backs from working all week in the tobacco fields. If there was any pain, the pain was in our hearts. Just as Otis Redding would sing it, "Pain in my heart, it won't let me be." If anything was missing, Otis could fill it with, "These Arms of Mine." We especially loved "slow dragging," we called it. When a slow song like "When a Man Loves a Woman" was played, the host's mother would walk through the crowd and touch the backs of those who she thought were dancing too close. That was your only signal before being told to go home! But by ten or eleven o'clock, the party was over anyway because most of us had to get up the next morning and go to church. I know I did.

Summer was also a time when I got to see my little sister Joyce. Joyce and Cleo lived in New York with my biological mother Christine. We didn't see a lot of each other, but some summers, she spent time in Winterville. Joyce and Jackie were about the same age, and Butch was two or three years younger. They were an active bunch. I sometimes looked after them. I wouldn't call it babysitting because I was just staying at home with them until aunt Nellie returned. Butch was

a hand full. Saying that he was only active wouldn't do fairness to the term childhood.

Butch today is a mortician. We always knew he would be. When he was three or four years old, he would set up little figurines of people in a church congregation format, and then he would conduct make-believe funerals. It was weird. Sometimes he would name the people he was funeralizing. After graduating from high school, he went on to mortuary school and became a mortician. He has been a mortician ever since. I don't understand it, but he loves it.

Joyce and Jackie were very playful and giggled all day long. They both were very talkative, but Jackie talked continuously! They got on my nerves just a little bit because I was a teenager. But it was cool watching all of them grow up. Things were starting to change, and they were growing up under different conditions than me. For example, both Jackie and Butch attend desegregated high schools. The county had integrated all the high schools when they graduated. So positive progress was happening. Today, Joyce is a retired nurse and college professor, and Jackie is a retired university librarian.

Living Under Jim Crow—Its Impact

As pointed out earlier, during the summer, I was doing the same work my enslaved forefathers did during slavery. Although slavery ended in the United States in 1863, former slaves were still not truly free. This is true because very soon after the Emancipation Proclamation passage, the Southern Confederate states passed laws to institute slavery all over again, but at the individual state level. These laws were called the Black Codes. So not much had changed for most slaves during this period.

Because of the Black Codes, the states had implemented to take away rights given to freed slaves under the constitution; the United States Congress passed the Civil Rights Bill of 1866. And I do mean the states had taken away the slaves' freedom. For example, in the North Carolina Constitution, Section 2 of the North Carolina law described the law's purpose as making freed slaves subject to the same laws as they were subject to before their Emancipation. Those laws, of course, were slavery. Below is an excerpt from one of North Carolina's Black Codes. Pay attention, particularly to Section 2.

> **Sec. 1**. *Be it enacted by the General Assembly of the State of North Carolina* that negroes and their issue, even where one ancestor in each succeeding generation to the fourth inclusive is white, shall be deemed persons of color.
>
> **Sec. 2**. All persons of color who are now inhabitants of this State shall be entitled to the same

> privileges, and are subject to the same burthens and disabilities, as by the laws of the State were conferred on, or were attached to, free persons of color, prior to the ordinance of emancipation, except as the same may be changed by law.

Section 2 is so important because it applies to all enslaved people who had been emancipated by the Thirteenth Amendment to the Constitution of 1863 which freed the slaves. But this new law enacted at the local and state level in North Carolina now took away those rights from all free persons of color and returned them back to the laws they had been subject to prior to their freedom. This meant that their rights had been restored legally back to a condition of slavery in North Carolina even though the Thirteenth Amendment to the Constitution had freed them. Don't think it can't happen again.

During the Reconstruction period, Congress had passed the Thirteenth, Fourteenth, and Fifteenth Amendments. These amendments to the constitution were called the Reconstruction Amendments because they ended slavery, guaranteed citizenship for all formerly enslaved people, including those in North Carolina.

And the Fifteenth Amendment gave male slaves the right to vote. This amendment was ratified in 1870 by Congress. Even though slaves got the right to vote in 1870, they still could not exercise those rights completely free of intimidation until over ninety-five years later with the passage of the Civil Rights Act of 1966.

Instantly after the ratification of the Fifteenth Amendment to the constitution in North Carolina and in most other southern states, free former slaves and White Republicans formed

Weak Start Unapologetic Present

voting coalitions. And overnight, they changed politics and the balance of power at the local, state, and federal levels. But this condition was short-lived. Because by 1876, just six years later, Reconstruction ended because of conservative Democrats and ex-Confederates' attacks. A White Supremacy Campaign was starting to rise in North Carolina and growing strong.

The White Supremacy Campaign in North Carolina impacted the political progress of Blacks in the state. But because of some state laws that were passed by the White Republicans, they were able to slow down its impact. As a result, in the 1898 state election, as many as 80 percent of eligible Black voters participated in the state election. This caused the Democratic Party to beef up its "White Supremacy Campaign" of targeting Black voters. This effort was similar to what we see the modern-day Republican Party is doing across the country with voter suppression, only then it was more intense and extremely violent.

The *News and Observer* Newspaper sponsored regular addresses and newspaper articles appealing to White voters about "Negro domination," Black men raping white women, and other fear-mongering. It was very much like what is done by Republicans today when they degrade African American voters by accusing them of cheating. Like the president tweeting mean, nasty, and demeaning things about most Black people in public, and much like him tweeting to praise White supremacy. It's all the same, just different people and times.

The Democrats even devised a plan to attack the city of Wilmington if Blacks were to be successful in keeping control of the local government in Wilmington. Wilmington then was the most populated city in the state. It had a sizable Black population and a Black newspaper. Consequently, the Black newspaper editor responded to the racist newspaper articles by *News and Observer* calling Black men rapists.

They responded through news articles accusing White women of initiating the sexual contact. This angered White Democrats greatly. Meanwhile, the white supremacy campaign of the Democrats was very successful and resulted in the party winning the overwhelming share of districts across the state. But in Wilmington in the 1898 election, Blacks and Republicans combined to control all local Wilmington elected offices.

In response to White Republicans' success and recently freed Blacks in Wilmington in the local election, the white supremacists on Aug 10, 1898, attacked and burned the office of the Black newspaper, *Daily Record*. The attack resulted in the killing of thirty-six Blacks. All elected officials were forced at gunpoint to resign and were run out of town. Democrats filled all local government positions with handpicked white supremacists. This event placed fear into the hearts of Blacks in North Carolina and would prove to impact voter participation for years to come.

Especially since both the federal and state governments stood by and watched this happen with no intervention at all. The "Wilmington Insurrection" was the name given to this historical event. They then pursued implementing a white supremacist agenda across the state, which they were successful in doing. This event led to the implementation of white supremacist laws and amendments to the state constitution, which established poll taxes, literacy tests, and a complete disenfranchisement of Black voters. I will talk more about that later.

This situation is so tricky because these laws still existed when I grew up in North Carolina. When I was a teenager, these laws were still on the books and were enforced. That is the reason I say I grew up under Jim Crow. Legally speaking, segregation ended with the passage of Brown vs. the Board of Education in 1954. But several Jim Crow laws still existed and were enforced. And they remained in place until Congress passed the Civil Rights Bill of 1966. Even with the passage of the Civil Rights Bill of 1966, segregation was still very prevalent. When I graduated from high school in 1968, Pitt County schools still had not been desegregated. Just think about it, Congress had already passed a Civil Rights Bill in 1866, a hundred years earlier to ensure that we had full rights as citizens, and a hundred and two years later, it had not materialized.

And shockingly, some traces of the Jim Crow laws are still present in the North Carolina Constitution even today in 2020. To be more specific, a literacy requirement for voting was placed in the North Carolina Constitution in the 1900s to deter Black men's voter participation. It was placed there two years after the North Carolina election of 1898 when 80 percent of eligible Black voters participated in the election. It is still there and has been there for 120 years.

Any reader can read the literacy requirement law in Section 4 of Article VI of the North Carolina constitution. It states:

> *"Every person presenting himself for registration shall be able to read and write any section of the Constitution in the English language."*

This literacy requirement is an example of just one of the Jim Crow laws and how it kept Black men from voting during that period. Most Black men could not read and write. In recent years there have been multiple efforts to repeal this law and remove it from the state constitution. But voters have rejected all efforts to do so. That tells us a lot about where we are today. I am not sure, but I would be willing to bet that North Carolina is not the only state that still has some remnant of Jim Crow in its constitution. Let's hope I'm wrong. I will address it further later in the book.

Reckless Eyeballing

When I was a teenager growing up in North Carolina, I remember our teachers warning us about "reckless eyeballing." I was a junior or senior then, which was especially important because of the social changes that were taking place. They were very concerned about us getting ourselves into trouble. For example, East Carolina University was just about five miles away, and a lot of young African American boys liked to hang out at the beer bars where the college students hung out. I emphasize beer bars, because liquor by the drink was illegal in North Carolina. Even if it weren't, we would have been too young to buy it. But these places were just places where college kids hung out and listened to music, etc. So as a junior or senior in high school, some could get in. Simultaneously, the "miniskirt" was becoming very popular, and the "micro-mini" even more.

Our teachers knew that because of the social changes taking place, there was an opportunity for different races to socialize together more. Almost all the girls who attended East Carolina University were White. And the majority of them were not from the local area but from other parts of the state or other parts of the country, where dating between races may not have been a big deal.

But our teachers wanted to keep at the forefront of our minds that we were living in eastern North Carolina during segregation. And they wanted us to be aware that by just looking at a White girl with perceived sexual intent, we could be accused of and charged with "reckless eyeballing." Like me, some of us had girlfriends, so that was not a problem for us. But for some, it was.

Our teachers could point to the most famous national case involving reckless eyeballing recorded that took place right there in North Carolina in 1951. It involved a Black man by the name of Mack Ingram. Ingram was charged with reckless eyeballing even though he never got closer than 75 feet of the sixteen-year-old White girl. The state still charged him with "reckless eyeballing." He served about two-and-a-half years in jail before the North Carolina Supreme Court reduced his charges from rape to assault and sentenced him to six months in jail. But by then, he had already served over two years in jail.

The judge instructed the jury that Mr. Ingram would be guilty if he used, "intentional threats or menace of violence such as looking at a person in a leering manner, that is in some sort of sly or threatening or suggestive manner...he causes another to reasonably apprehend imminent danger." Mr. Ingram was found guilty by an all-White jury.

Our teachers wanted to make sure that this did not happen to any of us. They knew that a lot of social changes were taking place while attitudes and laws remained the same.

Jim Crow Etiquettes

Believe it or not, there was actually a Jim Crow etiquette. This is because Jim Crow was so prevalent in the United States. This was true, especially in the southern part of the United States, even though Jim Crow did exist in other parts of the country. If Black people didn't follow it, they were subject to attacks—directly or indirectly—through their families, employment, physically, and any other way possible to be attacked. There is plenty of history to prove it.

The practice of Jim Crow etiquettes worked in conjunction with the Jim Crow laws. So there were the laws, and then there was the expected behavior. If this conduct was not adhered to, then the state applied the law. Sometimes White people not in authority took things into their own hands. This is what happened in the case of lynch mobs. When this happened, law enforcement either participated or kept hands off so that the mob could do the harm they desired.

Below are some examples of Jim Crow etiquettes:
- A Black male could not offer his hand (to shake hands) with a White male because it implied being socially equal. Obviously, a Black male could not offer his hand or any other part of his body to a White woman, because he risked being accused of rape.
- Blacks and Whites were not supposed to eat together. If they did eat together, Whites were to be served first, and some sort of partition was to be placed between them.
- Under no circumstance was a Black male to offer to light the cigarette of a White female -- that gesture implied intimacy.
- Blacks were not allowed to show public affection toward one another in public, especially kissing, because it offended Whites.
- Jim Crow etiquette prescribed that Blacks were introduced to Whites, never Whites to Blacks. For example: "Mr. Peters (the White person), this is Charlie (the Black person) that I spoke to you about."
- Whites did not use courtesy titles of respect when referring to Blacks, for example, Mr., Mrs., Mis., Sir, or Ma'am. Instead, Blacks were called by their first names. Blacks had to use courtesy titles when referring to Whites, and were not allowed to call them by their first names.
- If a Black person rode in a car driven by a White person, the Black person sat in the back seat, or the back of a truck.
- White motorists had the right-of-way at all intersections.

Stetson Kennedy, the author of *Jim Crow Guide* (1990), offered these simple rules that Blacks were supposed to observe in conversing with Whites:

1. Never assert or even intimate that a White person is lying.
2. Never impute dishonorable intentions to a White person.
3. Never suggest that a White person is from an inferior class.
4. Never lay claim to, or overly demonstrate, superior knowledge or intelligence.
5. Never curse a White person.
6. Never laugh derisively at a White person.
7. Never comment upon the appearance of a White female.

Modern Day Jim Crow Etiquette

During Jim Crow, African Americans, with few exceptions, adhered to Jim Crow etiquette when interacting with Whites. Whites expected this behavior and overwhelmingly embraced it. Today, most African Americans do not behave in a manner that is expected by some. President Trump demonstrates modern-day Jim Crow etiquettes and its expectation through the use of the offensive language we see him directing towards African American people. His behavior is motivated by his inability to force the ones he comes into contact with to behave as he wants them to. So when Congresswoman Maxine Waters asks him tough questions he cannot answer, he calls her dumb and unintelligent. During Jim Crow she could not have asked a White man a difficult question. Nor could she have made any negative statement about him publicly. When LeBron James builds and operates a private school to help improve the academic standing of minority students, the president sees this as something he would stop if he had the control to do so. Since he doesn't have that control, he calls Lebron the dumbest man on the planet. During Jim Crow, Donald Trump could have shut down the school. And believe me, he would have. But now, the only thing he can do is resort to modern-day Jim Crow etiquettes in an attempt to degrade him. But LeBron and other African Americans he attacks ignore such ignorance.

Jim Crow and the etiquette of Jim Crow operated on the premise that African Americans were inferior in intelligence and social status. This was true whether they were educated or professional people. It didn't matter. Today, the president and people who love and support his hateful and racist distasteful behavior engage in the type of verbal, shameful characterization of African Americans as he does. In their minds, they are savoring a time when society demanded Jim Crow etiquette.

Our president and some others still long for the day when Jim Crow was the law of the land. They cannot see African Americans as equals. This is true whether the person is the first African American president, first African American first lady, or with a specific distinction. It doesn't matter. Modern-day Jim Crow etiquettes, just as during the Jim Crow period, will not allow those Whites who subscribe to this practice to see African Americans as equals. And this is where the conflict comes in. Because with very few exceptions, African Americans will not satisfy White people's desires by behaving and thinking of themselves as inferior.

As for our president, he has degraded all African American women and African American men. This includes the one or two he has around him. But as I said earlier, there are a handful of exceptions of African Americans who will still adhere to the expected Jim Crow behavior. When Abby Phillip, a black journalist, asked the president a difficult question, he said, "What a stupid question, but I watch you a lot. You ask a lot of stupid questions." He would only make such a statement to an African

American woman. And his modern-day Jim Crow belief is that if she is African American, she must be asking a stupid question. He feels insulted by an African American woman asking him a difficult question because it doesn't meet modern-day Jim Crow etiquettes or expectations.

In summary, the president, other selfish individuals, and White supremacists practice modern-day Jim Crow etiquettes. But they practice this behavior without the participation of the overwhelming majority of African Americans.

Living Out Jim Crow Practices - The Whites-Only Counter

When I grew up under Jim Crow in North Carolina, I didn't really understand that some of the things we were subjected to were because of Jim Crow. It was a way of life for Blacks, particularly in the South. For the most part, our parents did everything possible to protect us from these practices. And I am very thankful to them for doing so.

I do remember, for example, as a young boy going shopping in Greenville about five miles away with my aunt Nellie, and shopping in White's Store. Now I don't know why it was named "White's." But that was its name. There was a food counter where hot dogs, milk shakes, sandwiches, and sodas were sold in White's. If you were Black, you could purchase at the counter but could not sit at the counter.

You had to purchase takeout and stand at the end of the counter while your food was being prepared. I saw other Black people do that so often that it didn't really seem like a problem.

But there was also a small window in the back of the kitchen where Blacks could purchase food. This was at one time the only place a Black person could buy food in White's. The hot dogs were very good. And when you first set foot in the store, the only thing you could smell was the aroma of freshly made hot dogs. So I do remember on a number of occasions wanting to buy a hot dog, but Aunt Nellie didn't really want me to. She would say something like, "I will make you hot dogs at home when we get back." I was a child, so my perspective was that it just wasn't the same as buying a hot dog in White's. So I would continue whining, "I want a hot dog. I want a hot dog." Sometimes she would just give in and allow me to have the hot dog. But it was very clear that she didn't want me to have it. I didn't understand then that she intended to protect me where she could from the practice of Jim Crow. You see, even though our parents hadn't experienced anything differently, they still knew it was wrong.

There were also other examples of situations such as this. I came to understand as I became a teenager that she had either tried to protect me or had done so.

White's was a clothing store. But Blacks could not try on clothes before buying them. Whatever you purchased, you had to keep. There was no return policy for Blacks. By the time I was a teenager and was able to go shopping for clothes on my own, that practice had changed. Additionally, the food counters had been closed. The "sit-ins" at Woolworth's food counter in Greensboro by four A&T students in 1960 changed the practice throughout the South.

Coping with the Anger from Jim Crow

Still a teenager and in high school, Jim Crow was not at the top of the list of things on my mind. But through lectures in class, demonstrations that were taking place, television, and personal experiences, I knew it was very much alive. As I got older and more aware, I became angry. That anger was about to be tested. I would be faced with a decision of how I was going to respond to it then.

One night, three of my friends and I were standing on the corner of business highway 11 and directly in front of Mr. Hart Hammond's store. We were all about fifteen years old. These were guys I had known since I was a toddler and had been playmates of theirs. They were all from Newtown. We were a little older now, and although friends, we were not very close friends. It must have been somewhere around 8:30 because it was not entirely dark. I was leaving Linda's house and on my way home. Linda lived just down the street from the store.

When I reached the corner where my three friends were standing, I stopped to join the conversation they were having. It was not uncommon for young boys from the neighborhood to stand there on that corner and just talk and sometimes even sing and act crazy and just have fun. We did that all the time.

So as we were standing there doing whatever we were doing, we could hear coming towards us in the footsteps of a person walking at a brisk pace. It caught our attention, so we stopped what we were doing to pay attention. In those days, it was the style for boys, at least in the South, to wear shoe taps on their shoes' heels and toes. It gave a tapping sound as you walked, so we could not ignore the sound coming from the person walking towards us. The person was walking in the street.

From the sound of his steps, we could tell that he was walking very fast and taking very long steps. It sounded like somebody in a hurry and just on the verge of running.

And suddenly he was close enough for us to see it was a White boy about our same age. Somebody from our group yelled, "It's a White boy, let's beat him up!" The other three boys in our group said, "Yea!" and started towards him, placing themselves in a position to attack the White boy. Just as he got close enough for us to see his face, and they reached out to grab him, I interceded by grabbing the person who had touched him first.

We wrestled for a short while, but just long enough for the White boy to run and get away. You see, the White neighborhood was only a block away in the direction that the White boy was walking from, and obviously, he lived on the other side of the Black neighborhood and was on his way home. It was very unusual for a White person to walk through the Black community. Not that it was a bad neighborhood or anything of the sort, but it just didn't happen in the segregated South.

After we had finished wrestling and the White boy had run and gotten away, my friend yelled to me, "If we were walking through their neighborhood at night, they would have beat us up!" That was his justification for wanting to beat up a White person he didn't know, had never seen before, and had never had any interaction with. There might have been some experience that he had that caused him to feel that way. I don't know.

All I know is that I understood that the personal anger that I felt for that time about the racial conditions we faced could not be resolved by beating up a White boy who I didn't even know. I wasn't sure what the answer was, but I knew that wasn't it. I would not stand by and watch an innocent person physically harmed, even if he was White. From that day forward, I don't believe I could count that person any more as a friend. We spoke to each other when we saw each other but never really had any conversation.

So I guess I would say that I dealt with my frustration and anger about racism by joining protest marches as I got older and educating myself on and trying to understand what was happening to us. Because at this stage of my life I became much more aware. But it wouldn't be until I would get to North Carolina A&T that I would have the in-depth understanding of our circumstance necessary for surviving them. I will talk about that later. I was just about to graduate from high school.

Graduating from High School

It is now the summer of 1967, and I am a senior in high school. I am still working in the tobacco fields, but I know those days are about finished. I didn't know then that I would still be doing that until I graduated from college. By now, Linda and I were spending a lot of time together. You might say we spent all our free time together. Yes, we were in love. Sometimes we would get together with some of our other friends at their houses. In those days, we spent a lot of time at our friend's houses as dating couples.

Aunt Nellie loved to cook, and she was an excellent cook! But long before women's liberation, she stopped cooking for us on Saturday. Everybody was on their own on Saturday. Most Saturday's, Uncle Winser would bring hamburgers for lunch when he came home from working a half-day on Saturday. He was a carpenter, and it was very common for him to work a half-day on Saturdays. He enjoyed seeing the children eat a lot. His philosophy was that if there was no food left, somebody didn't get enough to eat.

Another thing that stands out to me about Saturdays during that period is that the older men like Uncle Winser and his close friends, and several of the young men my age, would sometimes meet at a store we called the "Ducky-Lucky" and eat together. This was nothing formal at all. The men would just buy fish and the ingredients to make homemade cornbread, and they would prepare a fish stew. There was a jukebox there that would allow us to play all the latest hits. We would eat profusely and listen to soul music. We loved being with the older men because they had jokes to tell that would make us laugh uncontrollably. It was all good fun.

But on Sundays, Aunt Nellie would cook as if it was Thanksgiving. Actually, she would start cooking some things late Saturday night and finish up early Sunday morning before going to Sunday school and church. This was a southern thing that most people did every weekend. It was not uncommon for people to just drop by on Sunday and have dinner with Aunt Nellie. Or at least eat some of what she had cooked that day.

So a lot of Sundays after church, Linda and I would spend the day at either my house or her grandmother's house eating and socializing. I know it sounds like we did a lot of eating, and you are correct. We did. We also spent an equal amount of time at Aunt Bell's with our close friends, and my cousin Gin and friend Rander. Again, eating, listening to music, and enjoying ourselves.

Money for College

My biological mother's name, as I pointed out earlier, was Christine Patrick. She had moved away to New York when I was about 3 or 4 years old. She had gotten married and had another child by the name Joyce, my sister. We didn't see each other often, only during those times when my mother would come home. My brother Cleo had also moved to live with my mother, and I didn't see him often either. But I had remained living with Aunt Nellie and Uncle Winser.

Weak Start Unapologetic Present

Early on, when my mother found out that I was a good student, she told me and others that she had already started planning and saving for me to go to college. So when it would come time for me to go to college, I didn't have anything to worry about because it was all taken care of.

She would remind me of that from time to time when I spoke to her over the telephone or when she would come home during the summer to visit for a few days. That was all good for Aunt Nellie and Uncle Winser to hear, knowing that I didn't have to be concerned about the finance of attending college.

Winterville then had a population of around 1,500 people. About an equal number of Blacks and White inhabitants. Greenville was four or five miles west of us with about 60,000 people, and Ayden was about four miles south of us with about the same population as Winterville. The surrounding areas were all rural with crops growing everywhere.

Even though this was during Jim Crow, some poor Black and White families had socialized in illegal ways. Uncle Winser had told us that he and this White man in town when they were very young, worked in the fields together and even at times slept over at each other's houses. The White man had become a wealthy farmer and was the president of the local bank. As they got older, they didn't hang out together or anything like that, but they still knew each other.

The summer of 1967 was ending, and I was about to become a high school senior. I had watched several of my male and female cousins become high school seniors, graduate, and some go on to college. Now it was my time. My first cousin, Annie Mae, had been the most recent cousin to attend college. I was exuberant and looking forward to it.

I had started school, and it was around November. Uncle Winser and I were downtown picking up groceries when Uncle

Lester Patrick

Winser ran into an old friend of his on the street. It was the White person that he had been friends with when they were young. He had become the president of the local bank. They greeted each other and shortly after, Uncle Winser introduced me by saying, "This is my son Lester. He's graduating this year from high school and then going to college." He said so proudly.

The man responded by saying something like, "That's good, but don't you let him get none of those loans from the federal government. When he is ready to go to college, you come to my bank, and we will give you the money to go to school." Uncle Winser said, "OK, we will."

They ended the conversation, and we went our separate ways. But that wasn't that important to us because we both knew that my mother was already taking care of my going to college. But we were nice, nonetheless, in our response. After all, this was the Jim Crow south, and the etiquette required Uncle Winser to call him mister and him to call Uncle Winser by his first name. But they addressed each other on a first-name basis.

Meanwhile, now we are into spring, and I have gone through most of my senior year. And I have been told I will be graduating with honors. Man, I have gone from being in the slow section in grades 1 through 7 to bring my grades up to the point that would allow me to graduate with honors, about fifth in my graduating class. I was happy, to say the least. We had started to practice our graduation program. Because when I grew up, you didn't just show up and march down the aisle and receive your diploma. Marching in a high school graduation in those days was a big thing. Your relatives came from the North and everywhere else to see you march down the aisle to receive your diploma.

Weak Start Unapologetic Present

There was no such thing as not being in step to the music as you marched to "Pomp and Circumstance." That required weeks of practice to make sure that everybody's steps were in sync. On the day of the event, you could hear only the piano solo's sound as it thundered out the sound of "Pomp and Circumstance." You could hear a swaying sound that resulted from each step we took in perfect synchronization. And if you listened closely, you could hear the deep breaths that our parents and relatives took in fear that either of us might get out of step. Staying in step got almost as much attention as receiving your diploma. If you were out of step, you could be the talk of the town the following day. Consequently, it was April, and we were in the middle of practicing for our graduation ceremony.

That same month on April 4, 1968, around 6:30, I was on the phone with my friend Clint. As we were talking, he suddenly shouted, "They killed Martin Luther King!"

"Who?" I asked.

"White folks!"

I dropped the phone, and I could hear on the television coming from the other room that it was true. It was true; an assassin had shot and killed Dr. King. At the time, it was not known who had assassinated him. But cities around the country were going up in smoke as Black people took to the streets rioting.

The next day it appeared that teachers were only in school to console us. Those rooms that had portable televisions had them on all day. Our parents, the churches, the Black community, in general, were mourning. Many of us, at that point, felt hopeless. I was young, but I knew that this was very serious. Where do we go from here? It seemed like we were making so much progress. Even though most people didn't like Dr. King when he was alive, he was making a difference in the lives of Black and oppressed people here and around the world. Some of us could see that. We made it through watching the funeral, the riots, and newscasts on the theories of who had committed the assassination. Soon we were back to the regular school routine and practicing for the graduation.

It was now the end of May. My mother had come home for my graduation. The day before graduation, we were at one of my adult cousin's houses with my mother. His name was Jesse Ray. We were having a conversation about college and who was going to college and those kinds of things. Jessie Ray asked me where I was going to college, and I told him. He said, "Did you get any financial aid or scholarships?"

"My mother has already saved for me to go to college," I said.

Then, my mother interrupted. "Lester, I know I haven't had the opportunity to tell you this yet, but we had some financial problems, and I had to use the money I had saved for you to go to college," she said.

I could not believe what I was hearing. It was May, and the deadline for filing for financial aid had passed. I was graduating the next day from high school, and I am now finding out that I don't have any money to go to college. I know this is probably difficult for anybody reading this to believe, but I was not angry with my mother. But I was very disappointed.

Later, as we left my cousin's house, my mind was entirely on what my mother had said about there not being any money for me to attend college. I suddenly remembered Uncle Winser's White friend as we were being driven back home, and the offer he had made about giving us money for me to go to college. When I got home, I told Uncle Winser and Aunt Nellie what my mother had said. "Maybe we could go to your friend, Uncle Winser, and get the loan from him," I said. "We can do it next Saturday after I get off work," he replied.

Weak Start Unapologetic Present

I graduated the next day with honors. At the ceremony, I received a special award for completing twelve years of school with perfect attendance. I didn't miss one day from school. Aunt Nellie made sure I was there each and every single day!

The next Saturday, after Uncle Winser got off work, we rushed down to the bank to get the loan for me to go to college. We sat in the lobby for about five minutes before the receptionist motioned for us to go in to see Uncle Winser's friend, the president of the bank. "Good to see you, Winsler. What can I do for you?" he greeted us.

"I came to talk to you about the loan for my son to go to college that you promised," Uncle Winser said.

"Yea, I do remember that." He asked Uncle Winser if he had been keeping up with the stock market, the interest rates, etc? He even talked about collateral.

"Uh-huh," Uncle Winser nodded his head as if he followed what his friend was saying. Was this man serious? Uncle Winser didn't even manage his paycheck. When he got paid on Saturday, he bought lunch for us and brought the rest of the money to Aunt Nellie for her to manage. As far as collateral was concerned, Uncle Winser had collateral. He owned his own house. But you know, he didn't have any idea what that term meant. And his friend knew that.

After asking Uncle Winser all those embarrassing questions, he dropped the bomb. "Winsler, the time is not right now for me to give you a loan, but if there is anything else I can do for you, just let me know." This can't be happening! I thought.

We left the bank. Neither one of us said anything on the way home. When we walked into the house, Aunt Nellie was sitting on the couch with her arms folded as she did when she was about to engage in deep conversation. Her body slowly rocked from side to side as she asked, "How did it go?"

I knew Uncle Winser's supposed to respond, but I couldn't hold it, "He didn't give us the money!" I screamed.

Aunt Nellie's Determination

Aunt Nellie was silent for what seemed like a couple of minutes, as she let my comment sink in. She tucked her folded arms even closer to her body as she continued to rock from side to side. Then she raised her head and said, "I don't' care what he said. You are still going to college in September." I was silent, stunned, and pleased to hear her comment. I didn't have any idea what she meant by that, but I had seen that expression of determination coming from her in the past, and I knew that if she said it then she meant it.

She had a solid faith in God. Her whole life had been one of faith. But the level of determination she displayed did not start with her. I know she had inherited it from our forefather, Green Patrick. It was in her DNA.

Green Patrick was my great, great grandfather. He was born a slave in 1833. I don't know a lot about him, but the things that I know can only cause me to conclude that he was a very determined man. I know from documents that he was born a slave. My interpretation of another document is that by the time he was twenty-five years old in 1858, he was already a free man. This was five years before President Lincoln emancipated the slaves. I also know from documentation that by 1890, he also owned his house and farm. I don't know what this means, but he also had a twenty-one year old servant living in his household in the 1890 census. None of his children at that time were living with him.

Everything I have been able to dig up about him causes me to conclude that he was a very determined man. I could see that in Aunt Nellie. So if she said you are going to college in

September, then I was going to college in September. I felt good again and excited that in September, I would be going to North Carolina A&T State University in Greensboro, North Carolina. Man, I couldn't wait!

I couldn't help thinking about why Uncle Winser's friend didn't give us the loan. I am sure that he had had time to think about it and how it would look to the all-White board members. And he felt that giving us a loan for me to attend a Black college wouldn't look good for him, especially when North Carolina A&T was having such a significant impact on the civil rights movement.

But Aunt Nellie's attitude was that no White man, whether he was the bank president or what, was going to stop her son from going to college. Even if it meant working her fingers to the bone to send me—and she did.

As for my biological mother, Christine, she meant well. I can't help thinking, she was only thirty-five years old. I'm sure what she said was true that the family had a financial problem, and she had to use the money she was saving for me to go to school. Whatever the case was, it didn't have a lasting impact on our relationship. The subject never came up again.

PART II

Off to College

It was the end of August 1968 and it's time for me to leave home for college. Aunt Nellie had kept her word, just as she had said, "You are going to college in September." There I was ready to leave home for college. A couple of days before leaving, I ran into a person who was in the class before me in high school. His name was Kelly, and he was attending North Carolina A&T. He was starting his sophomore year. He informed me that he and another A&T student would be leaving for school the next day and invited me to ride with them. He explained the advantage of getting there a day early and getting a jump on registration over other incoming freshmen who would be arriving that Sunday.

I took him up on his offer and went home and prepared to leave. I packed my bags that night and also went to say goodbye to Linda. The next morning just before my ride arrived, Aunt Nellie gave me a check for my tuition. It was happening. That check represented the first of many that I would receive every semester to pay my tuition.

Aunt Nellie worked in the sewing factory, sewing shirts. So she was able to save her paychecks for my tuition. I realized in later years just how fortunate I was. Uncle Winser was a carpenter, so he was working except during times of inclement weather. The exciting thing is that by government standards, we were poor. But we didn't see ourselves as such. We had plenty to eat, for example, so we never needed assistance from the government to buy food. Uncle Winser owned his house, because when he worked for Uncle John as a carpenter, they would come together on the weekend and work on his house until it was built. Some others lived in homes built that way also.

Aunt Nellie always maintained a garden in the back yard where she grew collards, cabbage, beans, beets, and other vegetables. During the summer, she canned peaches, pears, and apples. She also canned tomatoes, corn, beans, and other vegetables.

Uncle Winser and other men during the fall would buy hogs, and sometimes a cow, and they would butcher them, make sausage, pork chops, etc., divide the meat and put it in the deep freezer. The bottom line is that even if there were days during the winter when Uncle Winser could not work due to the weather, it did not impact our ability to eat.

God had blessed Uncle Winser and Aunt Nellie to have steady jobs and the motivation to prepare when money was scarce. Even though we were poor by government standards, there was nothing poor about our parent's attitudes, desires, or survival skills. In these areas, we were very rich.

North Carolina A&T—Scott Hall

We arrived at A&T in the early afternoon. I was able to register and get a room in Scott Hall. I was already familiar in so many ways with Scott Hall through my cousins Dick and Skip's stories concerning life living in Scott Hall. When Scott Hall was built in 1951, it claimed to be the largest dormitory in the South. It housed 1100 men, and was built in the shape of an "H". It was very easy to get lost if you were not familiar with its design. Living in Scott Hall was like living in a small town. Each section of the dorm had its personality and was like its own little community. Walking through the dorm allowed you to experience those different communities with their unique personalities. It was a real experience. At first, I didn't think I would ever get any sleep. It was full of joyful sounds of all kinds most of the time, ranging from brothers playing the dozens, loud sounds stemming from card games, loud music, poetry being recited, brothers singing, etc. There had been some very famous people who had lived there. People like Elvin Bethea, Rev. Jesse Jackson, the Greensboro Four, and many others had all been students who lived in Scott Hall. Now I was moving in. At the time, Winterville, the little town I was from, only had about 1500 people in the entire town. So Scott Hall had a population about the size of my home town. It took a little getting used to, but I quickly adapted.

The campus was tranquil that day because there was hardly anybody there. It had a huge campus. I had been on the campuses of North Carolina Central, Elizabeth City State, St. Augustine's College, and Duke University. Still, I had never been on the campus of North Carolina A&T. I was very impressed. Later that afternoon, I found myself wandering around campus just exploring. I got lost, but I wasn't the only new student lost.

I ran into another student as I made my way across campus "Hey, bro, do you know how to get to Scott Hall?" he greeted me.

"No," I said, "but I have to get back there, too." We introduced ourselves, and I found out that he was from Detroit. We found our way back to the dorm and continued talking most of the evening. We had a very long and strange conversation. He was from a big city, and I was from a tiny country town. The kinds of things he talked about were foreign to me. And I am sure the things I shared with him were unfamiliar to him also.

This was my first time being away from home to stay other than visiting my mother in New York. I realized I had not had dinner because the campus was still technically closed. I was able to find some vending machines to curb the hunger, but at the same time, I realized that I no longer had access to Aunt Nellie's kitchen and wouldn't have access to her kitchen for a long time. So there were no late-night snacks to be had.

The next morning when I saw all the new freshmen standing in line, I saw what advantage it had been for me to have arrived a day early. Things were not computerized in those times, so registration was all manual. And if any of your information was missing or not correct, you had a huge problem. The process was prolonged. Some people were in line most of the day. I saw Earl, Monia, and Rander in line and stopped to see how they were coming along. After all, I had been there for almost twenty-four hours now. I was an expert in somethings they hadn't had to deal with yet. Rander and Monia were roommates, and Earl and I roomed together.

Classes started a few days later, after we had gone through orientation. There were students from all over the country and from other parts of the world. This was a new experience for me. I remember I called home every night to talk to Aunt Nellie and update her on what was happening. I also called Linda occasionally. The long-distance costs started to add up, but Aunt Nellie didn't say anything then because she knew I needed to make the calls.

The following week, classes were in full session. One of the first things I learned from the very beginning was that everybody there was smart. I mean I had been fifth or sixth in my class at Robinson, but at A&T, everybody had been good students in high school. Additionally, many students studied from high school curricula more rigorous than what we had at Robinson. A less rigorous curriculum was not a reflection on our teachers, but on the school board, and the influence of Jim Crow.

Student Activism—SNCC

There were a lot of activities happening on campus. This was still the middle of the civil rights movement, and A&T was already playing a significant role in the movement. The Greensboro Four, who were A&T students, had started the sit-in movement. They sat in at the segregated Woolworth's lunch counter and refused to give up their seats before being served. This movement started on Feb 1, 1960. They did not get served the first day, so they remained seated until the store closed. The next day they returned with about 300 students from A&T and other colleges. They continued the sit-ins.

By the end of the next month, about a third of the entire country experienced sit-ins at lunch counters, other segregated dining, and public facilities. The movement continued to expand across the country. But by the end of the school year, the students still had not been served at the Woolworth lunch counter.

During the summer of 1960, Woolworth integrated its lunch counter by serving four of its black employees at the counter while school was out. Woolworth's action instantly caused dining facilities, lunch counters, and some other public facilities across the south to become desegregated.

Additionally, Greensboro's *sit-ins* inspired local Black students in North Carolina and other locations to form an organization they named SNCC. It stood for the Student Nonviolent Coordinating Committee (SNCC). Its organization was inspired by the nonviolent nature of the Greensboro Four at Woolworth's lunch counters. SNCC then evolved to become a leader in the civil rights movement. It planned and organized the freedom rides through the South. White and Black civil rights activists rode buses to protest segregation in Whites-only facilities, bus terminals, and lunch counters. Even though the Greensboro Four sit-ins resulted in the integration of lunch counters and other segregated facilities throughout the South, not all states honored their efforts. So, there were still segregated facilities in the South and a need for the sit-ins to continue. And they did.

SNCC also organized the March on Washington in 1963. This was when Dr. King gave his famous "I Have a Dream" speech. But probably most importantly, it worked with the SCLC to force the passage of the Civil Rights Act of 1964. It was the Civil Rights Act of 1964 that legally ended segregation in public facilities and also prohibited employment discrimination based on race, color, religion, sex, or national origin. I was fourteen at the time, and I remember us discussing this in school and its impact on us. There were strong and active members of SNCC at A&T, so there was always protest literature passed out and protest gatherings taking place, etc.

So being at A&T, I was right in the center of civil rights activity. It was taking place everywhere and every day. That was one of the things that made campus life so vibrant and alive. It was that way every day and all the time. A&T, it seemed, was the epicenter of the movement on college campuses. Some students were powerful orators of the cause. It appeared that they had been placed at A&T for that specific time. They were in tune with everything happening in the world related to Black people, from South Africa to America and around the world. The student activists kept us informed on the cruel conduct against Black people worldwide, particularly here in the United States. Whatever negative treatment Black people experienced, we knew about it and were made aware of the solution. I experienced so much activism at A&T that it seemed as if my reason for being there was to learn about activism. Rallies were taking place every afternoon somewhere on campus. And I attended as many as I could. Some nights there were guests to speak about our roles as Black students and responsibility to the cause.

Of course, I was not there to learn to become an activist. My major was Business Administration. But current events and all the activism speeches I was hearing and the rallies I was attending were having a significant impact on my impression of who I was. And I loved it. My attitude was changing after just a short while being at North Carolina A&T. But my new awareness of who I was conflicted with my reason for being there. I had gone through a period from the first to about the fifth grade when I had not worked up to my full potential. But in the fifth grade, I had become focused, studied hard, worked hard, and tried to maximize my learning potential. I had developed and maintained that attitude through high school and was able to graduate with honors.

Now I felt myself drifting back into that past attitude of not doing my best in school, or at least not seeing school as the absolute most crucial thing in my life, even though I felt it should have been. I couldn't have this attitude because Aunt Nellie and Uncle Winser were making major sacrifices for me to go to college. And there were other people I would disappoint if I didn't do well, like my teachers at Robinson, my relatives, and others. The new freedom I had at A&T was another major stumbling block for me. We had non-compulsory class attendance. As a freshman, I misinterpreted what that meant. I wasn't the only one. It didn't mean that you never had to go to class, but it meant that if you didn't attend class the instructor could not dock your overall grade for not being there. But the reality was that if you were going to do well in a class, then you needed to be in class.

When I arrived at A&T, the Vietnam War was in full force and there was a draft. Most young men my age were eligible to be drafted. But if you were in college, then you had a draft deferment. That was good as long as you made the necessary progress every semester to keep your deferment. Because the schools had to report your progress to the federal government every semester, and if you didn't make the necessary progress, you would lose your draft deferment and possibly get drafted and sent to Vietnam to fight in the war. That alone should have been enough to motivate anybody in college to study hard. There were anti-war protests on campus. This was true even though we had a strong ROTC program for both the Air Force and Army. The war was not a concept embraced by A&T students. Students understood the concept of young Black men going off to war in a foreign land to fight and kill people they didn't even know for a country that didn't even consider them true citizens. During my freshman year at A&T, I was in ROTC because it was mandatory for all freshmen men, unless you had prior military service. So, I was in Army ROTC during my freshman year. The requirement was changed to be noncompulsory after numerous student protests. Consequently, I only served in Army ROTC one year before the administration abandoned the requirement.

 There are genuine reasons why civil rights were such an integral part of life at A&T. There was the Greensboro Four, who were A&T students that I mentioned earlier. Still, there was also the Reverend Jesse Jackson, a graduate of N.C. A&T, who went to work with Dr. Martin Luther King immediately after graduation, fighting Jim Crow and advocating for civil rights in the United States. Rev. Jesse Jackson was an upcoming influential civil rights leader who would become the first serious Black presidential candidate and the leader of other powerful nonprofits, "Operation Push" and "The Rainbow Coalition."

Guest Lecturers

During my freshman year, some of the guest lecturers significantly influenced me. These were guest lecturers who used to come to campus to address the student body. Speakers like Stokely Carmichael would address the student body occasionally. I remember being just blown away by Stockley's message of "undying love." He would emphasize that if we had not found something we were willing to die for, we were wasting our lives. His message was that we should have been willing to die for the cause of Black people. That was a new way for me to look at life, and it had a major impact on me. I was not looking for something to die for, but it did make me feel like my life should be about more than just getting an education. I was confused. Stokely Carmichael was a tremendous, convincing orator and a young civil rights leader. He was not that much older than us. He had graduated from Howard University, another Black university, so he could relate well to Black college students.

When he addressed the student body in my freshman year, he had served as the national chairman of the Student Nonviolent Coordinating Committee (SNCC). He also had been given credit or blame; however, one would interpret it as having changed the philosophy and direction of SNCC. Before his leadership, the organization subscribed to a nonviolent philosophy as the SCLC and Dr. King did. But when Stokely took over, he changed the organization's focus to a more radical view. That view saw violence as a viable defense against attacks from the White public and the police. When he was serving as national chairman of SNCC, he coined the phrase, "Black Power."

So when he spoke to us at A&T, that slogan was just kicking off and placed fear into the hearts of those not in touch with what was happening in Black America. This included both Blacks and Whites. This message initially only resonated with young Black college students and then it spread to urban cities. But it was misunderstood by so many. It was a message primarily embraced by young people. What Stokely was attempting to do was teach Black Americans that we had to be more responsible and take control of our lives.

In hindsight, I see how he could have delivered the message differently and enjoyed broader support. But still, he got the attention of the world for a while focused on Black Power. Dr. King referred to the term Black Power as an "unfortunate choice of words." But in reality, even Dr. King's nonviolent philosophy and approach did not enjoy broad support from America. It was met by White America with the same opposition in most cases as Stokely's radical philosophy.

So here I was, a freshman at North Carolina A&T in 1968, one of the hot spots of the civil rights movement, and it was having a significant impact on me. I didn't realize how much at the time my attitude was undergoing a significant change. I was starting to look at life a lot different than just a few months earlier. Before entering A&T, I was simply excited about the possibility of going to college and getting an education. Now, I was also becoming more aware of the impact that Jim Crow was having on me and other African Americans, and it made me angry. I had a lot of questions. I was on a Black university campus with a lot of very smart students.

There had been lots of smart Black students who had graduated from A&T and other Black colleges. Why were we not experiencing the same level of success as a race as were other races? There was no reason other than the fact that there were complete and deliberate efforts to keep that from happening. Now to some, it would sound like a radical idea to raise that question. I mean, my attitude was changing because that question was now at the forefront of my mind. And the only answer I had was that it was simply due to racism.

It was easy for me and many other young people to understand Stokely's message of "Black Power." Congress passed the Civil Rights Act of 1964 and the Voting Rights Act of 1965, but neither of those bills at that time had made a major impact on the average African American's daily life. Now I am not saying that they were not needed, because they were. But I am saying that in 1968, there was a separate fight that Blacks had to be engaged. The battle was necessary to get White America to recognize and respond as if these bills were law. The situation was very similar to what had happened in 1864 with the passage of the Civil Rights Bill of 1864, when most Whites ignored that Congress passed the civil rights bill. So I took a lot from Stokely Carmichael's message to us. That was my first time hearing him speak, but I got to listen to him speak a couple of other times while there.

Later that year, in my first semester, I also got to attend a lecture on campus given by Dick Gregory. He had been a comedian turned civil rights advocate and was a frequent university lecturer. His delivery was much softer than Stokely because he integrated his message with humor. Once after being jailed in Birmingham for protesting, he wrote, "It was the first real beating I have ever had."

Dick Gregory was a very active civil rights worker in the middle of many of the important civil rights events working along with Dr. King. He talked a lot about those experiences during his speeches. His message was nonviolent but still pointed out injustices, police abuse, and African Americans' economic disparities. In other words, some of the same inequalities that we are fighting for today. But the important thing is that he did also have a message and he was a prominent lecturer on both Black and White college campuses.

Dick Gregory spoke for two hours in Selma to the public two days before the voter registration drive known as "Freedom Day" on October 7, 1963. He was instrumental in the search for the three civil rights workers who vanished in Philadelphia, Mississippi by offering a $25,000.00 reward for information. Hugh Helfner provided the cash. The reward did work, and the bodies were found about forty-four days later by the FBI.

He engaged in several hunger strikes to bring attention to issues. In 1963, he was jailed while fishing with the Nisqually nation in Washington in a protest fish-in. He was protesting their rights under a federal treaty to fish in the location he was fishing and using the fishing method they used. He was still jailed, but he went on a fast for six weeks before being released from jail.

He shared with the student audience at A&T his philosophical views of what we needed to overcome oppression. He was a firm supporter of Dr. King, and it came through as he spoke about his work with him.

Attitude Change

Like other students, he left a very strong and positive impression on me. Now I had two very different ideologies I was wrestling with, plus material I was reading that either supported or challenged both—one, a radical approach to achieving freedom, and another, a nonviolent method of achieving freedom and justice.

This is so important because, as I mentioned earlier, my views about life and my existence was heavily influenced by what I was hearing coming from these lectures at A&T on social issues and related materials I was reading. I should also add that local students spoke at times on different social issues that could be extremely convincing. For the most part, student messages were all very radical. Their messages were revolutionary because they expressed views that demanded freedom now at all costs. They did not subscribe to a nonviolent approach whereby they would be spit on, hit, kicked, water hosed, and beaten without fighting back.

This was the general attitude of most Black college students then. We loved and respected what Dr. King had done, but felt that things were simply moving too slow for the most part. An abandoning of the nonviolent approach started to occur around 1966 when Stokely Carmichael started to lead SNCC. I was still in high school then. Most Black college students quickly gave up on the idea of nonviolence. I had become one of those. It was not that I wanted to see anybody injured. But neither did I see any logic in it being necessary for me to be injured, or harmed just because I wanted to live as a free human being and to be treated equally. What was wrong with that?

Ironically, even though I was on a Black college campus, not all students held the same view. When some of these lecturers would visit campus to give speeches, it always sparked heated discussions in the dorm between those who would attend the events and those who didn't. Those who didn't participate in and didn't subscribe to any of the philosophies simply felt that education was the way and civil rights advocates for them were more entertainment than substance. In contrast, those of us who were always in attendance were looking for the answer in addition to education. We were searching for the right leader with the message of how we would get out of the mess or overcome it. After all, they had already killed Dr. King for promoting his nonviolent philosophy. Little did any of us know that the period we were living in then was actually the end of that phase of the civil rights movement. I will address that later in the second part of this book.

Many other visiting lecturers spoke to students at North Carolina A&T while I was there, and many of whom I was able to hear. Some of the well-known ones included James Farmer, Jesse Jackson, Louis Farakhan, and some others. There is no time to visit all of these nor to emphasize each of their personal philosophies. But the one thing I can say about them all is that they shared one thing in common no matter how different their perspectives were. They all wanted freedom for Black people in America and around the globe. But in general, they had different approaches to getting there. And as students, we also wanted freedom and opportunity.

But even so, my attitude was being influenced by all of these people and other students on campus. Later in graduate school, I would learn the psychology behind the attitude changes that were taking place for me. The real question was how these changes would impact me as a person. Was I becoming a better person, a better student, or was I just becoming an angry young Black man? Would this help me or hurt me? Only time would tell.

On-Campus Entertainment

A&T was and is known for its academics, but sports and entertainment were essential also. In the late sixties and early seventies, we got some of the best music ever created from some of the most creative artists. Because of A&T's reputation as a robust Black college, these artists all loved to perform at N.C. A&T. Whoever was hot at the time, performed at A&T. Even *Super Fly"* made a stop at A&T on the same day the movie previewed. He was at A&T's homecoming to be with his brother.

Weak Start Unapologetic Present

Whether the performer was Stevie Wonder, James Brown, Joe Tex, the Delfonics, Archie Bell and The Drells, Kool and the Gang, The Last Poets, Nina Simon, The Modulations, Mariam Makeba, Jerry Butler, the Moments, the Chilites, or any other big name act, they all visited and performed for us to help complete the Aggie experience. If they were hot, then they performed for the Aggies!

We also had a solid sports department. In my first year, the school was a member of the Central Intercollegiate Athletic Association (CIAA), an all-Black conference. This conference, organized in 1912, was one of the oldest conferences in the country. It included most Black colleges on the eastern seaboard. Basketball finals and conference championship games were played at the Greensboro Coliseum. This event was a huge party that lasted all week long. Students and alumni from all the schools returned for the championship games. A&T had buses going back and forth to and from the coliseum throughout the week of events.

Most people didn't come back to watch the games, but rather to party all week long. Students and alumni sparsely attended most of the games during the day, but the parties went very strong. All hotels in Greensboro and the surrounding areas were always sold out for this event. This was when the number of people who attended the CIAA's national championship actually exceeded the number of attendees of the Atlantic Coast Conference (ACC) National Championship. Both tournaments were held at the Greensboro Coliseum then, and the CIAA had greater attendance. I remember attending the games to watch some of the players on teams from some of the colleges we didn't play during the regular season. But we still heard about the teams and their star players via the Black media. This was an exciting time and a delightful experience. Don't forget the football season. A&T had a very competitive football team and excelled in other sports such as baseball, tennis, track and field.

Former members of the CIAA Conference formed the Mid Eastern Atlantic Conference (MEAC) in my second year. This split the CIAA because several of the strongest teams became part of the MEAC. The MEAC conference members no longer played the week-long national championship games that had been previously played in Greensboro. They were played in select cities of the participating teams, so the location changed annually.

Academics

So far in describing my experience attending North Carolina A&T State University, I have primarily talked about campus life that included activism and entertainment. But I would be remiss not to discuss A&T's academic standing as an educational institution. After all, that is the reason Aunt Nellie sent me there.

A&T was, at the time I attended, and still is, an excellent academic institution. It is among the best universities in the nation. I am not just saying that because it is my alma mater, but it has been receiving academic recognition in different areas for a very long time.. For starters, it is the largest Black university in the country. There are so many rankings and recognitions that take place that I will not attempt to discuss any of them here. But to show just how prominent of an educational institution North Carolina A&T is, I will simply refer to the list of rankings below. I am also posting below a shortlist of some notable alumni.

Rankings, Recognitions, & Prominent Alumni

- Number 1 public historically Black university (HBCU) in the nation, as well as the America's largest HBCU for the sixth consecutive year. (*U.S. News & World Report*)
- Number 1 producer of African American undergraduates in both Engineering and Agriculture and in masters degrees in mathematics and statistics (U.S. Dept. of Education)
- Number 1 producer of degrees awarded to African Americans in North Carolina.
- Number 2 public university in America for combining research and classroom teaching. (*Wall Street Journal*)
- Number 3 online M.B.A. in North Carolina. (Online M.B.A. Today)
- Number 11 best online school nationwide in STEM education for women. (Guide to Online Schools)
- Most affordable of North Carolina's top universities. A&T alumni earn more in average early career earnings than those of all but two other UNC campuses ($51,800). (*Money Magazine*'s *Best Colleges for Your Money 2019*)
- In the top 3 research universities in the UNC System for more than a decade.
- Recognized by the Department of Electronics, Computer, and Information Technology as having one of the top online graduate Information Technology programs. (*U.S. News & World Report*)

Prominent alumni include:

- U.S. Congresswoman Alma Adams (D-NC)
- Kevin Wilson, Jr., Academy Award-nominated filmmaker
- Tarik Cohen, Chicago Bears star
- Walter Hood, MacArthur Foundation "Genius Grant" winner and landscape architect
- Janice Bryant-Howroyd

- The Rev. Jesse Jackson Sr., civil rights activist
- Dr. Ronald E. McNair, NASA astronaut who perished in the 1986 space shuttle Challenger tragedy
- The A&T Four: Jibreel Khazan, Gen. Joseph McNeil, the late Franklin McCain and David Richmond
- Henry E. Frye, former North Carolina Supreme Court Chief Justice
- Terrence J, actor/producer
- Michael Regan, North Carolina Secretary of Environmental Quality
- Alvin Attles, vice president of Golden State Warriors, NBA Hall of Fame
- Retired Brig. Gen. Clara Leach Adams–Ender
- Elvin Bethea, 2003 NFL Hall of Fame
- Janice Bryant-Howroyd, founder and CEO of ActOne
- Willie Deese, former president, Merck Global Manufacturing Division
- Lt. Col. Paul "Loco" Cruz, U.S. Air Force
- Ronald Penny, North Carolina Secretary of Revenue
- Addie Whisenant, White House director of African American media under President Barack Obama
- Donna Scott James, president and managing director, Lardon Associates LLC
- Dmitri Stockton, president and CEO of GE Consumer Finance for Central and Eastern Europe
- Zonya Johnson, Broadway actor and singer
- Former U.S. Congressman Edolphus Towns (D-NY)
- Retired Brig. Gen. Jimmy E. McMillian

From the partial list above and the accomplishments from all the research conducted at the university, you can see why I stated earlier that one of the first things I learned about A&T life was that all the students were very smart, not just a few. My first semester was pretty strenuous. I did carry a full load but ended up dropping one class. That first semester did require many adjustments that I am not sure I can say I was willing to make then. There were so many other nonacademic events taking place that it seemed like I was always being distracted.

Thanksgiving Holiday

By now it was time to go home for Thanksgiving. I hadn't been home nor seen anybody from home other than A&T students from Winterville since August. Just a few days before Thanksgiving, we jumped on the Greyhound bus and took it to Greenville. That was about an all-day ride because it stopped at every little town along the way. And then, of course, we had to wait for the bus to unload and load passengers. It would have only taken us no more than two and a half hours by car because it was only about 160 miles.

My first time taking the bus home seemed like forever. I couldn't wait to see my family and Linda. I couldn't wait to sit down at Aunt Nellie's kitchen table and have dinner. I remember getting home just at about the same time that Uncle Winser got home from work that day. It was a cold fall afternoon, so we could sit down together just as we always had before I went away to college and have dinner. That was a day I will never forget. I had not seen my family since August, and it was now November. I remember everybody saying to me, "You look different." Nobody ever told me whether it meant to be a positive or negative comment, and I didn't ask. I'm not sure I wanted to know. And I guess I did look different. Because now I only wore dirty jeans and a coat, a bush jacket, and an unironed shirt or a sweatshirt. So I think I did look a lot different.

Before leaving home to attend college, I was known for wearing starched and pressed light brown or tan khakis, a stiffly starched shirt, and colorful alpaca sweaters. That was the style in that part of the country. And don't forget the cordovan shoes, tassel loafers, and the big apple hat. Aunt Nellie worked in the shirt factory so that she could buy shirts almost for nothing. I had so many shirts. I couldn't wear them all. And every weekend, she would starch, iron, and press my shirts for me to wear to school the following week. She kept me looking my best.

When everybody in the family said that I looked different, I could only assume they were not so crazy about my new look. But they were still happy to see me. Just as happy as I was to see them. You see, it didn't take me very long after getting to A&T to know that I couldn't wear starched khakis and shirts there. It would have cost a fortune, and I didn't have a penny. But that was not a problem because the way I was dressing was the way everybody on campus dressed. Wearing jeans and bell-bottoms was the college way of making an expression, looking black and carefree, and being cool. It took a while, but they got used to my new look. That was what they meant when they said I don't look the same.

After having dinner that night, I rushed over to Linda's house. We had not seen each other since late August. That night might have been when I started to accept for the first time that we would probably end up marrying. Up to that point, we were just going steady. But it had become much more than that. We were really in love. We were not the only ones who knew it. Everybody else in town knew it as well. When anybody in town saw either of us, they expected to see the other. If I weren't with

Linda, even the grownups would ask where she was. About four of us were couples dating since high school and were still dating each other then. All four couples ended up getting married and are still married today to each other. So when I saw Linda that night for the first time since August, she embraced me and said, "You look different." But she was pleased with my new look.

It was good to be home for a few days. We spent the next several days reacquainting ourselves with each other and me telling her all about North Carolina A&T, the fun thing there to do, homecoming week, and about college life in general. I told her about the activism, guest lectures like Stokely Carmichael, student rallies and protests, and all the entertainment. She was excited about it, too, and was looking forward to graduating from high school and going to college.

Sunday came much faster than I thought. Before I knew it, it was time to go back to school. I said goodbye to Linda, my family, and about midday on Sunday, I took the Greyhound bus back to Greensboro to finish up the rest of the first semester. I would spend most of my time upon returning, preparing for finals. Then after finishing my finals, I would be returning home again for the semester break.

Back at A&T, I completed my finals and prepared to return home for Christmas and the semester break. I was exhausted because I had gotten behind in a couple of classes with term papers and had to study for finals as well.

Christmas

It was just a few days before Christmas, and I had finished up the first semester. I felt a sense of relief and at the same time, a sense of increased stress and some guilt. I felt relief, obviously, because I had completed my first semester of college. But I felt guilty because I knew I had not worked up to my potential. And I knew Aunt Nellie was sacrificing for me to go to college. There was also the stress of knowing that if I didn't pass all my classes and complete a certain number of credits, I would lose my draft deferment and instantly become eligible for the draft. And again, the Vietnam War was in full force.

I had no way of knowing then, but later during that coming summer, I would be one of the people selected to serve as a pallbearer for a recent Robinson Union High School graduate, who would be killed in the war. His name was Josephus Daniels.

After packing up all my things, I took the Trailways bus to Greenville, North Carolina, which is about five miles from my hometown of Winterville.

Aunt Nellie met me at the station. She was thrilled to see me, even though it had only been about three weeks since she last saw me. She had noticed how thin I looked when I was home for Thanksgiving and couldn't wait to feed me until I had meat on my bones again. So she started to work on that right away by cooking my favorite meals. And I responded as she expected me to. I ate everything she put in front of me. I still didn't gain any weight, but I enjoyed trying.

The following day, as expected, Linda and I got together. Linda lived with her grandmother, so usually, it was pretty quiet there as it was at my house. At my home, there was just Jackie and Butch. Jackie talked nonstop but was always very pleasant and polite. She was the ideal little sister. (By the way, Jackie grew up to become a librarian at a local university.) Butch, on the other hand, was a handful, but most of the time, he was maneuvering what looked like hundreds of little plastic men over the floor playing make-believe funerals. He had a desire to be a mortician, and practically everything he did centered on that.

At Linda's grandmother Miss Ethel's, it was usually quiet also, for the most part. But during the holidays it got pretty busy. This was the time when her relatives from the North came back south for a holiday. There were two significant holidays when Black people, for the most part, came to visit. Those holidays were Christmas and the Fourth of July. They came home for Christmas because it was a time when older and most Black women baked every type of cake, pie, and desert one could dream of eating. Some started baking directly after Thanksgiving and would continue until Christmas Eve.

The men would barbecue whole hogs over a pit. They would dig a pit about three feet deep and about five feet long. Then they would fill the pit with slow smoking oak wood. They then lit the oak wood, placed a wire screen over the pit, cut the hog down the center to open it up, and placed it onto the wire. This process usually started on the afternoon before Christmas Eve and lasted all night long. About midday on Christmas Eve, they would take the hogs off the pit and end the barbecuing.

Uncle Winser would bring his portion home, take a sharpened hatchet, and chop the meat into very fine pieces before seasoning it with a special sauce he had prepared a few days before cooking the meat. It was delicious. This went along with the greens, cabbages, chicken, potato salad, cakes, pies, and other deserts Aunt Nellie had prepared.

Whatever the case is, there was nothing humanly possible to  keep Black people from the North from coming home for Christmas to eat that good food. Only in North Carolina could you get this type of barbecue. And the Black people from the North would remind us of that with every bite they took. The eating usually started on Christmas Eve and lasted the entire week. There were lots of eating and drinking for those who did drink and in general family parties. So many people came home from the North that it seemed like most cars in the Black neighborhood had out of state license tags.

It seemed like she had about a hundred cousins, uncles and aunts, who came home from the North for Christmas at Linda's house. Her cousins crowded the place, but still, it was always a very festive time. Uncle Winser would have cousins who came to eat and talk about their times growing up, etc. They would talk about the hard times, things I couldn't even comprehend. And when they would leave, believe me, their stomachs were full. I can still hear them saying as they were packing up in their cars, "Cousin Winser, we sure did enjoy ourselves, and we look forward to seeing you next Christmas."

And of course, somewhere in the mix of all of the eating, we exchanged gifts. Even with all that was going on, this Christmas had a little different feel for me. Because in the back of my mind were my grades. I could not get them off my mind. Whenever

Weak Start Unapologetic Present

I ran into any of the community's adults, they would ask how I was doing in school. I would always say, "I am doing very well in school." Aunt Nellie and Uncle Winser would just smile.

Meanwhile, I would rush to the post office every day looking for a letter with my grades. Finally, they came. All I will say is that I didn't fail anything. That gave some sense of relief because at least I would be maintaining my draft deferment. But by no stretch of the imagination was I pleased with my performance because I knew I could do a lot better, but didn't. In hindsight, I probably would have felt better even if I had failed a class if I knew I had worked hard but simply fell short. That wasn't the case. I had done just enough to get by. I wasn't proud of myself, but it was Christmas, so I focused my attention on the time I had remaining to celebrate the holidays. Linda and I spent all our time together. Usually, we were either at her grandmother's house, my house, or at some of our friend's houses.

Christmas break went fast, and I was back at North Carolina A&T, ready to begin the second semester. Shortly after being fully registered and classes started, Rander came back to the dorm one day excited about having been hired for a part-time job. He said they needed another person, so I applied and was hired. We worked on the swing shift from about three in the afternoon until about eleven pumping gas at a nearby gas station. Many of the customers were A&T students, so the manager also felt very comfortable hiring Earl for the graveyard shift from eleven until seven in the morning. So, for part of the week during the second semester, we were partially running a gas station. When we were there, the manager hardly ever showed up because he trusted that we would take good care of everything. Now I had some spending change I could use to buy a Boss Webster's baloney sandwich when I had those late-night hunger pains but didn't have access to Aunt Nellie's kitchen.

Lester Patrick

Boss Webster's Grill

Boss Webster's grill was just across Market St. from A&T on the Block. He was known throughout the country by past A&T students and others from the Greensboro area for his baloney sandwiches. Boss Webster was a tall, stout, Black man who wore a white apron and hat while he stood in front of a hot grill flipping quarter-inch-thick pieces of baloney. He would cut a slice of baloney about a quarter-inch thick, throw it on the grill next to sliced onions, a big slice of cheese, and two slices of white bread all on the grill next to each other. Once the baloney was ready, he would place the onions and cheese on the baloney, then scoop it up and place it all between the two pieces of bread. When you grabbed the sandwich with both hands, hot grease slowly dripped onto your clothes if you were not careful. So you had to be very careful handling and eating a Boss Webster baloney sandwich. It required a particular skill set you would acquire over time. There was a secret to it. You had to carefully take a couple of napkins and wrap them around the bottom of the sandwich. This would stop the hot grease from dripping on your clothes and onto the floor. And once you had successfully mastered that part of the experience, it was good eating, especially for a very late-night snack. Boss Webster's grill was always full of A&T students.

We started to work at the gas station, usually three nights per week. That usually included the weekend. And we did that the entire second semester. The first semester was packed with campus activities, and the second semester started the same way. The football season was over, but we were coming upon the second half of the basketball season. There were still a significant amount of protests and student activism taking place on campus. Then, of course, there were my classes. I was taking a full load again, and had learned from the first semester that it was always best to take a full load. This was in case I needed to drop a class for some reason. In my case, if I had to drop a class, I could still complete the required number of units to prevent losing my draft deferment.

Dudley High School in Unstable Condition

I remember sometime around March, I believe, that the cafeteria workers were looking to get a new contract and were starting a negotiation for higher wages with the contractor. Basically, from what I remember, as students, we were doing everything possible to support them in their efforts. There was even a period in which we did not eat in the cafeteria to support the workers. At one time, I remember community organizations setting up areas on campus with sandwiches and other snacks to assist us in not eating in the cafeteria. There were protests to support them, and the focus was on us helping them to obtain their goals of receiving higher wages. This, along with some other protesting that was going on, led to general unrest and uneasiness on campus.

Shortly after, around the first of May, a dispute started to evolve at one of the local Black high schools. I don't know what happened at the high school firsthand, just what I was told and have read about it. I know firsthand that N.C. A&T students came to the aid of local high school students from Dudley High School. I do remember rallies on campus to inform students of the Dudley High School situation. It would become known as the Greensboro Uprising. A crucial point is that the Greensboro Uprising included N.C. A&T and Dudley High School. With the situation starting at the high school.

The Dudley High School incident centered on school administrators not allowing a student at Dudley High to become president of the student government even though he had received the majority of the votes cast. His majority came from write-in votes. It seems that the school administrators would not agree to student Claude Barnes running for office because of his suspect involvement with the Black Panthers and other groups representing the Black Power Movement. Barnes was a student-athlete and an honor student. He was also president of his junior class. The students at Dudley had several demands that the administration was not willing then to concede to.

Even though the school administrators would not allow Barnes to run for office, over 600 students wrote his name in on their ballots, thereby giving him a six hundred to two hundred win over the person officially allowed to run for office. But still, school administrators would not let him take office. Because of being denied the opportunity to assume the office, Barnes and a few other students walked off-campus. They went to nearby N.C. A&T to seek support in the matter. Nelson Johnson ran for president of A&T's student body and won. He was a junior at N.C. A&T. Barnes and Johnson knew each other because Barnes had served as a youth leader in a nonprofit that Johnson had organized. The name of the organization was "Greensboro Association of Poor People." Its objective was to help poor Black city residents fight for better housing and jobs and against racial discrimination.

In response to Barnes' request for support from students, Nelson Johnson, president of the student body at N.C. A&T, attempted to help settle the dispute. He arranged a meeting with the principal of Dudley. The principal was African American, but the school board, like most other school boards in North Carolina then, were all White. He was unsuccessful in his efforts to bring about a resolution that was agreeable to both parties. Both the election and the meeting took place on May 2, 1969.

Response to the Disturbance by Local Officials

The following week, school administrators suspended three Dudley students for leaving campus. In support of them, several hundred students protested by also leaving campus. A&T students had been involved all along. But now, hundreds of students marched from the campus of A&T to join the students protesting at Dudley High School.

Whether intentional or not, the all-White school board sent the district's White public relations person to the school to deal with the situation that made things worse. This only served to escalate the students' and the community's belief that the all-White school board was removing the Black principal's official responsibilities to handle a situation that had arisen at an all-Black high school. So, community members themselves came together and sought a resolution but was unsuccessful.

By now, the situation had moved into the second week of May. On May 13, Nelson Johnson, N.C. A&T's student government president, and two others were charged and arrested for interfering with a public school's operations. His arrest didn't de-escalate the problem as the officials expected it would. It only made things worse. The Dudley students continued to picket their high school. The city police arrested seventeen Dudley students on May 19. The school was closed early that day, but the picketing and protests continued on May 20.

On May 21, students continued picketing outside the school while community members inside attempted with no success to resolve the situation. In the early afternoon, the number of protesters picketing the school reached over a hundred people. Police were already present and joined administrators in asking protesters to leave. But they would only agree to leave if the police agreed to leave. Both protesters and police left the school, but within fifteen minutes, the students had returned. They threw rocks at the school building breaking windows. This caused the police to return. When they returned, they were suited in riot gear and released tear gas to disperse the group. The school was closed for the remainder of the day.

Greater Participation from AT&T Students

Upon hearing about what was happening at Dudley High School, student leaders initiated a protest meeting to inform the general student body. This resulted in several hundred A&T students marching over to Dudley High School from the campus of North Carolina A&T to provide support. Some protesters threw rocks at the police and the school.

This marked a critical phase of this uprising. Had the city government leaders, school board, and the school administrators simply listened to the students and made some attempt to negotiate with them, then the problem probably could have been resolved at this point. Instead, they relied upon the police to resolve the problem. Something very similar to what we are accustomed to seeing today. The police's actions caused the activities to expand throughout the community surrounding the school. Now, rather than the protesters throwing rocks and bottles at the police only, they turned their attacks against any White person driving through that part of town. The police escalated the problem way beyond what it should have been, causing several people to be hurt at this phase of the fighting. There was gunfire all over the city. And as night set in, the mayor of Greensboro asked the governor to send in the North Carolina National Guard. The governor responded by initially sending about 150 soldiers. The mayor's action of requesting

Weak Start Unapologetic Present

soldiers added fuel to a fire that was already getting out of hand because the mere sight of jeeps and armored vehicles all over that part of the city only further escalated the situation. Let's not forget the impact that the arrest of Nelson Johnson, student body president of N.C. A&T, and several Dudley students, too, had on this uprising.

By now, the anger and frustration of students were about to peak. There was gunfire all over the city and especially in the area surrounding A&T's campus. We could hear the sound of gunfire very clearly from the dorms. The pungent smell of smoke fumes also filled the air. Somewhere around six o'clock that evening, a lot of A&T students walked up and down a portion of Market Street directly across the campus called "The Block." There were several small mom-and-pop stores located there. Some of them were grocery stores, beauty products, etc. One of the stores owned by an Italian man named Cid was among the group. I believe the name of his store was Cid's Groceries. But don't quote me on that. The other stores were all owned by Black people. This was the Jim Crow South, and some local Black youth felt that his store should not be there. They felt all the stores in the area should have been owned and operated by Blacks. Of course, that was not the right attitude and did not justify what was about to occur. I heard loud talking or discussions among Black youth concerning this. Shortly after, I observed scores of Black youth bombarding the store to loot and destroy it. When it was all over, the store had been completely destroyed.

Only a few of the many youths on the street that night participated in the store's looting. A couple of cars traveling through that area driven by Whites were stopped and turned over. They then threw rocks at any vehicle driven by a White person coming through that area. This, I am sure, resulted from years of

Lester Patrick

frustration and pent-up anger and had finally found a way to be released. Dr. King said, "A riot is the language of the unheard" He made that comment in a speech he called "The Other America". He continued in that speech to ask the question, "What is it that America has failed to hear?" Clearly, Dr. King was not condoning violence, nor do I. But the situation that was taking place resulted from so many young local youths feeling that they had no voice. The only way to get the attention of those in authority was to engage in this type of behavior, so they thought. This behavior again cannot be condoned for then nor today. But we all should be asking the same question today that Dr. King has posed, "What is it that America has failed to hear?" And like then, we all should be seeking ways to listen and hear these unheard voices. The situation had gotten way out of hand. Within a few minutes, the police were called in again, but there were not that many police who responded. I remember being surprised that so few police had shown up and thought this must be a trick. A few minutes passed, and most of the youth involved with the looting left the immediate area. Shortly after then, as I was walking with another A&T student, we ran into Monia coming towards us. We stopped for a few minutes to talk about what had just happened. We were standing a few doors from Cid's Grocery store that had been looted. There were no policemen visible then. It appeared they had left the area. Even the crowd of students had thinned. We slowly walked west down Market Street while continuing our discussion. Monia was to my left, next to the storefronts. Another A&T student was on my right, walking next to the street, and I was in the middle as we walked. Just as we approached the front of Cid's store, a ballpoint pen was lying directly in front of the door, but still on the sidewalk. Monia said, "Oh, a pen," and he reached down to pick it up. As soon as he touched it, three cops came out of nowhere, grabbed him, handcuffed him, and arrested him. There was nothing that we could do except watch. He had done absolutely nothing. Youth from around the city had looted the store. I don't believe that Monia was even on the Block when the store was looted. And the pen that he picked up was lying on the sidewalk.

We went back to the dorm and told other students what had happened. By this time the shooting had escalated, and it was starting to be dangerous walking around on campus or in the dorms. There were rumors then that White citizens were driving by campus and randomly shooting on campus. Student leaders called a student body meeting and updated us on what had taken place up to that point. They told us about the National Guard's presence in that part of the city, the Dudley High School situation. Several students spoke and gave their perspective of what had happened. The meeting ended somewhere around ten o'clock.

Once the meeting ended, many of us went directly to the Block on Market Street. We joined hundreds of local youths from the city. By then, Market Street was being patrolled by National Guardsmen in full riot uniform riding in jeeps. Shots rang out. According to the police, they came from one of the men's dorms. So, the mayor gave the police permission to fire back. This is when things got bad. Students scattered to try and take cover wherever they could. Some male students ran to the girls' dorms because they were closest to the Block and Market Street. Running at a brisk pace with several other students, I safely ran to Scott Hall where I lived. By now, it was somewhere between eleven-thirty and midnight. Even though we were just a week away from final exams, nobody appeared to have been trying to get any sleep so they could prepare to take early exams. There was simply too much fear and excitement to rest. The later it got, the worse the situation became.

Willie Grimes Murdered

It was unsafe to walk up and down the hallways in Scott Hall because it was the object of the police fire. I lived on the side of the dorm that was receiving a lot of the gunfire. We could hear the sound of machine-gun fire and the bullets hitting the walls. Nobody was safe, and it was a miracle that no more students were injured.

At around 12:30, I went down into the lobby of Scott Hall to see what was going on then. Shortly after, I found myself wondering out on the back steps leading into the lobby. The doors were all open, all lights were on, and a few students were standing on the steps. Maybe three or four of us stood there. This side of Scott Hall faced the student union, and my thought was that it was safe to stand in that spot.

About ten minutes later, Willie Grimes and two other students with him came rushing down the stairs past us. When he saw me sitting on the rail, he stopped and came back momentarily. "Hey, homeboy," he said, "I will bring your sneakers back tomorrow." I said, "OK, I will be here." He then rushed off with the other two students he was with. You see, several days before that night, Grimes had stopped by my room to ask if he could borrow my sneakers. He was on campus and wanted to play basketball but didn't have his sneakers on campus. Grimes lived off-campus and didn't want to go all the way home to get them, so he borrowed mine. When he came back to return them, I was not in my room.

About ten or fifteen minutes later, one of the students who were with him came rushing back to the dorm. I was still standing on the steps. He yelled, "Your homeboy was just shot". I asked what had happened. He proceeded to tell me that when they got on the other side of campus past the student union, cops were hiding in the dark. When the police identified themselves, they all started running back to Scott Hall. According to him, Willie Grimes stumbled and fell. He was just a few feet away from him, hiding in the dark himself from the police. But he was close enough to hear Willie Grimes say, "Please don't shoot me." According to the student, the police then shot him in the head and left. He then ran back to bring the news. Some students were taking him to the hospital then.

The word spread quickly that the police had shot Grimes. None of us knew at the time that he had died. Almost as quickly as the word spread, did the shooting also escalate! That night there was so much gunfire between shooters in Scott Hall and the police that it was dangerous for us to sleep in our beds. I laid on the floor until morning. Going to the bathroom or anywhere else required us to crawl on our knees and hands or risk being shot by a stray bullet if we stood up.

The next morning after taking a shower, Earl, Rander and I, as I recall, went over to the campus infirmary to check on Grimes. We assumed he had been taken there for treatment. We didn't know at that time that he had died. We asked the nurse on duty if we could see him. The nurse informed us that he was taken downtown. I am not sure if they took him to the infirmary first or not.

I remember going back to my room and just thinking about what on earth had happened. I was tired and worn out from the stress of not having any sleep, being fearful all night of possibly being shot, and very angry. Willie Grimes had been shot and killed for no apparent reason. He was a very nice individual and did not deserve what had happened to him. Grimes was also my cousin. More importantly, he wasn't protesting, nor agitating the police. If I recall correctly, he was trying to get home from campus. The police have given their account of what happened, but I believe the version from the student who heard him plead for his life.

I called home to talk to Aunt Nellie, but they had already been made aware of what had happened by the news. At that time, she told me that Uncle Simon would be coming to pick up my cousin Dick and me that day. Dick was a senior then. When I talked to her, the president had not formally dismissed school, but many parents had driven to campus to pick up their children. I did not make her aware of this at the time. I just said, "OK." But I knew then; I was not going to leave until I had to. I just couldn't do it. In the previous couple of days, I had seen so much injustice that I simply could not leave then. I felt a personal commitment to stay.

That experience was causing me to realize that even though it was going to be an enormous advantage to have a college degree, it was just as crucial for me to know what I stood for. I was now starting to understand what Stokely Carmichael meant when he talked about "undying love" and finding something you are willing to die for. I saw what was happening at A&T and what I was experiencing to be directly related to my newfound understanding of my freedom as a Black man or the lack of it, and my self-respect. I had found something that I was willing to die for. And it was with me all the time, but the timing wasn't right for me to understand it until then. So I didn't tell Aunt Nellie that I wasn't coming home then. I just knew I wasn't and would have to deal with it later.

Situation Becomes More Intense

It was now Thursday. Willie Grimes had only been dead since the early morning hour of about 1:00 AM, and the fighting

Weak Start Unapologetic Present

between students against police and the North Carolina National Guard had ceased temporarily. That is the way it was. The gunfire would occur all night, but as soon as it was daybreak, it stopped. I am sure that the Greensboro police and the National Guard did not want the general public to see just how brutal their attacks were against us. By stopping the gunfire at daybreak, they could cover many things up just as they did for the Willie Grimes murder. Even as students gave their version of the story, they could still be disputed by city officials, police, and the National Guard because the worst part of the battles were taking place at night when there were no media there.

That was one aspect of it. The other part was that officials were embarrassed for it to be revealed that they could not overtake Scott Hall, where most gunfire was coming from. That became obvious after the battles were all over because one of the excuses that the police used for not taking over Scott Hall earlier was that the shooters were veterans trained for war. A&T had both a very strong Airforce and Army ROTC. And one accusation released to the media was that students had broken into the armory on campus and taken guns. And that these guns were being used to fight the police and National Guard. That was not true. It is not my place to say where the guns came from, but I know that account wasn't correct.

During the battles, several national guardsmen and police were shot. There was one situation whereby several police had been pinned down on campus and could not leave due to gunfire. They had to be rescued by the National Guard. The fighting was fierce. Some students who were military veterans at A&T then, had seen military action in Vietnam. Some said it was just as bad as some of the battles they had seen or had been in.

Now just think about that for a moment. Let that sink in. Here are the Greensboro police and the North Carolina National

Guard attacking students at A&T as if we were foreign enemies! That is the reality of what was happening. I am not saying this to be the case, but even if a few students had done some things that maybe they should not have done, the way the officials handled it was about as irresponsible as any disturbance has ever been handled in this country. But I cannot include the A&T administrators in this irresponsible behavior because they were victims themselves. The governor did not inform or consult with Dr. Dowdy, Chancellor of North Carolina A&T, before making any moves on A&T. Officials responded just as if they didn't exist. This was indeed the Jim Crow south. And the government, from the governor to the mayor, responded as such.

By midday, the campus was filled with bumper to bumper cars of parents picking up their children, taxis picking up students for the bus, train, and airport to leave Greensboro. Later in the early afternoon, Dr. Dowdy declared school closed and canceled the final exams for the next week. President Dowdy canceled everything except senior graduation that was going to take place in the first week of June. I knew Uncle Simon would be coming later in the afternoon to pick up my cousin Dick, a senior, and me. But I knew I was not going home until I saw this thing out. I didn't quite know why, but for me personally, I felt like if I left early, I was giving in to the White supremacist government of Greensboro. I took this very personally. Every action they had taken to this point was one of White supremacy. It was no different than what was happening to Blacks in South Africa at the time. I guess you might say I had become more self-aware. All I knew then was that I could not give in to it. Even if I got injured by gunfire in the process, I was not going home yet. So I conveniently made myself unavailable when Uncle Simon came to pick us up. I didn't want to have to explain to them why I was not leaving. The fact that Dr. Dowdy canceled school did mean that I would have to leave by close of business the next day anyway, which was Friday. There were a few hundred other students who also did not leave that day. But most did.

That late afternoon, just before dark, I went to the cafeteria for dinner with another student. This had to be before dark, before the shooting began. Little did we know at that time that this would end up being the worst night of all.

That night around nine o'clock as I recall, the shooting started again. I don't know if the first shots came from students on campus or the National Guard, but once it started, there were times when it was pretty much constant. I could hear the sound of bullets hitting the sides of Scott Hall and in some cases, the shattering of windows. Some of these bullets were coming from a gun mounted on a tank and directed at Scott Hall. I was told later by students living in Cooper Hall that it was also under attack. But there was no question about the attack on Scott Hall because after all this was over, you could see the bullet holes in the sides of the outside walls.

I remember going back to my room and lying on the floor because it was not safe to sit or stand up after the shooting started—any trips to the bathroom I had to make by crawling on my hands and knees. Earl, my roommate and Rander, like so most others, had left and gone home.

I smoked cigarettes then and realized I was freshly out. I wanted to go to the room of another student who I knew smoked to get a cigarette, but he lived down the hallway and in another wing. That was a long crawl, but I had no choice if I wanted a cigarette. So I set out to get a cigarette and returned to my room the same way. There I took cover again on the floor as the gunfire continued. At the foot of my bed, between the closet door and my bed's foot, was a two-student desk. I realized I could sit on the floor between the foot of my bed and behind a desk chair and at least feel safe because it was not in direct line of sight with the window. My dorm room was on the south side of Scott Hall. This was the side that faced towards Market Street if you were walking from the Block. It also meant that police, National Guard, or just angry White citizens could enter the campus via some other streets adjacent to Market Street without actually coming through campus. So this side of the dorm was especially dangerous then.

Guardsmen Bombard AT&T's Campus

The shooting continued throughout the night. It was more intense than the previous two nights. But at day break, it stopped as always. At about 7:15, I crawled from under the side of my bed on the floor. I stood up and collected my toiletries so I could go to the bathroom and take a shower. It felt good to be able to stand upright.

I then took my shower and was standing at the sink grooming myself when I heard an announcement over the intercom from a student, "National Guards are going to take Scott Hall." I immediately grabbed my toiletry bag, wrapped my half robe around my body, and started out of the bathroom. But before I could get into the hallway, I could hear the shooting, and it was very close. When I stepped into the hallway, I could smell the strong choking odor of tear gas and see National Guardsmen coming towards me in gas masks, with rifles

Weak Start Unapologetic Present

pointing at me. Some were shooting the locks off of unopened doors, kicking down doors, and using their rifles to destroy anything that looked breakable.

They broke stereos, radios, televisions, and any other electronic devices and didn't leave a room until they had destroyed it. I was ushered down the stairs at rifle point in my half robe and with no top. I had to drop my toiletry bag to keep my hands raised in the air. When I got downstairs and outside, there were probably about fifty other students standing with their hands raised.

A formation of guardsmen stood single file facing Scott Hall, and another formation stood with their backs to Scott Hall and facing the other group of guardsmen. We stood at rifle point, with hands raised, in between the two formations. I could not see this then, but  they had, at the same time, also invaded Cooper Hall, the senior dorm. Cooper Hall is shown in the picture above. A helicopter filled the air with tear gas it dropped as it circled the area. An army tank with a mounted machine gun was also pointing at us as we stood between the two formations of guardsmen.

They were very tense, and it made for an extremely vulnerable situation. Because as they stood guard over us, other guardsmen were searching for guns inside the dorms. Even after the guardsmen had taken over the dorms, there were still a couple of gunshots that came from Scott Hall. I was afraid that it might kick off a round of firing as we stood between the two formations of guardsmen.

They were only able to find about ten rifles in the dorm. There were many speculations by the authorities as to what happened to the guns and why they couldn't find more. One account was that they were smuggled out an underground tunnel under the campus before the dorms were taken over. I cannot officially say what happened to the guns before they invaded Scott Hall because I don't know. But what I can say is that students had short-wave radio communication access and knew the police's whereabouts and the National Guardsmen during this uprising. I am sure that had a lot to do with the guns not being there when the National Guardsmen invaded the dorms.

Somewhere between four and five hours of standing outside bareback with just a half robe covering my bottom, I, along with the remaining students under guard in front of Scott Hall, were released to go back into the dorm so we could pack up and leave. So I did that. I got dressed, packed my things, and made my way to the bus station. I was outraged, tired, and emotionally distraught. Later that day, the mayor of Greensboro declared that they had successfully taken Scott Hall. To me and all other students, that was not exactly a victory worthy of bragging.

During this period, jeans were not fashionable except for college kids. I remember standing in line to get on the bus and this young adult lady saying to me, "Oh, you look so relaxed in your jeans." I said, "Thank you." If she only knew what I had been through over the previous three or four days and what was going through my mind, I am sure she would never have made the comment. But she was just referring to the relaxed look that jeans could give you. Looking back at the situations now, I am sure we all needed counseling.

On the Way to Winterville

Now I was on the Trailways bus and was on my way back home for the summer. I had officially finished my freshman year at North Carolina A&T State University. This was not exactly the way I had expected it would end. But it was 1969, I had changed, things around me had changed, and this was only the beginning.

After getting on the bus, it was full. I chose to take it still because now I was anxious about getting home. After a while, my thought was that there would be a seat available for me to sit down. We had traveled probably about half the trip stopping at every little town in North Carolina and some small places that weren't even towns just picking up people. It seemed like very few people were getting off. So there was never an empty seat. I was utterly exhausted from not sleeping over the last several days and hardly eating.

At about halfway the trip I woke up after having been taken off the bus and laid out along the side of the road. I had passed out and hit my head against a metal part of a seat, and had created a pretty deep gash over my eye that was gushing blood when I woke up. The bus driver asked, "Do you want to go to a hospital?"

"No," I said. "I want to go home."

"OK," he said. After giving me a bandage for the cut, we were on our way again.

I eventually arrived home. Aunt Nellie and Uncle Winser picked me up at the station and wanted to know why I had not come home with Uncle Simon. I tried to explain, but as I expected, they didn't understand. I then proceeded to tell them the whole story of what had happened and how the National Guardsmen had treated us, students and citizens. Aunt Nellie had been born in 1930 and Uncle Winser in 1914. So they both were very familiar with the Jim Crow ways. But even her and Uncle Winser couldn't understand why the governor, mayor, and National Guardsmen responded the way they had. They did not buy what some were reporting on the news, that students just wanted to get out of class early, so they started a riot.

Willie Grimes was a Robinson Union High School graduate, like Earl, Rander, Monia, myself, and two or three other A&T students. The following week, his funeral was held in the gym at Robinson Union. There were a lot of people in attendance, including a lot of students from N.C. A&T. He was a member of the "Pershing Rifles" fraternity. They were all in attendance as well and participated in the funeral. The entire town had the question of how a nice young man like Grimes could go off to college and just get killed for no reason. Those of us who were there had the same question but no answers.

Building upon a Lesson Learned

The following week, Uncle Charlie came over to the house and asked me what I would be doing during the summer. As you would have expected, my response was that I would be working in tobacco when it came time to do so. He told me that there were some vacancies where he worked, and he would advise me to apply. He worked at a factory that manufactured modular campers. The units were portable box-like campers that folded up and could be pulled behind a car or truck, whatever your preference was. Once you reached your camping destination,

Weak Start Unapologetic Present

you could open it back up. There were three different sizes. I believe the largest size would sleep three people.

The next day, I put in an application. Obviously, they did need people because they asked if I could start the next day. I said, "Yes," and I did. Along with Uncle Charlie, about five other Black men from Winterville worked at the plant, located about twelve miles from Winterville on highway 11. Four of them commuted together daily. I joined them the next morning. The work was very tedious and repetitive. It involved working on an assembly line creating the individual parts for the modular campers. At the very last stage, the individual components were assembled to create the camper. There must have been about fifty men working there, and no women. Around eight of them were Black, and all the rest were White. There was never any interaction, for the most part, between the White men and the Black men. During the breaks, the Black men had a little place outside the side door where they assembled for fifteen minutes and held brief conversations, and the White men assembled in multiple groups throughout the building. They both repeated the same format during lunch for thirty minutes.

There was a foreman that kept things going on track. He was a White man that stood about 6ft. 6in., and towered over most of the men. He had a thunderous voice, so when he asked a person to do anything, the entire plant heard it. This was true even with all the machinery running. I noticed the very first day the difference between how he addressed White men and the Black men who worked there. With the White men, he would simply tell them what he wanted to be done. But for the Black men, he spoke to them in an angry tone of voice. He spoke as if he had already asked them to do something, and they had done it wrong the first time. But from what I could see, that was never the case. When I observed this happening, the first thoughts that went through my mind were whether I was misinterpreting what I was seeing. I couldn't help asking myself if I was over sensitive in my way of thinking about this. Could the fact that I, less than two weeks before, just left an environment at N.C. A&T where, as a Black student, I had been shot at, tear-gassed, and just simply oppressed by White supremacist have something to do with my view of this? Or could it be just what I was seeing?

When I saw this happening, it took me back to a time two years before, when I was in high school. I had a part-time job in high school, working at a senior citizen's facility. My job was to get to the facility early in the morning and also in the afternoon to help the ones who needed help to the dining room, bathroom, and other places within the facility where they needed to go. I was also responsible for cutting the grass.

One Friday afternoon, I went to the facility to pick up my check. When I arrived, one of the African American women was standing by the rack where I had to pick up my check. She said, "Do you see the note on your check?"

"Yea," I said. "It says, my check is being docked eight dollars for the welcome mat that I cut."

"So what is your response?"

"My check has already been docked, so there is nothing I can do," I answered. We ended the conversation, and I left and went as I always would have done to cash my check.

When I got home, Aunt Nellie asked what happened at work. I said, "Nothing, but I got paid."

"Did you get all the money you were owed for the hours you worked?" she asked.

"No, because my check was docked for cutting the welcome mat."

"Did you cut the welcome mat?"

"No, I didn't'.

"Then you cannot just allow them to take your money for something you didn't do. If they don't correct your check, you have to quit," she said. I didn't want to quit, because this part-time job gave me some spending change. The woman who managed the place was adamant about me paying for the mat. So I had to quit my job.

My aunt Bell, Aunt Nellie's sister, also worked at this facility. So when she came to work, she was told about my check being docked for cutting the welcome mat. The women who worked there knew that I didn't cut the welcome mat because they saw the owner's husband cut it the week before when he cut the grass. So, Aunt Belle called Aunt Nellie to make sure that I dealt with it. That was a precious lesson for me. From that experience, I learned that my integrity and self-respect were much more valuable than the money I was making there. Because had it been left to me, I would have just ignored it and continued working as if nothing had happened.

Now I was a couple of years older, and listening to civil rights leaders discuss Black people's inequities. I had just experienced massive oppression by the national guard and government leaders in Greensboro. These experiences combined to add to the lesson that my aunts had taught me about speaking up for myself. After careful consideration about my observation of how the Black men were being treated, I made a decision. I decided that if the foreman approached me in the demeaning tone of voice he used towards the Black employees, I would not allow him to address me in that manner. I decided that I would be as polite as possible, but I would not let that happen.

Additionally, I decided to politely tell him that I didn't mind performing any of the job tasks he assigned me as long as he respectfully addressed me. But keep in mind this was still the

Jim Crow South. So I was not quite sure of how he would respond. But as a Black man, it was something I had to do. All of these things went through my mind.

Discussions with Willie Grimes' Father

The first day I was at work at the camper facility, I learned that Willie Grimes' father, Mr. Joseph Grimes, also worked at the facility. This was a surprise to me. Like all the other eight or so Black men who worked there, he assembled in a small group just outside the side door for break and lunch. I remember the very first break. He asked me what I knew about how his son Willie had died. I could feel the pain he showed as he waited for my response. It was a very, very difficult time for him. I wanted so badly to say something that could console him and could help him deal with the grief he was experiencing. But I could only tell him what I knew, which was not enough to help him understand what had happened. I relayed to him that I had seen Willie about ten minutes before he was shot. He had stopped momentarily to tell me that he would be bringing my sneakers back the following day. He was wearing my sneakers when the police killed him. I was not looking forward to getting them back after this happened, but I remember his younger brother George returning them to me one night during the summer.

I told Mr. Joseph Grimes what the student, who was with Willie when he had stopped to talk to me, had told me shortly after they had left. I told him that the student relayed that when they got over past the student union, where it was very dark, there were police hiding there. And when they saw them, they ran, but Willie stumbled and fell. I also told him that the person said he heard Willie beg the police not to shoot him, and then he heard the shot. That was not an easy thing to say to a father who had lost his son to this senseless shooting in just a few prior weeks. We had the opportunity to talk about it numerous times during the breaks and lunches while working there. But I was never able to tell him anything new. Neither was he ever satisfied with what I had said or with the information others had given him. I remember one day him saying, "I just don't understand how nobody can know the story of what happened." I also share that same concern, how could nobody not know the full story of what happened? Or how could the officials not accept the stories told by students about the police shooting Grimes?

After working at the camper facility for about three weeks, finally, the day came. Shortly after the afternoon break, as I worked in the area I had been assigned to work, the foreman came over to reassign me to another work area. He pointed his finger at a nearby location and yelled in a loud, angry, and demeaning tone of voice, "Move these items over there so they can be used!" I stopped what I was doing and gently said, "I don't mind moving the items, but I would prefer when you address me that you would not speak to me in such a harsh tone." His response in an equally loud, abusive, and demeaning way was, "You are fired, go punch out." I left the floor and punched out.

Meanwhile, I went to the car that we all commuted in to wait for the other four Black men. I sat there and tried to assess the situation. Was it wrong for me to demand to be treated with respect? Should I have done what I did after my uncle had given me an inside lead on the job? How would my action affect the other men? Could I have dealt with it differently? All these things went through my mind.

After about two hours, the other men came out of the shop because it was time to go home. At first, they were silent. Then one of them said, "I am so glad you stood up to him." Before I knew it, the other men, including my uncle Charlie, congratulated me for speaking up. Then I remember my uncle Charlie saying, "You don't have to take this because you are getting a college education." I thought, is it going to be that simple by just getting a college education, or will it become more complicated? I felt good by their responses and encouragement. The only thing was that quitting that job would result in me working during the summer in the hot, nasty, stinky, horrible tobacco fields. It was improbable, I was going to find another summer job out of the tobacco fields. But it wouldn't be that way forever.

So I did work that summer in the tobacco fields. The working conditions were just as horrible as always. But everybody else, for the most part, was doing the same thing, so that helped a little bit in dealing with it. But this was an unforgettable summer. Linda had graduated from high school and was expecting to go to college that fall also.

Internalized Racism and Oppression

This period for Black people was a very complicated one. Not only did we have to deal with the impact of Jim Crow brought on by White people. But there was also an impact of Jim Crow brought on by Black people who subconsciously practiced some of the negative behavior of Jim Crow against other Black people. This is so important to note here because, unfortunately, it was not uncommon for some Black people who lived under Jim Crow also to adopt some of the behavior of those who kept Jim Crow in place. This is not to say that Black people were not supportive of each other during these times, but merely recognizing the role that Jim Crow played in Black people subconsciously mistreating each other. It still happens today. Consequently, over time we would have to learn how not to routinely participate in such harmful behavior.

Weak Start Unapologetic Present

This situation was and still is too sensitive to cite a specific example. Because no Black person wants to be thought of as hurting other Black people, whether intentionally or unintentionally. But there were situations whereby some students didn't necessarily get the support and attention required to attend college. Many Black high school students of that time were the first in their families to graduate from high school prepared to attend college. Or even with the hope of attending college. Consequently, when students who fell into this category didn't get the support from their schools, then it was inevitable that they would experience a delay in attending college. Because after graduating from high school they usually had to figure it out on their own.

There were a couple of reasons for this situation. But one of them can be attributed to what some psychologists call internalized oppression. Internalized oppression is a concept whereby an oppressed group uses the methods of the oppressing group against themselves. In other words, they treat other members of their group poorly, in following with the pattern of mistreatment they experience or have been taught or have observed from the oppressing group. This is usually done without the oppressed group even realizing they are copying the oppressor's negative behavior.

It happens a lot in the Black community and also with other minority groups. It occurs when one group views itself as unequal to and not as valuable as the oppressing group. And that oppressed group has a strong desire to be more like the oppressing group by adopting the oppressing group's value system as much as possible. This was very common during the Jim Crow era because White people have always been the oppressor and Black people have always been the oppressed in the United States. Black people had not developed in the minds of

Lester Patrick

many a value system of their own. So they copied the behavior of Whites in certain circumstances. And a lot of that behavior could harm members of their own group. And in this case, other Blacks.

To be clear, we all were victims. It was not uncommon for school counselors of that time to primarily work with those students who they were told had people from their families who had gone to college or whose family members were likely to attend college. Some had developed an image of students who matched their ideas of a college student. If you didn't have that person in your past, then it was unlikely those in charge were going to spend any real-time working with you. Now there were exceptions, but that generally was the way it was. This was just one of the many areas of our lives where internalized oppression manifested itself as a result of Jim Crow.

The internalized oppression could also evolve into internalized racism. Internalized racism occurs when a group member knowingly or unknowingly takes racial action against a member of its own group. This happens when the targeted group has lost its identity. As Black people, we had no real official identity. Or an identity that was respected by society in general. We lost that when we were brought here from Africa as slaves. Members of the oppressed group who exercise discrimination against the ethnic group it belongs to are usually suffering from a lack of self-esteem. This happens when the person internalizes the oppressive prejudices and biases about the identity group to which he/she belongs. Most times the person is not even aware. I could say more about this, but I won't here. The point being made is simply, that this behavior was very prevalent during Jim Crow and is still present to some degree today.

We also see internalized oppression play out today through Black politicians, and in some cases, African American citizens who support political policies that can hurt them, their families, friends, and other African Americans. One specific example would be African Americans who support a party that openly pursues a policy to suppress the right to vote. African Americans have been fighting for the right to vote without any interference or intimidation since the 1800s. For whatever reason, some African Americans have joined forces with those who actively hinder our ability to vote. Those same African Americans have also joined forces with the same people to support policies that eliminate health care for millions of the poorest Americans. African Americans are disproportionately impacted negatively in both of these cases. These are the best examples I can cite of internalized oppression involving African Americans.

This is why it was so important for Black people to make a special effort to develop an identity of our own, not one that we were taught.

For example, "Black is beautiful" could not be copied from the White oppressor. It was something that was uniquely ours and that most of us could identify. We had been taught that black skin is not beautiful, and that only white skin is beautiful. This was the standard that was forced on us and that many Black people bought into before we understood how to exercise respect for ourselves. But when a SNCC leader introduced the "Black is beautiful" campaign, we started to see fewer Black people doing things like using skin lightening products to lighten their skin, Black men straightening their hair, etc. We began to embrace an Afro-centric look that included the Afro, braids, and African attire for males and females. We started to develop our own identity, and it is still evolving today. The lack of an identity strongly influenced Black people in authority significantly because negative behavior was simply passed down to the next generation to influence their attitudes about themselves. If no unique attempt had been made to break the cycle of negative and low self-esteem, then it would have just continued to repeat itself. To reemphasize, this was a major Black societal, cultural problem. Other ethnic groups also experience and deal with the same issues of internalized oppression and internalized racism.

Educational Redlining

Another problem that African Americans experienced during this Jim Crow era was one of "educational redlining." If it wasn't enough that Black people themselves participated in conduct that hurt each other during the Jim Crow era, things were further complicated by the federal government implementing discriminatory policies in Black communities when it came to distributing financial resources. This was done in the form of a practice called redlining. Redlining is a practice of denying financial funding to specific locations and communities based upon the race of the people living in those communities. It started with the Federal Housing Administration in 1934 to ensure that housing in America remained segregated. So banks and other agencies and lending institutions followed these guidelines. In this case, redlining focused on housing. But banks used the same maps that were drawn up to support redlining in the housing industry for the redlining of Blacks and other minorities for financial support to attend college.

This practice was at play when many African Americans graduated from high school in the sixties and seventies. This potentially influenced some counselor's behavior in their selection of the ones they chose to support in their pursuit of funds to attend college. Because of the redlining practice, there was only so much money available for Black students in any given area of the country to attend college. This influenced some Black counselor's behavior even without their awareness of the practice of redlining. They only knew that only so many Black students were going to get financial aid. They didn't know then what we know today about redlining. So they didn't even understand that this Jim Crow practice was influencing their negative behavior of other Black people. Educational redlining today continues. But in a different form. Today, the money is made available to Blacks for attending college, even to students from the country's redlined areas. The difference is that Black students are redlined by the college they attend. If you attend a Black college or university, your interest rate for your student aid will be higher for the same amount of money borrowed than if you attend a predominantly White college. Some studies show this. So these two conditions combined to contribute to a lot of African American students being delayed in, or not even attending college.

Returning to North Carolina A&T

I had spent the summer working in the tobacco fields and doing many of the same things I usually did during the summer. Only this summer, there was the memory I had about what had happened at A&T. I could not put the memory aside. If it started to drift from my mind momentarily, it was only a matter of time before I would run into somebody who would ask me, "Are you planning to go back to A&T in the fall? I would always say, "Yea." They would usually follow up with, "You don't think it's dangerous there?" and I would always respond with, "No, not really." The truth is, I was not afraid, and I was looking forward to it even more so than before my freshman year. This period of history was plagued by riots, protests, sit-ins, boycotts, and demonstrations. Some of which took place in both urban and rural settings. It was all designed to fight Jim Crow. But I was starting to realize that most of this activity was supported by and was largely the work of young Black college students. College students were at the center of the civil rights movement practically on a daily basis. This was true whether through direct participation, or through support of those who were leading the way. So I could understand why there were so many people thinking that I would consider not going back because civil rights were viewed differently by Black college students as opposed to Black citizens in general.

So when it was time for me to return to N.C. A&T, Linda also prepared to leave for New York in search of a job. She wasn't there very long before she found a very promising job. But her heart was set on attending a Black college and having the experience that most other young Black college students she knew were having. She intended to work one semester until she was prepared for college, but it turned out she worked two semesters and started college the following fall.

I returned to N.C. A&T as a sophomore. It was good to be back. I noticed several apparent things upon returning. The college maintenance crew had repaired most of the bullet holes on the outside walls of Scott Hall. But on the northeast side of the dorm, there were bullet holes that remained. I believe they were left there to remind students and the general public of what can happen when the United States government decides to attack its own citizens. Those bullet holes were there when I graduated. I am told they remained there until the dorm was replaced in 2004. All the dorm rooms had been repaired, and there was no sign of the damage the guardsmen had done. The second thing I noticed upon my return to A&T that fall was the absence of several students known to have been leaders on campus. There were rumors about several of them not being allowed to return and transferred to other colleges.

I registered with a full load but was unsure if I wanted to change my major. My sophomore year started out differently for obvious reasons. I was not a freshman this year as I was the year before, so I was familiar with the college routine for the most part. I didn't have the same roommate because Earl had decided not to return to A&T for his sophomore year. He had found a job in New York that he liked during the summer and had decided to stay there for the time being. My new roommate's name was Roy Harris. Roy was a very nice person and easy to get along with. I could not have asked for a better roommate. We roomed together in my sophomore and senior years. Our junior year, Roy decided to move off campus but moved back on campus for his senior year. During my junior year, I roomed with Eddy Shaw, another good person and good roommate.

Linda being in New York meant that we would have a long-distance relationship. To some degree, we had a long distance relationship in my freshman year because I was at A&T, and she was a senior in high school. But this was different because we both now were young adults. And there was a difference in the distances between Greensboro and New York as opposed to Winterville. So we did the best we could under the circumstances. We communicated via phone, and we saw each other during the holidays. On holidays, Linda would come home to Winterville, and we kept things going that way.

Meanwhile, college life at A&T was still very active. Many of the same kinds of things happened like in my freshman year, but without the National Guard invasion of campus. At the end of the year I went home for the summer. Linda also came home from New York so she could be prepared to start college at Livingstone College in Salisbury, North Carolina in the fall. Livingstone College was about forty miles from Greensboro. So we could see each other often. Sometimes she would come to A&T for special events like homecoming, etc. We had agreed that we would not get married or start a family until we both had a college degree. We had observed some young African American adult couples, who were a few years older than us, whereby both spouses had a college degree. It looked like they were doing pretty good to us, even for the Jim Crow period. That was a commitment we both were solidly in agreement on.

In the winter of 1972, I graduated from North Carolina A&T, with my B.A. Degree in Business Administration. The economy was in a major recession. After hanging around home for a while and not getting a job there, I moved to New York to live with my mother, stepfather, brother, and sister in Sheep's Head

Bay. After leaving college that spring to live with her mother and brothers, Linda also went to New York for the summer in Brooklyn. I found a job working for the city monitoring the activity of about thirty community centers to assess how the funds were being used and monitor children's attendance, etc. It was not exactly what I had spent four years in college to prepare for. So at the end of the summer, when Linda prepared to leave to go back to Livingstone College, I left New York and went back to Winterville. Shortly after being in Winterville, I enlisted in the United States Navy. The intent was to allow time to just pass for a couple of years until the recession was over. My life was about to change drastically. But that was OK, because I needed some real structure in my life at that time.

PART III

Being Sworn into the Navy

In October 1973, I traveled to Raleigh, North Carolina from Winterville to be sworn into the United States Navy. That was a real experience because I reached a point just before the swearing-in when I was wondering if I was doing the right thing. We were taken to the airport and put onto an airplane for Chicago later that day at about 4 PM. This was my first airplane ride. I remember trying not to let it show that I had never been on a plane, but the other guys with me made that problematic. None of us had been on an airplane before. And from the way they were behaving after a while everybody on the plane knew it also. They were yelling things like, "Look down. Do you see the little people looking like ants?" How can you ignore that? But I did until the captain announced that we were about to experience turbulence. At first, that didn't mean anything to me, but when the plane started to bump and rock, that got my attention. But we landed safely and were immediately taken to the Navy base at Great Lakes, Illinois.

Great Lakes Navy Base

When I left North Carolina, it was a very mild sunny and chilly fall day. But when I arrived at Great Lakes it was extremely cold. It was so cold I couldn't believe it. The first day I was there was spent getting a haircut, going through personnel processing, getting Navy issue clothing, and those things. I had a very nice Afro one minute, and the next minute I was utterly bald. Some of the White boys had very long hair and looked like hippies, but a minute later, were bald. Pretty soon, we all were completely bald. We took an incredible number of shots. Until that point, I thought there was a limit to the number of shots a person's body could safely handle simultaneously, but not the Navy. In two or three days, they gave me several shots everywhere there was a place I could be poked. I questioned the fact that they never even asked anybody, what shots they may have had before they joined the Navy. That wasn't important to them.

The later it got in the fall, the worse the weather got. Some days we got blizzards. We got thunder and lightning, snow, and high winds all at the same time. For the ones of us from North Carolina, it was unbelievable. Every morning they would wake us up with an announcement on the intercom saying something like, "It is 45 degrees below freezing in Fairfax, Alaska, but with wind chill factor, it is 60 degrees below freezing here at Great Lakes. Good morning". They did that to irritate us first thing in the morning.

Boot Camp

Boot camp began as a real experience. It was different from what I had envisioned. There were probably about a hundred recruits in the group I was in. Of that number, I think there might have been six or seven of us who were Black. Three of us were from the South, but the rest were from the North. Of the White recruits, almost all of them were from the Midwestern states and states that annexed Illinois. They were pretty accustomed to the weather, but the ones of us from the South were in shock.

The weather dictated the entire boot camp program. This period was during the Vietnam War, and the base was swarming with recruits. So there was never enough indoor space for the majority of us to do physical training. Consequently, the majority of the training took place inside the barracks and in classrooms

Weak Start Unapologetic Present

before lecturers. The only time we got to exercise was if we really messed up and was required to work off some demerits. Then we were sent after dinner to a gym for physical exercise or punishment— however, you viewed it. Most of us didn't view it as punishment, rather an opportunity to get a good workout and to get away from your company. Because other than that, there was no physical exercise, because outside you could get frostbitten quickly. This was the first time in my life that I gained weight because my physical activity was almost nonexistent. I mean, we woke up and had just a few minutes to use the bathroom, shave, make up our beds according to Navy standards, shower, get dressed, and get into formation to be marched to the cafeteria for breakfast. Once we had finished breakfast, we were then marched to a classroom for our daily eight-hour lecture. Of course, there were breaks for lunch, but in general we were in training all day long. We covered the Navy's history, Navy battles, ship types, safety aboard ship, and just a total Navy indoctrination.

We completely covered our faces and hands when we traveled to the cafeteria. The only thing exposed was our eyes. We were also able to volunteer to shovel snow for fifteen minutes at a time to keep the sidewalks clear and safe, but not more than fifteen minutes. I quickly learned that I was not able to shave every day. I developed a severe rash after a few days of shaving. After being sent to the doctor, the doctor wrote me a "no-shaving permit." So I didn't have to shave during boot camp and the rest of my stay in the Navy. So as a recruit, I had a beard. That wasn't so unusual for a sailor because you were permitted to wear a beard once out of boot camp, but it was uncommon for a recruit to wear a beard. The Navy culture was a bit difficult to get accustomed to. There was a Navy language, and much of it involved cursing. It was just routine. It was so much part of the communications that I overlooked that many times I was cursing while engaging in conversation. I guess that is where the phrase comes from, "cursing like a sailor." It was simply built into the regular communication of how you referenced things and relayed your thoughts to others. It was used in the classroom, conversations between sailors. It was just part of the Navy. I understand that the Navy has made special efforts to change that part of the culture in recent years, but when I was in, it was an integral part of the culture.

Another thing that is so important to mention here is that even though Jim Crow was legally over, Jim Crow practices were still alive. And as such, both Black recruits and White recruits had come from segregated environments. This was true no matter what part of the country you had come. Chances were your involvement with people other than your race had been very limited. We spent much time learning how to stay out of trouble and adapting to Navy life. So the first couple of weeks didn't lend itself to the opportunity for many conversations between us.

After that period was over, there was time in the barracks after class time for us to get to know each other. We learned early on that almost none of us had had personal interaction with members of the other race. Some of the White sailors even said they came from small towns or communities, whereby they had never seen a Black person in their town. Almost all of them had never talked to a Black person. All they knew about Black people was what they had seen on television for the most part. And believe me, that was not much because it was rare during Jim Crow to see a Black person on television.

After several weeks, we all became accustomed to the routine. And around the fourth or fifth week, we were given Saturday and Sunday off. That didn't mean that we could leave

Weak Start Unapologetic Present

the barracks, but we could do things that could be done in the barracks like watch television. We did have to still get into formation at certain times during the day to march to the cafeteria, our shoes had to be shined, etc., but we didn't have to go to class. And unless you had messed up somehow and had to work off some demerits, then you also would not be going to the gym. But we could write letters, prepare for Monday morning, and watch television. And this is when our one and only race relations conflict became apparent.

This was the fall of 1973. We had just come through a period whereby the only Black person that you would see on television was Bill Cosby in *I Spy*. I think it aired for around three years until 1968. Prior to that was always the *Little Rascals* with Buckwheat and Stymie. Then around 1968, the TV show *Julia* aired with Diahann Carol starring. But before then there was only *The Amos and Andy Show*. This show aired between 1951 and 1953, officially. It was so degrading to Black people that the NAACP led a boycott against it. The networks took it off the air for that reason. But when I grew up, the show was still being aired on the local networks in Winterville and Greenville because White people loved it. This degrading depiction of Black people was how many of them, with no interaction with Black people, developed their opinions about us. *The Amos and Andy Show* also helped them to be more comfortable with the reality of Jim Crow. And it enhanced their belief that helping to keep this system in place was necessary. And that they had to do their part to make sure that it happened. It was very damaging to us as a race of people. And equally detrimental to the progress of the country as a whole.

When I grew up, seeing Black people on television was so rare that if there was a Black person on TV, people would call each other in the community and say, "Turn to channel 7. There

Lester Patrick

is a Black person on TV!" Or they might just run next door or down the street to carry the message. But whatever the situation was, they wanted to make sure that everybody could see that person. Usually, the person would appear on a program like *The Ed Sullivan Show* on Sunday night. He was known for giving Black talent media exposure, allowing Black people to appear before a national audience. Had it not been for him, a lot of Black talent would probably never have been nationally known. But in 1971, a show named *Soul Train* aired for the first time. It would go on for over thirty years and was hosted by Don Cornelius. He filled the program with dance, the latest Black artists, and fashion. But before *Soul Train*, there were hardly any Black people on TV at all. So when it appeared with the combination of dance and music, it was an instant hit with most African Americans.

We were now in about our fifth week of boot camp. We were a group of young men who had come from at least two different backgrounds. Those two backgrounds being one that was predominately White and another that was predominately Black. Despite that, we got along very well. There had not been any conflicts between the two races. But now we were getting time off on the weekend, whereby we could socialize and watch TV together. One Saturday morning, about 11:00, as I recall about seven of us African Americans made our way to the TV room to watch *Soul Train*. When we entered the room, we noticed it was almost filled with White boys also getting comfortable to watch a hockey game. One of us asked for the remote control so he could find the program. But he got an instant response from a person standing near the TV that he and several others were about to watch a hockey game. This was the first opportunity that any of us had since being there to watch any TV at all. The African American recruit was not pleased because he had already checked the schedule and *Soul Train* would be coming on shortly. So he said, "But we planned earlier this morning to watch this program." The White boy said, "That's too bad because I am the one who has the remote control, and we are going to watch hockey." Things were starting to get tense because several other White recruits got up and stood in front of the TV with their backs to the TV as if they were going to block us from the TV. When they did that, all of us African American recruits stood and positioned ourselves in front of them.

Believe it or not, as stupid as it was, we were about to fight over the TV. Now we were vastly outnumbered, but at that point, it didn't matter to us. We were not going to back down from what we felt was our right to watch the program we desired to watch, and neither were they. Just as the conversations started to get loud, another recruit came into the room and observed what was happening. He said, "Hey, I want to watch hockey, too, but it's coming on again later on another channel. We can watch it then." Just like that, the mood changed. I looked around, and all I could see were dumb sailor expressions on everybody's faces. We all looked really, really dumb. So we watched *Soul Train*. And some of the White sailors watched it with us, and enjoyed it. The point here is that we were just moments from fighting. We were still in boot camp. There wouldn't have been any justifiable reason for keeping us in the Navy. If we couldn't get along with members of the opposite race in a boot camp environment, we definitely wouldn't have been able to do so on board a Navy ship or submarine. There is no doubt all of us would have been put out of the Navy with a bad conduct discharge for fighting.

Shortly after watching *Soul Train*, we all got into formation and made our way through the cold winter snow to the cafeteria. What could have been a very disastrous situation for all of us was de-escalated by just one level-headed thinking recruit. After this was over, everything returned to normal, and we never had any more conflicts between the races. I think we all learned a precious lesson that day. We should always look for ways to de-escalate the problem. Unfortunately, though, I would learn later once I was out of boot camp that some sailors in other parts of the world had not been quite as fortunate as we had been that day to have a level-headed person present when a conflict arose. Consequently, I would learn later that at least one race riot had occurred aboard a major aircraft carrier, and the ship had to be stopped in the middle of the Indian Ocean. For anybody who would not be familiar, aircraft carriers are ships that provide support for fighter jets to take off and land in the ocean on the ship's flight deck. Think of it as a traveling air force in the ocean, operated and supported by the Navy. If an aircraft carrier has to make an unscheduled stop in the ocean, it becomes a national security issue.

Boot camp continued for a few more weeks. But before its completion, a couple of times we were granted weekend passes to go to Milwaukee and Chicago for the day to party. At least all the partying we could get in before nine o'clock that evening because that was the curfew. It doesn't sound like much, but when you have been locked up for weeks in a barracks and get the chance to spend all day away from base you take advantage of it. So we did everything we could do without getting into trouble while still getting the bus back to base by nine because we were so close to graduating from boot camp. Most of us were discussing what we would be doing after graduation. Some would be going directly to a ship. Others would be going to Navy stations in the United States and some out of the country. But several of us would be leaving boot camp and going to school.

Weak Start Unapologetic Present

I remember talking about the school that I would be attending to some other recruits. I knew nothing about the school. Another recruit heard our discussion and interrupted by sharing that his father had attended that school. That was the school that he wanted but did not get selected because he didn't qualify. He emphasized he would continue applying until he got in because that was his career goal. He had been encouraged by what he knew of his father's work. His father loved it, and he knew he would also. I had no idea what the school involved. I had based my perception of it on the job title. The job title was "Radioman." I envisioned the job activities of people who handled walkie-talkie's, police dispatch systems, and that kind of thing. I had no concept of what it was. He tried to explain to me what was involved, but I didn't get it then. I had never even seen a ship except on television. So it was challenging for me to picture what he was trying to describe about the job. Nevertheless, it got my attention. You see, I didn't care at that point what the job involved, because I had joined the Navy temporarily until the recession was over. So my attitude was that I would do anything for twenty-four months until the economy improved. After all, I was getting paid, and it wasn't working in the tobacco fields. So I was happy for the time being.

To the best of my recollection, boot camp was about ten weeks. When it was over, each of us got orders to our next duty station. My next duty station was Radioman A School in Bainbridge, Maryland. But before reporting there, I had thirty days of leave that allowed me to go home. After graduating, we bid each other farewell, and most of us were on our way to the airport headed for home.

Linda was at Livingstone College and was a senior. Knowing that I was coming home, she came home and was there by the time I got there. It was good to see her. I remember her saying when she first saw me, "You gained weight." I had. Due to inactivity, most of the time, I had gained weight for the first time in my life. I had picked up about ten pounds, and she recognized it immediately. But even with all the eating I did after being back home and sitting at Aunt Nellie's table, I didn't keep the weight on. In just a few days, I had lost it, and I was back to my average size, about the same weight as I am today. I had gotten home after New Year. So Linda was home on semester break. That worked out well.

After thirty days, it was time for me to leave for Bainbridge, Maryland for Radioman A School.

Introduction to Technology

I arrived at Bainbridge, Maryland for Radioman A School. The base was out in the middle of nowhere. I mean there was nothing else there except a very small town nearby. I was assigned a room in the barracks where all students lived. As I recall, the rooms didn't even have doors on them. The campus had been a World War 2 base during the war and converted for use as the training center. There were quite a few students there, with each class being about a week ahead of the next. I attended my new class the following morning. Two of the people I was in boot camp with were also in the class. There were about twenty people in the class. Several people had come from other boot camp training centers like Orlando or San Diego.

The first morning was spent with the instructor giving us an overview of the entire curriculum with an emphasis on week one, which he was teaching. The program was a twelve-week program, as I recall, and usually, we got a different teacher for individual classes as we moved through the program. Some instructors did teach multiple classes.

Weak Start Unapologetic Present

We were given an overview of what we would be learning and how we would apply it once we had graduated. I quickly learned that my perception of what a radioman did had nothing to do with my original thoughts. The job had nothing to do with walkie-talkies, audio dispatching, etc. as I had visualized. This training had to do with the most sophisticated communications in use at the time. The entire program was twelve weeks long, and each week would become progressively more technical and challenging. The Navy dedicated the last three weeks to put the theory we would learn during the previous weeks into practice. The Navy called that three week period of the class, Prac Deck. We were in class eight hours each day, with fifteen or twenty-minute breaks in the morning and afternoons, and an hour lunch. Each Friday, we were tested on the material studied during the week, and every student was expected to make weekly progress. If you didn't pass the test you couldn't continue on until you had done so. We started with a very detailed look at what we would be qualified to do once we had graduated from school, the locations of our duty stations, and other related information. We then went directly into learning about the Navy's communications organization. The instructor introduced us to and covered communications security, and the handling of classified material, and related subject matter. Each of us was required to have a top-secret clearance. Some students were dropped because something came up in their background investigation that would prevent them from eventually getting a top-secret clearance.

Every day proceeded very much as the day before. There was a lot of studying and preparing for the following day and for the test on Friday. We continued with a different subject each week, with each week's course material building upon the previous week. We covered the message format in detail and learned the procedures for commercial traffic and distress communications. This is a very interesting part of the class because it covered the electronic message format used between the joint Army, Navy, and Air Force services. And it also covered the electronic format for the Navy. The military agencies needed to communicate with each other using electronic messages. These were the message formats used to do that. After World War II, an assessment of how the Navy traditionally patrolled the seas was made. Traditionally, Navy ships traveled together in given parts of the world patrolling the seas. After introducing nuclear weapons, the Navy determined that ships that traveled closely together posed a grave security risk to the country. These ships could be attacked all at once and greatly impede the country's ability to respond. This is where the importance of telecommunications emerged. By using telecommunications between ships afloat, all ships could have communications between themselves in dispersed locations in the world.

Telecommunications capability reduced the probability that one nuclear strike could disable several ships simultaneously. The method by which this communication was done was through electronic messaging over connections established using radio frequency transmission. In a nutshell, that is what this class was all about. It is worth noting here that it was around 1971 when the first commercial email message was transmitted. It was transmitted between four universities—Stanford, and three others. It was not transmitted over a radio frequency network like the one I was learning in training school, but over dedicated, connected telephone lines that connected the four universities. This effort was part of the ARPANET project sponsored by the federal government, which evolved into today's Internet.

Weak Start Unapologetic Present

Messages were created in 1973 using teletypes. Another device that was a component of the teletype was used to then transmit and receive the message. So naturally, we spent a significant amount of time becoming familiar with teletype procedures and the equipment. One of a radioman's primary duties was to handle messages, so a week was spent on covering traffic handling procedures. There was focus on the ten or so components of a communications center and the prescribed handling of messages for each area. Additionally, appropriate Navy publications of importance were also referenced where necessary. The next two weeks we covered more operational procedures and administration.

The next few weeks became very technical. We then covered antennas and radio wave propagation theory, emphasizing the characteristics of radio waves, frequency, wave length, wave polarization, and the effects of propagation waves. We also covered the details of several other aspects of antennas and radio wave propagation during the week. We covered the structure of the ionosphere, the stratosphere, and the troposphere and transmission conditions. The Department of Defense and the Navy in particular, were amongst the few organizations then using radio frequency communications. I will talk about this later, but the Navy was using radio frequency transmission to communicate with ships in the ocean, between ships and shore stations, and between shore stations.

Naval communications facilities were interconnected using radio transmission technology as the transmission method. This formed a private network between Navy entities. One way of thinking of this radio frequency network is by looking at today's Internet. Today's Internet is a public network that interconnects computers and servers using both wired and wireless connections. What I was being introduced to in 1973 in the

Navy with radio frequency transmission was an early application of wide-area wireless networking. Commercial connections such as those cited above with ARPANET used to connect the four university sites operated over wired connection. The Navy used wireless connections to connect ships afloat and shore stations via radio frequency waves, and wired connections to connect shore to shore Navy sites. The remaining weeks of the class consisted of learning about the actual equipment that made up shipboard communication aboard a ship and communications equipment at shore stations. We covered the operations of the equipment, maintenance, and specific required safety guidelines.

Before going into the Prac Deck section of the training, we had a week of typing to prepare us to become certified on typing. To perform the job of a radioman, we had to type at a high rate. My typing skills were nowhere near where I needed to be to certify. That part of the class was conducted as the previous weeks. We sat at a desk with headphones over our ears and typed audio messages that were transmitted to us by the instructor. So we sat there eight hours per day, typing each message as they were transmitted to us. At the end of the message, the instructor would say pass your paper to the front of the class, and then transmit more messages while he graded the paper you just turned in.

Towards the end of the day, he would select one of the tests we would pass forward to be used as the final test for that day. That test would determine whether you had qualified for typing certification or whether you would have to come back the next day. If you did not certify that day, then you were given one hour to have dinner, and then you had to report back to typing class until nine that night, continuing your attempt to certify. If you didn't certify during the extra hours, you were required to

Weak Start Unapologetic Present

return the following day. This was usually enough time for most people to certify. It took me all week long, day and night, but I was certified in time to move on to the next and final phase of training, which was Prac Deck.

Finally, the training program was completed with a three week exercise called Prac Deck. This was the most important part of the class, because up until this point, the class consisted solely of theory. On Prac Deck, we had to execute everything we had learned the previous ten weeks. Prac Deck was organized, set up, staffed and implemented just as a communication deck onboard a ship. So a section of the room we were in would be the "USS whatever" ship with all the appropriate communications equipment. Another room was set up as another ship. Then there was a room set up as a shore communications station. Again, each room was furnished with appropriate communications equipment, including transmitters, receivers, transceivers, patch panels, crypto equipment, monitoring and diagnostic equipment, oscilloscopes, amplifiers, attenuators, antennas, and other communications equipment.

Once the Prac Deck was initiated, it operated twenty-four hours, seven days per week. So each student was assigned to a ship and a shift. We worked each day according to our work schedule as we would if we were aboard ship. When we were not on Prac Deck we were expected to be either studying or sleeping. Prac Deck was fun, because it really was just like being at work on board a ship. The only difference was we were being observed by an instructor and was graded throughout the shift based on how we performed. Live traffic was transmitted over the network notifying us of a given frequency that the ship needed to be set up to receive traffic, etc., so we had to go through every step we would need to go through just the same as if we were aboard a ship. The majority of the points for the class came from Prac Deck. It didn't matter how well you had done in the theory portion of the class. If you failed Prac Deck, you would fail the class.

Charleston Navy Base

After completing this class, I received orders to go to Charleston, South Carolina to attend another school. About five of us were selected to attend. But first, I had thirty days' leave of absence to go home for rest and relaxation. So I went home first for thirty days. Linda would come home on the weekend, and we were able to spend time together.

This class was a class I would never have expected to have attended. It was a Morse-code class. Even then, the Morse code was outdated. But the Navy had ships afloat at all times, and it also had submarines afloat. There were certain war conditions whereby submarines could not communicate using traditional means, so it was necessary to use Morse code in those situations. Therefore even though the technology was very old, they needed Navy radiomen who could transmit and receive Morse code at high speed in case of emergency. The class was extremely difficult to complete. The Navy had established transmission and receive speed rates beyond most people's capability. The failure rate was very high. The success rate was so low that, as an incentive for passing the class, we were given our first choice of duty station anywhere in the world. All we had to do was complete the class.

On the downside, if you did not successfully complete the class, you were instantly given orders to a ship docked there in port. Every morning as I walked to class I could see people hanging over a ship chipping paint on the side of a ship about eight or ten stories high. They looked to be hanging on the side, dangling on the side of the ship. To me, that was all the incentive I needed. I knew I could not do that.

This class operated very much like the week-long typing class I went through in Bainbridge during Radioman A School. The instructor sat in front of the class at an elevated desk overlooking all the students. Meanwhile, students sat at a desk wearing headphones and listening to Morse code eight hours per day for three or more months. The instructor would say pass your papers forward because that was your test for that day. You were expected to make a certain amount of progress every week. If you had not made the necessary progress on Friday, then that same day at the end of the day before class was dismissed, you were given a set of orders with an assignment to a ship. This was significant because, in many cases, we would see that person on Monday morning hanging along the side of a ship chipping paint or painting the ship while hanging multiple stories up in the air in the hot sun. Wow. Again, I could not do that. But I saw this happen to several students because most students simply did not complete it successfully.

Hitchhiking to Charleston

Charleston was, for the most part, an excellent place to be. Unlike Bainbridge, there was something there to do. But additionally, I could jump on an Amtrak train on Friday afternoon and go home. So a lot of weekends I did that. The trip was about six hours one way. Over some time, it got me into more trouble than what I would have liked. The Amtrak train has a reputation for always being late. It didn't matter when you took it.

In most cases, it would be late. I usually took the train leaving Wilson near my home at about 10:30 p.m. on Sunday. When accounting for its late arrival in Wilson, it should have been arriving in Charleston at around 6:30 a.m. That should have been enough time for me to change my clothes and get to class. But in most cases, it just simply didn't get there on time. So on several occasions, I was late. But I could not be late again. The last time I was late, the chief told me that I would be put out of the class if it happened again. I thanked him for not putting me out of class, and I assured him I would not be late again.

The next Sunday night, when I got to Wilson, the Amtrak train left the station as I was being driven up. So obviously, I missed it. And that was the last train of the night. The next train to Charleston wouldn't arrive until the following day. I jumped in a taxi and asked the driver to catch up with the train at the next station. The next stop was about 20 miles away. He said, "No. I don't think I can catch it. Where are you going?" I told him I was going to Charleston. He said, "All I know to do to help you is, take you to the freeway, and maybe you can try hitchhiking." At first, that sounded crazy, but then I thought, what do I have to lose? The next train is not until tomorrow morning. I cannot be late again, or I will get put out of the class. So I said, "OK, take me there." The driver took me to the freeway, and I got out. It was pitch dark along the North Carolina interstate highway. I do mean pitch dark. I couldn't even see my hands. There was no light anywhere! No cars were passing on either side of the freeway. I don't recall which highway it was, but I couldn't see anything at all. I was wearing my dress blue sailor uniform that night for some reason. I stood there for about fifteen minutes, and still not one car passed by on either side of the freeway. And then I saw a car coming on the side of the highway I was standing on. With my right arm, I extended my hand and thumb to indicate I was hitchhiking. The car slowed up and slowly came to a stop shortly after it passed me. It then backed up to where I was standing, and the driver rolled down his window. "Where are you going, sailor?"

"Charleston," I said.

"Get in, I am not going to Charleston, but if you drive, you can drive yourself there. And wake me up when we get there."

"OK," I said and threw my bag in the back and jumped in, and started driving. The person who had stopped was a White sailor driving from Connecticut to Miami to reach his next duty station. He was stationed on a submarine and didn't have to be there for another week. So he had plenty of time. This was the only time I can remember when I had worn my uniform on my way back. It happened this time because I didn't have time to change before rushing to the Amtrak station. It is very likely that if I were not wearing my Navy uniform, the sailor would not have stopped to pick me up. This was still the Jim Crow South, and he would not have taken that chance.

Sometime around 6:30 that morning, we arrived on the Charleston Navy base. I woke the sailor up, thanked him for the ride, and he was on his way to Miami. I quickly rushed to my room, changed clothes, and got ready for class. That was a close call, but I had made it back on time. I remember saying I am not going home this weekend. I'll just stay here because it is too big of a risk. I just couldn't risk getting put out of class. So I didn't go home the next week. But the following weekend I did.

Jumping Off a Moving Amtrak Train

It had been two weeks since I had been home. I told Linda about my experience the last time I had come home. She thought what I had done was dangerous; me hitchhiking back to Charleston. At the time, I didn't agree with her. All I knew was that I had pulled it off and was looking forward to getting to the Amtrak station on time with the hope of getting back to base on time. The train came. I boarded and was able to get some sleep. At about six the next morning, I was waking up as we were pulling into Charleston. I was dosing as we were pulling in, but I could see the signs that read Charleston. About ten minutes later, I woke up and the train was moving. I had fallen back to sleep. The signs were still reading Charleston! I jumped up and asked the porter what was going on. He said, "We are now leaving Charleston."

"What! I have to get off here!" I said.

"I am sorry, but the only way you can get off this train is to jump off, because it won't stop again until it gets to Georgia," he said. I quickly thought about it, and made a split decision to jump. I grabbed my Navy bag, and I jumped off the train onto the tracks. Just as I moved off the tracks, another train was coming in the opposite direction and just missed me. I was bloody from the scratches I received on my legs, arms, hands, knees, and ankle. My clothes were torn practically off and my shoes were busted. But believe it or not, I was alive! At first, I couldn't believe it. As I got up to collect my scattered things everywhere, I could see this White man sitting on his houseboat fishing. He momentarily stood up with his fishing pole in his hand and just stared at me in shock. "Did they throw you off the train?" he asked.

"No. I jumped." Then as I limped over to where he was, I asked if I could use his phone to call a taxi to get to base on time.

"I don't have a phone, but I have a truck, and I can drive you to base," he replied. We were only about ten minutes away. So he came down off his boat and drove me to base. As we left the area, I could see that if I had waited a minute later to jump, I would have jumped directly into the water because we were in the "marshlands."

He rushed me to base. I had just enough time to take a shower and get to class. But I was still bleeding from some of the scratches on my hands and cuts on my arm. And by now, my ankle had swollen big, and I was having a problem walking. When we got into class attendance formation, the chief walked by to do a visual inspection to make sure we all were in full uniform with Navy jeans and belts on, with our names stenciled on our shirts, etc. He stopped in front of me and asked what had happened to me. I could hardly stand up, and my hand was still bleeding and throbbing from pain. "I had to jump off the train, or else I would have been late again," I told him.

"What!" he exclaimed. He then ordered two people to take me to sickbay for treatment. I was on crutches for a few days, but I didn't get put out of class. This time I really meant it. I was not going home again until I graduated from this class. I only had about three weeks left.

Selecting My Next Duty Station

The suite I lived in was a three-person suite, but only two of us lived there most of the time. Both of us were attending school. The suites were very much like college dormitories. If you took away the Navy uniforms and replaced them with street clothes, you couldn't tell the difference. And even with that, if you were to enter the barracks after regular working hours or on the weekend when sailors had their music blasting and were wearing their street clothes, you really couldn't tell the difference. I guess one difference would be the beer machines. Because in the barracks, rather than having soda machines, there were beer machines, which many sailors started their day. Other than that, there were no visual differences. So anyway, my roommate and I got along very well. He was a White sailor from the Midwest who spent most of his out of class time partying.

Lester Patrick

The Charleston Navy base was very busy. There were always people arriving for temporary duty for a few weeks, either waiting for their ships to come in, returning from overseas duty, or sometimes waiting for permanent room assignments. Because we had a vacant bed in our suite, sometimes a sailor would be assigned to our suite on a temporary basis. I was about at the end of my stay in Charleston, because I was very close to certifying. In order words, I knew I would certify within two or three weeks. So I had a huge decision to make. And that decision was, where in the world do I want my next duty station to be because the incentive for passing the class was that we got our first choice of duty station anywhere in the world.

We were not yet in the information age, where I could just google locations around the world and compare in order to make a decision. So in my search, I started to make frequent visits to the on-base library and bookstores to purchase and read tour guides of countries that interested me. But the best resource I had was from the sailors temporarily placed in our suite as the third person. For about a month, a Turkish officer was rooming with us. His whole conversation was all about Turkey. He almost convinced me to select Turkey as my next duty station. His best friend was a Greek Navy officer. The odd thing was that when he roomed with us, Greece and Turkey were in the middle of a conflict. And the United States was training officers in Charleston from both countries. Their countries were in conflict, but they were the best of friends. We all spent a lot of time together in our suites after class. And they both attempted convincing me to select their countries as my preferred duty station. After my Turkish roommate left, he was replaced for about a week with a person just returning from Haiti. I had never been to Haiti. I had never been outside of the country, but it didn't sound like a place I was interested in staying for a couple of years. But then our next roommate was a sailor, who was just returning from Morocco. I had never even heard of Morocco. But he explained to me it was in North Africa and couldn't stop talking about how much he loved it. His enthusiasm and expressive descriptions of life there really got my attention. I went to the library to research Morocco in the encyclopedia. The material was all very basic, but enough to further my interest. I also purchased a tour guide from Morocco and Spain. That was what sold me. It attracted me as a place I wanted to go and stay for a couple of years. So I requested my next duty station orders for anywhere in Morocco even though there were only two places I could be stationed there.

Graduating from School–Orders to Morocco

I successfully met both transmit and receive requirements for the class and was awarded a certificate and orders to Morocco. I immediately called Linda to inform her that I had graduated and had received orders to Morocco. I also brought to her attention that we were at a place we had talked about since high school when she was a sophomore, and I was a junior. We had agreed that we would not consider getting married until we both had graduated from college and had college degrees. I had already graduated from college, and Linda had just graduated that spring. She had just been hired by a new company in the accounting department. The company was in the process of moving to Greenville. She was one of the first to be hired, so she was getting in at a perfect time. We had stayed out of trouble and kept our agreement of not having children before being married. The timing was right. So I asked her if she would marry me. She said, "Yes. When?"

"What about next week?" I said. I can come home for the weekend, and we can get married on Monday." She agreed.

Getting Married

I arrived in Winterville on Thursday evening. We had a lot of work to do that Friday to be prepared to get married on Monday, but we were able to get it all done. Then on Monday evening, we had a small ceremony at Linda's house conducted by her pastor, Reverend Elliott. When the ceremony was over, I had to jump in a car and get to the Amtrak station to be back that next day for class. I had qualified, but I still had to stand formation for attendance.

Briefing for Morocco about Spies

Once I had received my orders to Morocco, I was required to attend indoctrination briefings. I don't recall how many days these briefings lasted. I just remember they lasted several days. I think there might have been three of us in the class. We all were going to duty stations in different parts of the world. The thing that we all had in common was that we were all radiomen. We all would be stationed in very politically sensitive locations and would be handling very security-sensitive materials. According to the person briefing us, by the time we would reach our duty stations, the Russians and other adversaries would already have a file on us. That was hard for me to believe. Why would the Russians care about me or want a file on me? The briefings walked us through the ways in which spies would approach us once we were there. We covered our responsibilities as American citizens and what our responses should be. They gave us warnings of what our behavior should be like and what would get us into trouble. Each of us would be stationed in Muslim countries. So we covered the things that we might do that could cause us to get into trouble, and things we could do that would offend the citizens of the country we were going to be living in. After several sessions of these briefings, I was starting to wonder if I had made the right decision selecting Morocco as my duty station. The sailor who had been my roommate for a couple of weeks didn't mention anything of these things. I mean, the thought of another country having a file on me, possibly being approached by spies, etc., didn't give me a warm fuzzy feeling. But it was too late now because in a few days I was going to be packing up my things, going home for thirty days, and then on my way to Morocco. I was very excited about being a newlywed and about getting orders to Morocco. I was looking forward to seeing my parents and my wife. About two days from then I packed up my things and returned home to start my month-long vacation before leaving for Morocco.

Returning Home Before Leaving for Morocco

I arrived home late in the afternoon. It was good to be home. This homecoming marked a significant milestone in my life. I had joined the Navy, gone through boot camp, gotten my first real exposure to technology by completing Radioman A School, and completed a very difficult Morse-code class. I had also gotten married and received orders to my first permanent duty station in a location that was my first choice. I had not planned this life for myself. I had thought I would finish A&T, Linda would finish Livingstone, we would get married and just live happily ever after right there in Winterville or somewhere in North Carolina. But that was not what God had planned for her or me. And I could see already that the way my life was starting to shape up was better than what I could have planned for myself. I would learn over the coming years that only God could have placed me in the location I was in at the time to allow me to gain the experience and exposure to technology that I would receive. There is no way I could have planned it myself.

Nothing much had changed at home. My parents and Linda were happy to see me, even though I was just there a couple of weeks prior. That made me feel good because they were all very proud of me. Not that they had not been proud of me before, but now I was starting to show them that the faith they had in me all along was not in vain. One big change that had taken place was that Linda had moved into my parent's house with my family. Aunt Nellie had really gained a new daughter. We were now all one big family.

Linda and I spent the month visiting friends, socializing, planning, and talking about Morocco. The time went very fast, and before I knew it, it was time to leave for my new duty station. So my family and Linda took me to Raleigh to the airport, and I boarded a plane to Morocco.

Arriving in Morocco

I arrived in Morocco at the Casablanca International Airport. Saying that it was a cultural shock would be stating it very, very mildly. As I walked through the door to enter the airport, on both sides of me as I walked down the corridor was a line of soldiers pointing machine guns directly at me. There were two sailors there from the base to meet me. Of course, they were not in uniform because the American uniforms could not be worn in Morocco. There were only a handful of Americans in the country, so we were pretty much invisible.

We left the airport, and I could see the city of Casablanca. It had a very mystic beauty about it. The whole country did. And a fragrance that you can only experience there. As we drove through the city, I could see a modern part of the city, and a medieval-looking part. They called that part of the city the "Medina." It consisted of the markets, very narrow streets, and white stone buildings without windows. People were everywhere, and this being an Arabic country, most people wore Arabic clothing that I was familiar with only through television.

Another thing that stood out was that this was a Muslim country, but one of the major exports— whether legal or not, I don't know—was "hashish." The odor of hashish was all over the country. I think this was one of the things I had been briefed about in Charleston.

Casablanca is about fifty miles from the capital city of Rabat. The view between Casablanca and Rabat was breathtaking. And the view was equally beautiful between Rabat to Kenitra.

The countryside in many areas looked like we had stepped back into time by thousands of years. Morocco was in history one of the areas that were conquered by the Roman Empire. So on our way to Kenitra, we passed several abandoned Roman ruins. I would take the opportunity later to come back and visit them up close. Between Rabat and Kenitra is a place called Sidi Bouknadel. This is a small town where I would be working. It is about eight miles from Kenitra.

Once we reached Kenitra, I was assigned a temporary room for a couple of days on the Moroccan Air Force base. It was Sunday, and nothing on base was open except the Navy barrack, which was not very large. There were not very many Americans stationed there. Morocco indeed was as mysterious-looking as the tour guides had described it. To grab a quick bite to eat, a couple of sailors took me to a takeout grill to purchase a Moroccan brochette. This sandwich consisted of very freshly cooked, delicious French bread, hot onions, mustard, and shredded horse meat, with some Moroccan French fries. Moroccan French fries were excellent. They came in a small paper-wrapped cup-like holder with a touch of vinegar and a sprinkle of salt. The meat was very spicy but good. This grill became a frequent stop of mine.

Sidi Bouknadel Morocco

The next morning I was shown where to catch the bus to Sidi Bouknadel, where I would be working. The small town of Sidi Bouknadel was just outside of Kenitra, about eight miles. But the Navy Radio Transmitting

Facility was a little further. The bus bypassed Sidi Bouknadel, and after two or three miles, we made a left turn onto a very narrow paved desert road.

From the bus I could see Moroccan nomads herding sheep in the fields of the desert. It looked like a scene from thousands of years ago, or like pictures you might see in the Bible. Men stood in long robes (called *jillaba*) touching the ground, watching over sheep as they grazed. Some leaned on long sticks about their same heights for support. When the sheep had eaten all the grass in their area, they moved on to another location.

Navy Radio Transmitting Facility, Morocco

Once on this road, we traveled about five miles into the desert before making another left turn. After making that left turn, we were on the premises of the United States Navy Radio Transmitting Facility. There was no sign or anything to indicate we had arrived. This was the home of about fifteen married families, ten or twelve Marines, and about ten sailors. The married people had a section of houses to the left just as we entered the gate. About a thousand feet further was the Navy and Marine barracks. Sailors lived on one side of the barracks, and Marines lived on the other side. The Navy club or bar and a tiny convenience store were between the family housing area and the barrack. To the left of the barracks was a very small cafeteria for the single sailors and Marines. Down a little further was a garage where the military vehicles were housed and repaired when necessary.

I should add there were no children on the base. The people living there were utterly isolated out there!

Continuing straight on the same street for about two miles was the Radio Transmitting Facility. You couldn't miss it. It could be seen as soon as you passed the housing area. The building was a huge white concrete building further in the desert. It was the only one there, and it stood out. It was in the middle of the desert with just a few desert weeds or plants covering the terrain. But a couple hundred yards from the building was the antenna field that surrounded the building. It was populated with a group of 800 -feet antennas mounted on very large steel stands. After I started working, I would learn that I would be electronically manipulating the antennas to rotate them into specific positions for the best transmission efficiency to ships in the ocean as I set up networking capabilities for them.

But further on the same street facing us was the large white solid concrete building. A guard neatly dressed in full uniform Marine, stood at the gate before we approached the Radio Transmitting Facility. He checked our ID and waved us in. Later after the Marines learned who I was, I didn't need even to stop unless I wanted to talk. Directly in front of us was the building.

It was secured by a very large steel door that made a thundering sound when opened and closed. But during the day, it was unlocked. About a hundred feet from the front door was another door that led to the floor of the Radio Transmitting Facility. This is where the console room was. This door was also a very large, heavy steel door that could only be opened with a combination. No combination, no entry. Whenever it opened or closed, the sound of it could be heard throughout the entire building. This was even over the noise of all the transmitters on the deck. A thick layer of glass enclosed the console room.

From the console room we could see out onto the deck where most of the equipment was located. A door from the console room provided access to the deck. All the radio transmitters, and transceivers were located on the deck. The diagnostic and monitoring equipment, patch panels, teletypes, crypto equipment, etc. were located inside the console room. The setup was extremely impressive. It looked like something from a science fiction movie. And there I was about to start working in that environment. And by the way, we could not wear military clothing in Morocco other than on the base. So if you commuted as I did, you had to bring your Navy clothes and put them on once you were at the facility. Then you had to change back into civilian clothing before leaving for home. We all received a monthly civilian clothing allowance.

Additionally, we were not allowed to fly the American flag anywhere on base. And that meant nowhere in the country. We could not make any display of anything American. So your bumper sticker that said "Sailors have more fun" had to be removed if you had one.

A Secret Duty Station

A bizarre thing had happened that captured my attention when I arrived in Morocco as I was being driven to Kenitra. After the two sailors had picked me up, we were just leaving the Casablanca airport when one of them said, "I hear you will be stationed at the secret location at Sidi Bouknadel."

"Well, I will be at the Radio Transmitting Facility," I answered.

"I know, you can't talk about it," he said. And then we moved to another conversation. I wanted to talk about the country and what I was seeing at the time. But the truth is, I had no idea of what he meant about a secret base. But I learned later that it was a secret site. It was so secret that the U.S. Congress didn't even know that it was there and operational. They thought the facility was located in Rota, Spain.

This takes much time to explain, so what I am doing here is giving a brief description of what happened when the Senate learned about this base. I am also posting directly below this general explanation in the two pages immediately following this explanation, a copy of the original article published in *New York Times* in July 1970, for anybody who wants to know more about how this situation evolved.

First of all, there had been an air force base located in Kenitra. But there had also been a Communication Station in the country. The United States was supposed to have withdrawn military personnel and closed all bases in Morocco in 1963. They did close the Air Force base, and it was turned over to the Moroccans. But the Communications Centers that were established and operated by the Navy were not closed. Congress was told that it was closed and moved to Rota, Spain. There was a receiver site that was opened up in Rota, Spain, but the site in Sidi Yahya was never closed. Congress learned in 1970 that it had not been closed. This is pointed out in the article below. But the interesting thing is, there is no mention of Sidi Bouknadle. For Sidi Yahya to operate it had to have a Radio Transmitting Facility within approximately fifty miles. That is where Bouknadale came in because it was the Radio Transmitting Facility. In 1963, the Pentagon was supposed to close down the communications bases, but instead, they entered into a secret agreement with the Moroccan government to keep the communications centers open. But at the same time, they opened up a Receiver Site in Rota, Spain.

So when I arrived, about three years after Congress had learned that the bases existed, the Radio Transmitting Facility at Bouknadle was still in that agreement with King Hassan II.

To make things even more complicated, when officials from the Pentagon testified before the Senate Foreign Relations Committee, the Department of Defense would not answer specific questions relative to the two communications centers. They feared that King Hassan II would demand that the bases be closed if it was made public that the United States had bases there. So in a nutshell, for that reason, it was a secret that we were there. And we had to be invisible. We could not get into any trouble. The Navy issued me a diplomatic passport that I was required to keep with me at all times. And under no circumstances could I wear any Navy clothing off base or display anything else that would even link me to the Navy.

The federal government also granted a top-secret clearance that was necessary for me to perform the duties of my job. Later I was awarded a "special category top-secret clearance." Not everyone gets one of those.

Senate Unit Finds U.S. Has Secret Base In Morocco for Navy Communications

By John W. Finney Special to the New York Times
July 28, 1970

> See the article in its original context from
> July 28, 1970, Page 4

About the Archive

This is a digitized version of an article from The Times's print archive, before the start of online publication in 1996. To preserve these articles as they originally appeared, The Times does not alter, edit or update them.

Lester Patrick

Occasionally the digitization process introduces transcription errors or other problems; we are continuing to work to improve these archived versions.

WASHINGTON, July 27—A Senate Foreign Relations subcommittee has discovered that when the United States withdrew its military forces from bases in Morocco in 1963 it entered into a private arrangement with the Moroccan Government to retain a large naval communications center.

Meanwhile, according to testimony received by the subcommittee, the Pentagon, anticipating loss of the Moroccan base constructed duplicate communications facilities at Rota, in Spain. Both communications centers have remained in operation, although Senate testimony indicates that they are performing essentially the same mission.

The existence of a communications center at Rota, a large naval base for Polaris Submarines, is openly acknowledged by the Pentagon. But the communications center in Morocco, at Sidi Yahya, some 50 miles northeast of Rabat has been kept secret by the Pentagon and the State Department for seven years as part of an understanding with the Moroccan Government.

Defense Department spokes men refused today to answer questions about the Sidi Yahya base or even to confirm its existence. The Pentagon referred inquiries to the State Department, which in turn re fused to discuss the base because of what a spokesman described as the sensitivity of the arrangements with the Moroccan Government.

While neither the State nor the Defense Department would comment formally, officials whom would agree to be identified only is "official sources acknowledged that the Navy was operating a communications center at Sidi Yahya. These sources said agreement to operate

Weak Start Unapologetic Present

the communications station was reached by the two Governments in 1963 when the United States was closing its bases in Morocco.

The base arrangements were discussed in closed-door testimony taken last week by the Subcommittee on Foreign. Commitments, headed by Senator Stuart Symington, Democrat of Missouri. The outlines of the testimony on the Moroccan base were provided by a sub committee member in an interview.

Now that the United States has been compelled to leave Wheelus Air Force Base in Libya, the Sidi Yahya communications center is the last remaining American military base in North Africa. According to State Department officials, this contributes to the "sensitivity" of the issue.

If public attention is drawn to the American military presence at Sidi Yahya, these officials explained, It might embarrass King Hassan II of Morocco, who is regarded as a moderate in the Arab world. The Pentagon was said to be fearful that publicity might provoke the Moroccan Government to demand American withdraw al, just as the new military Government of Libya recently demanded that the Air Force shut its large base at Wheelus.

Fulbright Critical

Members of the Senate Foreign Relations Committee, including Senator J. W. Fulbright, the chairman, maintain that the Administration has made no attempt to inform Congress on the nature of the secret arrangements it may have entered into with the Moroccan Government. The voluminous State and Defense Department "justification" document for the military aid program, for ex ample, contains no mention of the communications base in Morocco.

During the subcommittee investigation, it was established that the United States main tains major military bases in three countries with which it has no military treaties. They are Morocco, Spain and Ethiopia. In Ethiopia there is a communications center somewhat larger than the one in Morocco.

The maintenance of the communications base at Sidi Yahya apparently dates from an agreement reached between President John F. Kennedy and King Hassan in March, 1963. In a communique issued after a meeting with the Moroccan King, President Kennedy declared that evacuation of the American bases in Morocco "would take place" as provided for in a 1959 agreement between President Eisenhower and King Mohammed V. who was succeeded on his death in 1961 by Hassan, his son.

Big Base Complex Closed

The 1959 agreement provided for withdrawal of all American forces from Morocco by the end of 1963 and the closing down of the $400-million complex of bases that had been built to handle Air Force strategic bombers as well as Navy planes at a naval base at Kenitra.

At the time the 1963 communiqué was issued, there were suggestions by "informed sources" that some Americans might remain behind to train Moroccan forces in the use of the bases and equipment. According to Senate sources, this "training mission" was part of the "cover story" to conceal the continuing existence of an American base in Morocco.

Under the same Navy command as the Sidi Yahya station, the United States does maintain a training mission at Kenitra, about 20 miles away. Naval personnel assigned to the command total about 1,500 plus 1,500 dependents.

The sources said that the naval personnel were assigned to Kenitra "primarily to train Moroccan personnel in communications work but they also operate the communications facilities at Sidi Yahya."

The sources said that the communications station at Sidi Yahya was designed to "service the Sixth Fleet," stationed in the Mediterranean, while the communications facilities at Rota "provide support for ships operating near the base."

Meeting with the U.S. Ambassador to Morocco

When I arrived at the Radio Transmitting Facility that day, I was introduced to all the other radiomen on site. On a regular shift, there were usually three people operating the site. There usually were two radiomen and one electronic technician. I was able that day to meet the couple of people I was going to be working with. And I was given a very brief overview of my role there and a tour of the facility. Then I was introduced to the commanding officer, the senior chief, and a couple of other people who worked in the front office. I think four people worked in the front office, but they were only there during normal working hours. One of the sailors was named Foster. When Linda arrived, Foster and his wife, Teko, and Linda and I became friends and hung out together. So after these four people would leave the building, there were only three people on site. This was true on the weekend also. One of the things I was told when I met with the senior chief was that I had been scheduled to meet with the ambassador the following day. The ambassador met with every sailor who came to work there. That sounds like a lot, but there were not very many of us there.

The next morning I boarded a van in Kenitra provided by the Navy, leaving from the barracks and destined for Rabat, the capital of Morocco. It is about thirty miles from Kenitra and took about an hour. There were three of us to make the trip. We were taken to the Ambassador's house where we sat down and had a lengthy conversation with the ambassador and his wife over tea and cookies. We talked about everything, from politics to sports. He wanted to know everything about us, our families, schools, hobbies, etc. Our conversation lasted over two hours. During my conversation, I shared with him that I was a recent graduate of N.C. A&T State University. He was very familiar with the university. He had met the past president, and he also had an alumni of N.C. A&T currently working for him at the embassy. So we walked over to the embassy and took a tour. In the process, he introduced us to the A&T graduate. He was nice, but I never saw him again.

After the embassy tour, we walked back over to the ambassador's house, where we finished up our conversation. It appears that the ambassador had saved his real message to us until the very end. He had not just invited us there so he could welcome us to the country. When we got back, he explained to us in detail the things that we could not do while in the country. He even named some specific areas of the country he warned us to stay away from. One of them was Marrakesh, a very popular tourist attraction. At that time terrorists were roaming the countryside who were exiled from other Arabic countries, and there had been some instances with them taking Americans hostage.

Additionally, we were warned to under no circumstance go into Algeria. Algeria borders Morocco. That was a no-no for the same reason. He then proceeded to discuss with us our behavior while there and the way we should interact with the Moroccans.

He warned us about spies and people who might attempt to befriend us for reasons other than friendship and the importance of keeping a low profile. But to sum it all up, his final warning to us was, "If you get into any trouble at all, there is absolutely nothing that the United States government can do for you. If you get into trouble, you will be on your own." That last phrase, "on your own," got my attention. And I listened carefully to what he said, thinking all the while who in the world would not follow the warnings he was giving us and stay out of trouble. Well, I didn't know at the time just how easy it was to violate one of these warnings accidentally. But I would find out in a short two or three months. We thanked him for his advice and hospitality, and shortly after, we were on our way back to Kenitra. But I would be going back there soon because while I was there, the ambassador told me about one of his employees leaving the country soon and had a Volkswagen to sell. He knew I was just getting there and needed a car. I ended up going back a couple of weeks later and purchasing the car.

My Job at the Radio Transmitting Facility

I don't think that the Prac Deck training at Radioman A School could have better prepared me for the job. Just a couple of days after the lead radioman on my shift gave me some hands on instructions, and I was tuning the transmitters with the proper power being requested to the requested frequency, setting up the receiver to monitor the frequency tuning transceivers. Then I was patching in an amplifier, the crypto equipment, setting up the monitoring equipment, and the oscilloscope to look at the sine wave's quality being transmitted. Additionally, I was positioning the antenna at the exact degree requested by the ship via the receiver site and then, depending on the type of service being provided, listening to the transmitted signal on a loudspeaker. So I was answering requests coming over the teletype from start to finish. It was almost like being on Prac Deck at school, only this was real time, and there was a lot more there to learn. In addition to setting up a frequency network connection for a ship to transmit over, this site also broadcast Radio Free Europe throughout Europe. We supported all of the circuits belonging to the embassy in Rabat, gave support to submarines, and provided secure encrypted voice communication for high-ranking admirals to talk to embassies, other DOD officials, other admirals aboard ship, or to shore stations. We also transmitted facsimiles of weather maps to airplanes in the Mediterranean and more. We provided communication beyond what I could ever have imagined before arriving there. It did not take very long to understand firsthand just how important this work was to the United States' security and why it was so secret.

Changing Encryption Keys

Every day at the same time across the world, all DOD networks were taken down or out of service to change over to the new day's encryption key. This way, all networks, no matter where they were located in the world, were up and using the same encryption key. One of the things I did and all radiomen were responsible for was setting up and testing the encryption equipment with the updated key, and then bringing the network back up after testing OK in a back to back test configuration. This meant using an encryption key list to make the one to one cable to pin cross-connections until it was completed. There were a lot of pin cross-connections to make.

Sometimes when the system was brought back up, there was a suspicion that the Key had been compromised. The suspicion was that an enemy somewhere in the world had access to the Key. All the world networks would then have to go back down, and a new key configuration set up, tested, and then brought back online. Once the network was brought back up, the old Key list from the previous day and the one that had been compromised when that happened had to be shredded and placed in a secure burn bag. Then the secure burn bag had to be taken to the incinerator and burned. This had to be done by two sailors. One sailor placed the burn bag in the incinerator while the other sailor watched. After we were sure it had been burned, then we both had to sign a register that this particular key list had been destroyed. This was so important because if that key list got into the hands of the enemy like Russia or China, then they would be able to decipher all DOD communications, between any top-level government officials, including the president and anybody working out of the White House.

I should also add that as isolated as Sidi Bouknadel was, we were still being monitored by the Russians. And maybe some others, but definitely the Russians.

Russian Jamming Tactics

I mentioned earlier that this was a secret base, and we had to behave as if we were not there by not displaying flags, wearing Navy clothing off base, and anything that would indicate American presence. On the other hand, Russia had a small site just about a mile on the desert from the Radio Transmission Facility. They were not invisible and did not have to be. They were there for one reason. That reason was to make every attempt possible to interfere with our ability to provide communications support to the fleet. Sometimes they were very successful in doing so. Some nights and days, we would spend practically the entire shift trying to get two or three frequencies operating properly. The Russians would engage in what is called jamming.

We were taught about jamming in Radioman A School, and it happened just as we were taught. It works by the enemy having equipment to monitor frequencies that we were tuning transmitters to. Once they were able to identify and monitor the signal, they would then set up a transmitter on the same frequency and increase the power extremely high. This technique created interference strong enough to prevent a ship from transmitting legible data by interfering with the transmitting signal. When this happened, we simply had just to keep trying to get a good usable frequency up. Sometimes we would even set up multiple frequencies on multiple transmitters so the ship could get a transmission through before the Russians were able to interfere with it. They were more successful during certain times than at others. But that was part of the job.

KamiKaze-Like Mission

One of the first things that was introduced and discussed with me on my job was the emergency procedures for destroying the crypto equipment and key lists. It sounds far-fetched, but it wasn't. The procedure was established to handle any foreign invasion of the building that might result in the stealing of the crypto equipment and crypto keys. To be more specific, the Russians were only about one mile away from us across the desert. So it was very possible that they just might one day decide to forcefully come in and take the equipment and the keys. There were only three people on site most of the time, and we were all communications people and not soldiers trained to shoot guns. Obviously, it would result in war, but they knew that.

In 1968 North Korean forces overtook the USS Pueblo in the international seas to steal the crypto equipment. The Pueblo was a spy ship, and it was equipped with the same crypto equipment and keys that we were using. So it wasn't far-fetched

Weak Start Unapologetic Present

to think that the Russians would do the same thing at a Radio Transmission Facility.

Whatever the case is, directly in front of the teletype, which each of us used to respond to the receiver site and any other electronic communication we engaged in, was a glass case. The glass case was mounted about six feet high directly over the teletype. Inside the glass case was a very strong stick of dynamite and an electric lighter. Next to the glass box was a red hammer. Each of us were briefed on, and were required to sign a statement that, if at any time while we were at work and it became apparent that the crypto equipment and crypto keys were in danger of being compromised, we would light the dynamite and destroy the items. Each time I approached the teletype throughout my day at work, I could not help from looking at it when I was typing a response over the air because it was always right there directly in front of me. Most of the time I did not think about it, but there were times when I did. And it could be stressful knowing why it was there. Blowing up the crypto equipment also meant blowing yourself up!

But one thing that bothers me today is when I hear some Americans criticizing the people from other countries who are so dedicated to their cause that they are willing to blow themselves up as a war act. Some of us, Americans, have also been asked and agreed to do the same thing while serving our country. But most of the people criticizing have never served or sacrificed for the country one day or a second in their lives. But they have categorized themselves as being so patriotic. What hypocrites!

Linda's Arrival to Morocco

I eventually was given a room in the barracks at Sidi Bouknadel. It was very close to work, but it was isolated. The only people I saw were the sailors I worked with. There was no real interaction with the few families who lived on base. But after work, there was a bus that went between downtown Kenitra and Bouknadel. After work, and sometimes on weekends, we would go into Kenitra for recreation and interact with other people even though they were all Moroccan.

I was all settled in as far as work was concerned. And at that point, work was my life. Prior to leaving for Morocco, Linda and I planned her to meet me in Morocco as soon as possible. Shortly after my departure, she proceeded to obtain her passport, purchase her ticket, and resign from her job. Our primary means of communicating was by mail. I think we may have spoken by phone two times. Meanwhile she prepared to leave for Morocco. Consequently, I got a letter from Linda on a Thursday, and in her letter, she said she would be arriving in Casablanca on Sunday. Anyway, I told my friend Foster just in conversation, and he told the senior chief. The senior chief called me into his office and said, "I understand your wife will be coming this weekend." I confirmed that she would be coming. He continued with, "Are you aware that your tour of duty does not authorize you to have your wife accompany you?"

"No, I didn't," I said.

"Where do you plan to live once she gets here?" he asked.

"I am off tomorrow, so I will be looking for an apartment in Kenitra," I replied.

"I see." At that time, somebody came to his office door and needed to speak with him, so we ended the conversation. "I will get back to you on this," the senior chief said. So I left and went back to the deck and continued working. Later that day, Foster came onto the deck, and he handed me a sticky with a name and a number. This was a contact in Kenitra for on-base housing. I contacted the person and he assigned me to temporary housing for two in Kenitra. I was able to move into it the following day before Linda would arrive that Sunday. I think the Navy knew it wasn't a good idea to live on the local economy alone.

Sailors were living in Kenitra, but in all cases, two sailors lived together, or a sailor living married to a Moroccan girl who knew the culture. But it wasn't a good thing for us, with neither one of us speaking the language and with Linda just arriving in the country. Besides that, on those nights when I would have to work, she would be in Kenitra in an apartment alone with all foreigners. We lived in French Morocco, but the Moroccans spoke several languages. They spoke French, Arabic, Spanish, and a little English. We, on the other hand, only spoke English. At times we had to work very hard at communicating verbally.

Linda arrived that Sunday early in the afternoon. Unfortunately, we were a little late arriving at the airport. By the time I got there, she had already experienced the shock of walking through the two rows of soldiers pointing machine guns at her as she walked through. But I was there shortly after and found her sitting in the lobby waiting for me to arrive. Her culture shock continued as we made our way away from the airport and on our way to Kenitra. There was more shock when we arrived at the Moroccan airforce base where we lived. We had only been married a little more than three months, and this was our first house living together. We did not have furniture yet, but we did at least have a bed to sleep in and a stove. So that was good for the time being. By that time, I had picked up the car from the embassy employee in Rabat and commuted daily from Kenitra to Bouknadel.

Arabic Terrorist Captured in Front of Me

One morning, shortly after Linda was there and I had moved to Kenitra, where I had to commute from, I had been stopped temporarily for what I thought was a traffic inspection. The Moroccan Royal Police was known for setting up roadblocks whereby they stuck spikes in the road and checked everybody's ID. The Royal Police are the King's bodyguards who police the entire country. They ride motorcycles, dress in light blue uniforms with their pants tucked inside black knee boots, with a black tam covering their heads. They carry machine guns, and they don't play around. When they initiated these roadblocks, everybody did everything in their control to cooperate to the fullest. And we had been coached on how we were to respond when stopped by them.

Usually, when they set up one of these roadblocks, they walked over to your car and asked for your ID while another Gurdurn pointed a machine gun at your head. It was a very nerve-racking experience. But usually, once they had checked my ID and had seen that I was carrying a diplomatic passport, they would just wave me around the spikes, and I would be on my way. But this morning, after they checked my ID, they kept me sitting there in my car and proceeded to check the IDs of the people inside their cars behind me. There were four or five cars ahead of me, and nobody was moving. Suddenly, machine-gun fire started to echo in front of me. Some people in their cars dropped down, so I did the same. I could see probably fifteen or twenty men running from the roadblock into the desert. Some ran and were shot. But most of them fell to the ground and were taken by the Royal Police. I was just a little bit shaken. As a freshman at North Carolina A&T, I was shot at by the National Guards. But I had not experienced anything like this. Shortly after, they waived the rest of us through, and I continued to work. When I got to work, I told people what had happened, but nobody seemed that excited about it.

Weak Start Unapologetic Present

When I got back to Kenitra that night, I finished my last day of work for the week and didn't have to work the following day. I was over one of my friend's house by the name of Fred. Fred and his wife Kacy were friends of ours. They were one of the few people there who had a child. I told Fred what I had experienced that morning. He was aware of it. What had happened is that about twenty Arabic terrorists had been sent to Rabat to assassinate King Hassan II. But the Royal Police had identified them in the roadblock I was in. He knew about it because the ones they had not shot and killed in the roadblock, they brought back to Kenitra and placed them in front of a wall in the middle of the city, and executed them in the middle of the day. There was no jury trial, no plea bargaining, or anything, just death.

After Linda had been in Morocco for about a month, an accounting job came open in Kenitra on the Moroccan airforce base where we lived. She applied and was hired. So now, she had something to do all day long. Meanwhile, I worked a schedule that gave me a lot of time off. I worked for two days, had one day off, worked two nights, and had four consecutive days off. I could take four days of annual leave of absence and have nine days off. It was an excellent work schedule, but they wanted to be as accommodating as possible because the sailors who were there sometimes traveled to other nearby countries while on leave. Additionally, it was also a very stressful working environment for most. They wanted to relieve the stress as much as possible.

Purchasing Furniture in Rota, Spain

Linda had only been in the country a little more than a month. We had not addressed the furniture problem. There was no school in Kenitra for the few American children of Navy people who lived there. Consequently, they were flown every morning to Rota, Spain for school and picked up that afternoon to be brought back to Morocco. The advantage for us was that we could get a hop to Rota, Spain, as long as there were not more people who needed to take the plane there for business officially. Linda and I decided to go to Rota to purchase furniture. We went to the nearby airport on base to catch the flight. At the last minute, Linda was bumped because this was one of the days when there were several people who needed to go to Rota for official business. So we decided I would go to Rota alone and pick out some furniture. I went to Rota and I was amazed at the Navy commissary there. It was almost like being at a mall. My first store was a stereo store. Rota is one of those places with ships coming in, bringing in sailors who purchase a lot of stereo equipment. So they brought in equipment from all over the world. I stopped there for a while to just look at what they had. Before I knew it I had bought a complete stereo setup. I looked to see where I needed to go next to look at the furniture. By the time I found my way there and collected all the stereo equipment boxes, it was time for me to get back to the airport to catch the plane. I had not bought one piece of furniture, but I had a BOSS stereo setup with Kenwood speakers, amplifier, receiver, turntable, cassette player, reel to reel, and a big stack of albums.

When I got back to Morocco, the van drove me up in front of the house and stopped. Linda saw us drive up, so she rushed to the door as we were unloading the boxes. There were so many boxes. She came outside smiling and said, "All the boxes I see look like there is stereo equipment in them. Where are the furniture boxes?" I said, "Let me tell you." Before I could finish my statement, she had briskly rushed back inside the house and slammed the door to the bedroom. I did have an excuse, but she didn't even give me a chance to give it to her. I moved all the equipment inside the house and started to unpack it. I took everything out of the boxes and then proceeded to connect it all. At 2 a.m., I had everything connected. I then took a deep breath and took one of the albums from the stack of albums I had purchased and put it on the turntable. It sounded great! It sounded just as good as the one I had heard in the stereo display room. I went to the door of our bedroom and cracked the door. I could see that Linda was not sleeping, so I said, "You want to dance?" She looked up and said, "You are crazy. Why did I marry you?" I only had a couple of hours before getting into the shower and then getting ready to drive to work.

When I got to work, I was telling some people about my new stereo. Somebody said, "So when is the party." I said, "Well, I hadn't thought about it. Tonight!" So people showed up to hear music and dance. We didn't have any furniture yet, so we went into the market in Kenitra and purchased big thick pillows in case anybody wanted to sit down. Everybody had a good time.

I was enjoying my job and learning a lot. I had a lot of time off, so sometimes Foster and I would go out into the desert and visit with the Moors and nomads. The Moors are very dark skin black people of Arabic, Spanish, and Berber ethnicity. They would invite us into their tents and sometimes we sat in front of the tent on the ground and drank hot mint tea with them. They would dance for us, and sing folk songs. It was all very interesting. They were very hospitable. But what was of real interest to them was that I always had a fresh case of Boone's Farm in the back of my Volkswagen hatchback. The duty in Morocco was very stressful for most Americans. So the Navy tried to help the situation by being very flexible with the work schedules and being very liberal with liquor and wine. We all received a liquor rationing card each month.

With that card, a sailor could buy more liquor and wine than any one human being could ever drink in one month. And it was incredibly cheap. It was as if they were giving it away. So I always kept a full case of Boone's Farm in the back of my car. The Nomads loved it. And when I would drive across the desert to work, they would see me and start running toward the road, hoping to stop me. And I would stop if I was on time for work and give out a few bottles of wine. So whenever they saw my car they started to run towards it, expecting a bottle of Boone's Farm. Of course, I wouldn't do that today.

The Back Road to Rabat
Linda generally worked from eight in the morning until four-thirty in the afternoon, Monday through Friday. But I had a lot of time off. So I would wait for her some days and pick her up from work, and we would go out for dinner. One day, I picked her up to go to Rabat for dinner and dancing. I had heard about a back road to Rabat that was a little closer and had an even better view than the main highway. By the way, if I didn't mention it, in Morocco, they drive on the left side of the road. My steering wheel was on the left side of the car, but I had to drive on the left side of the road. That was a little awkward.

We left Kenitra, and I started driving the back way down a narrow concrete road. Then the road became gravel but still narrow. It turned into all rocks, big, little, sharp, round, and all kinds, and sizes of rocks. After about fifteen minutes of driving over the rocks, I felt the left side of my car bumping. I got out and confirmed my fear of having a flat tire. It was now starting to be dusk dark. I rushed to get the tire changed so that I could get away from that area. There was nothing out there but desert-like terrain on both sides as far as I could see. In the far distance to my left, I could see some nomads herding sheep.

Weak Start Unapologetic Present

I took out the jack, set it under the bumper, and attempted to change the tire. By now the part of the road that I was on, and had been on for a little while, was just sand. So when I attempted to jack the car up, the jack just sunk into the sand. I got back into the car. Linda was starting to become frightened. I wasn't sure what I was going to do yet. We were way too far out of town to try to walk back to Kenitra. And even if we tried, it was almost dark. We would not have been able to see well enough in the dark even to walk back. Not to even mention the snakes that we could be certain were out there. There was nothing between the location where we were and the city but desert-like terrain. What am I going to do? I thought. Crazy thoughts started to creep into my mind. We had heard about gross things in remote places in Morocco where people's heads were cut off, and that kind of thing. I am sure it was only folklore, but still, the stories went through my mind.

Just as I had about managed to put the crazy thoughts out of my mind, I heard loud voices coming from the left side of the car across the desert. I looked, and the voices were coming from about fifteen nomads running towards the car. Some were carrying Moor sticks. I couldn't understand what they were saying. I locked all the doors, and Linda grabbed me holding on as tight as she could. I tried to comfort her by wrapping my arms around her for protection. They reached the car, and suddenly the noise stopped. I looked through the rear mirror, and I could see them, but I couldn't tell what they were doing. Then I felt the back of the car being lifted up. I got out of the car, and to my astonishment they were lifting the rear end of the car and changing the tire. I couldn't believe it. I felt terrible about the way I had responded when I saw them approaching the car. I had locked the doors because I feared they would harm us, and they just wanted to help us. How often do we do things like that and never take the opportunity to get the feedback to know what people's true intentions are? I was fortunate in this situation that we did know instantly what their intent was.

They changed the tire. We could not communicate because they spoke Arabic, and I spoke only English. And then one of them gave a great smile and said, "Muhammad Ali." That was their way of communicating to me, an African American. And I balled my fist and repeated it back, "Yea. Muhammad Ali". I then remembered I had the Boone's Farm in the back of the car. I opened the back of the car and started to hand them bottles of Boone's Farm. One of them opened his bottle and took a swallow. Based on his expression and his response to the others, he must have liked it. Because they all then opened their bottles and started to drink as they left, walking back across the desert. I could see them drinking the wine and conversing very loudly. I had given them the entire case of wine. Meanwhile, Linda and I continued on our way to Rabat, and had a nice Moroccan dinner and entertainment that evening.

Welcome to Algeria

I had worked my shift for the week and was on my first day off. I got a call from Foster inviting me to ride to a location a long way from Kenitra to see a site that he had wanted to see since he had been in Morocco but had not taken the time. So I said, "Yea, I will be here. Linda is working anyway, so let's go." He picked me up in his car about a half-hour from then, and we were off to visit the site that he was interested in seeing. We drove for about three hours, and we were in the mountains. This was a part of Morocco I had not seen before, and it was breathtaking. We were traveling around the mountain and could look off across an expansive green valley. The valley was covered with fruit orchards, which I had never seen in the part of

Morocco we lived in. We even stopped in a tiny town that was a Jewish town, inhabited by only Jews. That was a real surprise. Nobody would have ever expected to have seen a Jewish village in the middle of an Arabic country living peacefully without any attention to it at all. We learned from communicating with some of them that they had been there for hundreds of years, if not longer.

We continued on the narrow and rugged mountainous road. We didn't see any people at all until we saw this man sitting on the side of the mountain. There was no traffic that we could see. At least we had not run into any traffic on our way up the mountain. So we stopped in the middle of the narrow road, and tried to make contact. Foster tried to ask him about the site we were looking for. After many attempts at trying to communicate, we concluded we were not going to be able to. Foster spoke a little Arabic because he had been in the country for more than one tour and worked at learning to speak the language. But he was unable to find any common phrases or words at all to communicate with this person. So we got back into the car and continued our drive up the mountain.

Finally, after about a half-hour later, we reached the top of the mountain. We came into this beautiful little town with several streetside restaurants. The climate was mildly warm and dry. It was a fairly busy little town and appeared to me to be a tourist town. I don't know because we couldn't communicate with anybody. But we decided to sit down at one of the streetside restaurants and have some lunch. We looked at the menus but could not read anything. They were all written in Arabic. We both thought that was pretty strange, because usually the menus were written in Arabic, French, and sometimes Spanish. We tried communicating with the waiter, but with no success.

As we attempted to communicate with the waiter, a person walking by overheard and stopped to assist. We couldn't understand him either, but he did say something that caught Foster's attention. He was able to make out that the person was saying "welcome." And then in a few words later, we both heard him say "Algeria." We jumped up and repeated, "Algeria?" while pointing to the ground. He nodded his head continuously as he smiled and said, "Algeria".

Well, it was pretty clear then that we were in Algeria, but didn't know it. The worst thing was, we didn't know how long we had been in Algeria. There were signs coming up the mountain tacked on to a stick post with handwritten Arabic words. But we couldn't read what they were saying. Then we realized that the man we stopped to talk to further down the mountain was also welcoming us to Algeria. This was one of the primary places where the ambassador had warned us not to go. He emphasized so clearly that if we got into trouble or were taken hostage, there was nothing the United States government could do for us. We were on our own. Whatever the case was, there was no time to have lunch. We knew we had to get out of Algeria immediately!

We jumped in the car and hurriedly started back down the mountain. We had no idea how far we had to go before we were back in Morocco. We just knew we had to hurry. We had not seen any cars on our way up the mountain, but we saw traffic coming towards us after about half an hour. It was a group of about five truckloads of soldiers. We cautiously continued on our way as we drove past them, trying not to raise suspicion. About a half-hour later, we were at a point where we could speed up. And Foster did. Ironically, shortly after we had speeded up we ran right into a Moroccan Royal Police roadblock with spikes in the road and a lighted torch burning. We were not looking forward to seeing the Moroccan Royal Police, but at least we knew we were back in Morocco. We were driving way over the speed limit when we ran into the roadblock. They looked at our IDs and then had us pull over on the side of the road. They took Foster's license for a gentle punishment and made us sit there for about an hour. Then one of them came over, gave Foster his license and said, "Zid." Zid means to go in Arabic. So we "Zid." They had let us go. We were OK with that. It was gooood, to be back in Morocco!

Experiencing the Culture

Linda enjoyed the work she was doing, and I enjoyed my work. But even with both of us working, we had the opportunity to experience a lot of Morocco. Linda had not been there very long when I came home one night, and told her that we had been invited to dinner by one of my coworkers, another sailor. He was married to a Moroccan woman about our age. So I came home that night, picked her up, and we drove over to his house. He lived in Kenitra in a villa. We sat down on the floor, or should I say we laid down on the floor on our sides. The host then placed a very large bowl with "cush cush" covering the bowl, some lamb, vegetables, and some small pieces of bread. Then everybody started to eat by sticking their hands in the bowl and rolling some "cush cush" closest to them along with portions of vegetables and meat. Everybody was well on their way to eating and enjoying themselves before Linda decided this would be it. She realized she had better go ahead and dig in because they would not bring out forks or spoons. I forgot to tell her that we would be eating with our hands. She probably would not have accepted the invitation if she had known. But she enjoyed herself. We had a big laugh later about how she responded after we left, but we all had good fun.

Tangier was one of my favorite places in Morocco when I was much younger. It sits directly across the Mediterranean from the Rock of Gibraltar. It is a spectacular experience sitting on a street-side restaurant having a meal and looking out over the Mediterranean Sea at the Rock. Tangier is a city that never sleeps. It's beautiful at night. At 2 a.m., you might see a wedding ceremony that had just taken place moving through the streets with its accompanying noise. There were people there from all over Europe and Africa. It was an exciting place to visit, and reminded me a lot of Las Vegas.

This was the time of discos and Moroccans were discoing big time. That was such a surprise because we were living in an Arabic country. But we were very young then and we used to go out downtown Kenitra for dancing with other couples at the Moroccan disco tech. Moroccans have this belief that Hercules was a real person. They believe that he was a Moor. We visited his cage on the Mediterranean. Moors have traditionally carried Moor sticks. I was told that the Moor stick was used in the past as a fighting tool. When I was about to leave Morocco, one of the nomads in Bouknadel gave me his Moor stick. This was a great honor. That was an act of appreciation, maybe for the

Boone's Farm I used to provide them with. I still have my Moor stick.

Going Home

There is a lot more to talk about as it relates to our experiences in Morocco. But time will not permit me to do so.
I had experienced my very first job working with the technology of the day. This was just the beginning. I cannot explain it, but throughout my career, God has placed me at the right place at the right time to give me opportunities to work with technology that most people simply have not been exposed to. The Radio Transmitting Facility in Morocco was one of those opportunities. From my interaction with many technical people over the years, I know that most people, due to no lack of action on their part, have simply not had exposure to the variety of technology I have been exposed to. Now, I realize that some of it has had to do with me being in the right place at the right time.

While I was in Morocco, I re-enlisted. My re-enlistment incentive was my choice of duty station and a cash bonus. My first choice of duty station was the Philippines. So leaving Morocco, Linda and I went to the Philippines for two years. But we first went home to North Carolina for thirty days.

Back to the United States

Our time was up in Morocco. The movers came over to our house about two weeks before we were scheduled to leave, packed all our things up, and shipped them to the Philippines. We had bought some furniture by now. A few days before leaving, I turned my car into storage to ship it to the Philippines. So now we were about ready to leave.

We said goodbye to anybody we needed to. The following day, Fred and Kacey drove us up to the Casablanca airport. It was a bizarre feeling. We had been out of the country for two years. It was not easy to keep up with anything that was going on in the United States. I didn't quite know what to expect. We had a television in Morocco, but it was Arabic television. Most of the air time consisted of King Hassan II addressing the country. It was more of a propaganda vehicle than an entertainment device. And even that was in Arabic. So we didn't watch TV basically for two years. But there was also military radio. We did listen to some programming being broadcast by it. But it catered more towards military-related issues than civilians. Now at work, there was a continuous news feed coming over the order wire, but you had to stand there and read it as it came over, or else you would have a challenging time finding a story that you might have had an interest in. We were not very informed about how things were moving along in the states. Especially with African Americans.

Changes Had Taken Place

We left on time and arrived on time at JFK. My step father, Robert, picked us up at the airport. My biological mother, Christine, didn't live very far from the airport. They lived in the Sheepshead Bay section of Brooklyn. Linda's mother also lived in Brooklyn, and several of her aunts and cousins lived in Harlem. So we spent a couple of days there visiting relatives. And then we left New York to go home to Winterville, North Carolina. Home sweet home.

When we arrived in Winterville, it appeared at first that not much had changed. To be more specific, my parents had not changed much. Linda's grandmother, Miss Ethel, had not changed much. Butch and Jackie were two years older, and that took a little getting used to. Amazing how much of a difference two years make in the life of teenagers. But the situation of African Americans, in general, had changed quite a bit. There had been definite social changes that had taken place at home within the two years we had been gone. For example, there were more integrated housing and apartments than before we left. Some of the people of our age range were experiencing mobility in their jobs. That was good to see. And there were definitely more African Americans who were in more professional positions. Some of them had attended the local community college to acquire the skills required for the workforce. Most people now were no longer just waiting to get out of high school to move to the North looking for a job. They were able to find jobs there at home or in nearby locations. The bottom line was that the Black middle class was on the rise. And it was undeniable. If you had been out of the country for two years, it was especially noticeable. I got a powerful positive feeling about that. But there was something very much missing. I had a suspicion of what it was but could not put my finger on it at first.

One different and major thing was that Linda and I had changed. I mean, we had changed a lot. We left home as very young, naive country kids from Winterville. We had matured a lot because of the things we were exposed to living on our own in a foreign Arabic country. Yes, we were only two years older, but those two years had come at a very critical point in our lives. We had just gotten married before going to Morocco. We had set up our first house there. We had learned how to even live as a married couple there. I am certain we would not have matured at the rate we did had we spent those two years living at home or near relatives and friends. We were completely separated from the lifestyle that we had known. And in most ways, the American lifestyle for two years. And now that I was back home, it became so clear as to how much it had impacted my view of life. I then understood the old adage, "You can never go home again." So even as we were told very often by people who we ran into that we had changed, we both knew it was true. The questions were, what do we do with it? How do we use it to our advantage?

But the other major change was the "spirit" of the movement that existed before we left. Before we left the country, there was an enthusiasm amongst African Americans as a whole. After being at home a few days, I simply didn't detect that. It appeared that everybody was working very hard, were trying to get ahead, and had forgotten about dedicating any time for the struggle. At first, I thought it was just me. But the second weekend I was home, my childhood friend Rander came home. We had a very long conversation about this very issue. He felt the same way. We were asking each other what happened to the spirit of the movement. We both had attended N.C. A&T together and had both experienced the movement. But now it looked like it was over. To us, it looked like it had been over since about 1971 or 1972. From what we concluded, African Americans who had had an opportunity to get a good job had decided that they simply needed to spend their time preparing themselves to keep their jobs. They felt that somebody else would deal with the movement. Based on what I have observed in recent years, we were correct. The movement was over. But as all can see, it was not complete. Because institutionalized racism against Blacks still exists today, the movement to fight it continues. My question is, where would we be today had we not let the movement die? Will we allow it to die again?

We had a great time in Winterville visiting our relatives and friends. I took all kinds of video footage of Morocco, and I showed them to many people. They were amazed at some of the movies I took, showing things that I have not mentioned in this book. But after thirty days of rest and relaxation, it was time for us to leave for the Philippines.

Off to the Philippines

The vacation was over and it was time for Linda and I to leave our hometown, Winterville, North Carolina, for a different way of life. This time it was the Philippines. We both were very excited about the trip. We had heard a lot about the Philippines and were looking forward to it. Aunt Nellie and Uncle Winser drove us to the Raleigh Durham airport. It was hard to say goodbye but we had no choice.

We boarded the plane destined for the Philippines. Our first stop was San Francisco. We spent two days in San Francisco at the Travis Air Force Base before we left for the Philippines. We flew from San Francisco to Hawaii, where we made a very short stopover. From there, we flew to Okinawa, Japan, with a brief layover there, before flying directly into the Manila International Airport.

Arriving in the Philippines

Finally, we were there. The entire flight was about eighteen hours. After arriving, we boarded the bus for Subic Bay. The Philippines is a beautiful country. It has a different type of beauty than Morocco because its tropical. Since it is near the equator, the climate and seasons are different than those in the United States. There are only two seasons: dry season and rainy season. But the temperature changes only by a few degrees from season to season. It's almost as if it is always summer. There are a few days during the winter when it is a little cooler than during the summer, but there is never a time when you can comfortably wear a sweater or even long sleeves at Subic Bay. The one exception would be up in the mountains of Baguio, a city in the northern part of the country. If you wanted to wear long sleeves there, you could, but you didn't need to. As far as time is concerned, the Philippines is fifteen hours ahead of California. So when it is Sunday in the United States, it is Monday in the Philippines. That took a little getting used to when coordinating a time to call home for birthdays, holidays, etc.

By bus, the trip from the airport was a little more than two hours. The Philippines consists of about 7,000 islands. The largest is the island of Luzon. The Navy issued me orders for the island of Luzon. There were three Navy bases in the Philippines in Luzon. There was Subic Bay, located in the city of Olongapo. The city of Olongapo today has a population of about 240,000. There was Cubi Point, also located in the city of Olongapo. The two bases were connected to each other. You would never know they were two separate bases unless you were stationed there. Then there was San Miguel Navy Base located at San Miguel, a town about twenty-five miles from Olongapo.

My Job at the Naval Communications Station Cubi Point

I received orders for Naval Communication Station Cubi Point. We usually would have received housing at Subic Bay. But when we arrived, there was a waiting list for housing at Subic Bay. So we were given temporary accommodation at San Miguel. This meant that I had to commute from San Miguel by bus to Subic Bay when I first got there. Riding the bus to work in the Philippines was a real experience. I didn't know it at the time, but my car that I had shipped—I thought I had plenty of time for it to have arrived before I got there—would be delayed by about two months. The reason for the delay was that the ship that transported it was taken hostage by the Cambodian Navy on its way to the Philippines. So I couldn't get my car until the Cambodian government released the ship. So, for the time being, my only mode of transportation was going to be the bus.

As a radioman stationed at a message center, several of my primary duties were to handle different classes of messages, ranging from government messages and official messages to replies of the Department of Defense and U.S. government departments. My duties also included handling messages other than those of the Department of Defense, broadcast messages of ships of all nationalities, messages dealing with special services such as weather, hydrographic data, and even personal messages for Navy personnel.

The messages we were required to handle consisted of numerous types of specific services such as movement reports.
It involved an up-to-the-hour report of every vessel location in the United States Navy. Hydro messages transmitted navigational warnings that were widely distributed around the world to entities having a need to know. These messages included information relating to the Atlantic, the Mediterranean, and the Indian Ocean. We also handled messages containing notices to airmen that addressed aircraft safety in different parts of the world. All these messages contained information that our enemies would find very useful and extremely difficult to acquire on their own. Then several different types of messages provided more general-purpose information. The bottom line is that this was a very busy message center. This was just my second duty station. As a radioman, there were a number of facilities I could have been assigned to that are part of the overall Navy Communication System. This was an example of one of the more common facilities radiomen might be assigned. But this

Lester Patrick

type of assignment could also be at an equivalent location onboard a ship.

    I worked at the message center probably for about a month. I quickly learned that once you learned how to handle the messages according to prescribed Navy regulations and became proficient with logging, filing, transmitting, receiving, etc. the job became repetitive. Now for a lot of radiomen, they absolutely loved that part of the job. Because there was this thing about having access to knowledge concerning current national and international events that you could only know by working in a message center. This was information that the average person doesn't know. And a lot of people really loved that. For me this was not the type of job that excited me at that time. I had just left a Radio Transmitting Facility where everything I did was very interesting and exciting. The message center just was not what I wanted to do then. There was nothing about the job that caused my adrenaline to flow.

    One day, I saw a radioman come into the message center who troubleshot the network and determined whether a bad teletype, printer or other equipment needed to be repaired or replaced. How involved he got with the equipment's actual repair was basically up to him because they had a Filipino crew at the repair shop to perform the repairs. But this person did troubleshooting at the message centers at both Cubi Point and Subic Bay. I said to him, "Your job sounds like something I would like to do." So the person gave me a contact, who I could talk to about a possible transfer to that department. They needed a person right then, so they were glad to have me join them. But it got better.

    As part of troubleshooting, the person performing the job had to be very familiar with the operations of teletypes, printers, and devices that transmitted messages to isolate problems. So they had to know in detail the specifics of how they worked, etc. Consequently, a class was starting that next week to cover the operations and repair of teletypes, printers, transmitting devices, and other related components. Best of all, is that the class was being taught at San Miguel. That meant that I did not have to now commute daily to Subic Bay. What a blessing!

The class was about twelve weeks as I recall. By the time it was over, we had been offered military housing at Subic Bay. It worked out almost perfectly. So my job was to provide the troubleshooting for these devices for both Subic Bay and Cubi Point. My official work location was Cubi Point once the class was over, and I had moved to Subic Bay. I was on call from the message centers if there was a problem. I liked that much better. I did that for the entire two years I was there.

I need to take time to put things in perspective relative to the technology I was dealing with then in the Navy and what was taking place in the commercial environment. This was 1978. Intel introduced the 8086 processor that summer. Apple introduced Apple DOS 3.1, the first operating system for the Apple computer. Additionally, Epson introduced the first successful dot matrix printer. This is what was happening as far as computers are concerned. The information age had not kicked off yet. But the first electronic message had been sent across the Internet. That point is an important one to emphasize because the Navy had been transmitting electronic messages around the world between its facilities for quite a while already.

But in 1978, TCP was introduced. TCP is the acronym for Transmission Control Protocol. This changed a lot as far as the transmission of data is concerned. One of the major changes is that, in the networking environment I have been describing, it was all done manually. In other words, we had to create the message with the proper routing information in the header of the messages for the destination addresses, etc.

With the implementation of TCP, this was automatically handled by associating addresses with the equipment or device. In the manual environment that existed before introducing TCP, if there was an error in the transmission of the message, the operator had to detect the error and either retransmit that portion of the message or the entire message. The receiver would usually request a retransmission. The TCP protocol was designed with error correction and detection when it was introduced. So if there was an error in the message, the equipment protocol itself was smart enough to know to request retransmission and correct the message. I won't go any further into how critical the introduction of TCP was to the information technology networking industry. I will end by simply saying it was a significant step forward. I would start working with one of its first implementations at my next duty station.

A Typhoon Hits San Miguel

We got to San Miguel right at the typhoon season. One day, within the first couple of weeks we were there, we were told to prepare for a typhoon. We didn't know what that meant exactly, but we made sure we were at home and out of the way of the storm. That was all we knew to do. San Miguel was probably located a thousand feet from the beach of South China Sea. All the houses were on stilts. There was a "lanai" at the bottom of the house, with a very large pull down heavy shade to block the sun. Our house had a vast picture window view of the beach. That night it started to rain extremely hard. The wind was very strong. It rained so hard that the walls were soaking and the pictures on them were peeling off. But about 1:00 a.m., the wind blew the big heavy shade from downstairs through the big picture window. There was a loud explosion, and glass splattered everywhere all over the place. Then our house was completely exposed to heavy rain and wind, with no power. We closed the door to the bedroom to lock ourselves off from that part of the house. Then we got down on the floor in our bedroom for safety. After several hours of being pelted by heavy wind and rain, the worst part of the storm was over.

At daybreak, we could see the flooding and damage. The typhoon had flooded most part of Luzon. We thought we had fared badly, but Filipinos, most of whom were reliant upon the local economy, had suffered greatly. Hundreds of people drowned, and many were stranded on rooftops and in their homes.

It was very similar to what happened a few years ago in New Orleans during Hurricane Katrina. Only this affected the entire island. After the water receded, things on base quickly returned back to normal, but for people out in the surrounding towns, it took a very long time to return to normal. The situation was also made worse by wild creatures like snakes. I will talk about that later.

Martial Law and Nightlife

When we lived in the Philippines, martial law was in effect. There were still signs in some of the bars that read, "Hang your gun on the wall." You had to be off the streets by 10:00 p.m.. You might ask, how do you manage thousands of drunken sailors under martial law just coming in from having been at sea for sixty or more days? The answer was, if you got caught on the streets after 10:00 p.m., you went to jail, no questions asked. I personally don't know anybody during the two years we lived there who violated or even attempted to break that law. Everything as far as nightlife was concerned was adjusted for martial law. Filipinos were known for discoing. All the clubs and discos opened up at 3:00 p.m. The lines usually started forming at the doors at that time. And they closed down around 9:00 p.m. to give everybody time to get off the streets. Curfew was over at around 5:00 a.m. So there was plenty of time for nightlife.

There were hundreds of night clubs, or discos on one street that led up to Subic Bay Naval Base. There was a section that was called the "Jungle" where the African American sailors hung out. All of the clubs and discos in that area of the MacSiSi catered to African Americans. They played music by African American artists. All of the live acts only sang soul music. Believe it or not, all of the bands were Filipino, and they were excellent! They were able to represent any African American band or group, from the Commodores to the Temptations.

On another part of the same street was a section that ca-tered to White sailors. Notice I didn't say "Whites only." These clubs and discos only played music by White artists. And their live acts imitated White American bands. So there was something there for everybody, including country and western. Filipinos did an outstanding job of representing them all. All activities had to be adjusted according to martial law except on base. The base was governed by the policies set up by the Navy. So activities on base could go on as long as base authorities allowed them to.

The description that I have given here of the way the night clubs were operated might give the impression that I was describing a practice of segregation. But that was not my intent or experience. Filipinos simply concentrated their services and talents on the audiences they had resources to satisfy. However, it might appear to have been a deliberate sign of social separation of sailors that might have been motivated by race. But that was not the case when I was there.

Moving to Subic Bay

I completed the class at about the same time a housing vacancy came up at Subic Bay. So I took advantage of it by Linda and I moving. Shortly after we moved to Subic, Linda started to work for the Navy Exchange in Subic. She worked as a News Editor of the Navy Exchange for Subic, Cubic Point, and San Miguel. So she regularly made television and radio announcements advertising Navy Exchange merchandise imported from around the world. She worked a regular day of eight to five schedule.

Subic Bay was a huge and busy naval base. There were ships in port at all times who were on Westpac cruises. These ships would bring in thousands of sailors alone. The United States government had an agreement with the Philippine government that it would provide a certain number of jobs for Filipino nationals. That meant that for every Navy position, practically a Filipino national was also hired for the same position. The exception would be in situations whereby they might come in contact with classified materials. For example, if there was a hard to repair printer problem at a message center in Subic Bay that required a lot of time, a radioman could de-install the printer and take it into the hallway for a Filipino to repair. The Filipino national was getting paid to perform that task, but he could not go inside the message center due to classified materials. After the repair was completed, the radioman would then reinstall the equipment. Because of this agreement between the Philippine government and the United States government, thousands of Filipino nationals worked on the base.

Then you add the sailors who were stationed there and their families, and the thousands of American civilian contractors who were also stationed there, you end up with a very large population at Subic Bay. It was like its own city within the city of Olongapo. Area-wide, it was enormous also. Subic Bay was complete with several very good restaurants, two or three clubs, a library, a Radio and TV station, two hospitals, a movie, supermarket, beauty and barber shop, and more. The club would sometimes bring entertainment like Ray Charles, Peaches and Herbs, the Soul Train Gang, and others. It also had a Navy Exchange that was larger than some malls. Subic Bay also had a football team that traveled up and down the western part of the world playing military football. They also had home games.

Living and Working in the Jungle

I both lived and worked in the jungle. There were wild animals all over the base. There were enough wild animals on the Navy base that the base created a zoo and populated it with animals captured on base by animal control. It was not uncommon to hear of very large snakes like boa constrictors being found in a person's yard. There were times when boa constrictors swallowed people's pets. There were all kinds of other snakes as wells. All over the base, colorful signs and posters displayed different snake types and gave strict guidelines on how to proceed if you came into contact with them. Large iguanas were very plentiful, too. Some of them were so large they looked like alligators. Then, there were the enormous lizards. Geckos could not be kept out of your house. You just had to live with them the entire time you were there. Geckos were so much a part of the landscape that they were always somewhere in your house. They usually were positioned at the top of the ceiling, where they were safe from us. The noise at night of all the animals and insects was amazing. It could get very noisy from all the different sounds of the jungle animals and insects sounding off together at the same time. In my backyard, monkeys would sometimes raid the trash cans. The backyard was tiny, with just enough space for a patio that butted up against the jungle.

The base in general was located in a jungle, but where I worked was even more so. The Navy construction team had built the building that I worked out of by merely clearing a narrow road about three miles long through the jungle. They then extended the primary road to the left through the jungle up a hill, with just enough jungle cleared for the building. The building sat on top of the hill overlooking the whole bay. As a routine, when I worked during the day, I always took my jogging clothes to work with me. When I was off work, I would jog through the jungle down the hill and return up the hill to the building. On most occasions, monkeys would sit on the side of the jungle and watch me. Sometimes a whole family would cross the road in front of me. When I saw them crossing the road, I would always stop and allow them to cross. I was told that if I didn't come in between the family, they would never attack me. It must have been true, because I was never attacked, and they were there almost every day watching as I jogged by.

The main road continued straight about two miles where they had built a very small hospital or clinic. Both buildings were built in the middle of the jungle, and there was nothing else there but wild animals. The view overlooking the bay was breathtaking, seeing the ships lit up at night and sitting in port at Subic Bay.

The same view revealed in its background a look of the South China Sea with waves splashing as far as you could see. You could also see where the South China Sea butted up against big mountainous rocks further down the bay. It was beautiful!

Beauty was one thing. But at night in the jungle, there was no light at all. It was so dark that when I drove down that stretch of road at night, it was like I was feeling my way. Usually, I was driving a Navy jeep that was open. So many times, I got a creepy feeling when I got a call at one or two o'clock in the morning that required me to drive down the hill to Subic Bay. Unless I was working during the day shift, I was alone at the building at night in the middle of the jungle. Sometimes, that wasn't a very comfortable feeling, especially with all the ghost stories told about the building.

The Story of the White Lady

I had not planned to tell this story, but I have to. When I moved to Subic Bay and started to work out of Cubi Point, one of the people who worked at the building during the day time asked me if I knew about "The White Lady." I said, "Who is The White Lady?" He proceeded to tell me that there had been this Navy WAVE who had fallen in love with a sailor there at Subic Bay some years before, and they were supposed to get married. She got all dressed up in her wedding dress to meet him at the chapel in Subic Bay, but he never showed up. She learned later that he had been sent back to America unexpectedly. And he didn't even bother to tell her that he was leaving. So she left the altar and started walking.

She walked through the jungle up the road towards Cubi Point near the building that I worked. But as she was walking, a taxi which was taking somebody to the medical clinic driving in the same direction did not see her on the road because it was so dark. He ran into her, and killed her near the turnoff that led up the hill to the building I worked. Since that time, numerous people claim to have seen "The White Lady" walking up and down that part of the road dressed in her wedding dress. It was a big tale when I was there, and from what I heard then, it was a story being told all over the Philippines. I drove up and down the road hundreds, if not thousands of times at night during the two years, I worked there. I can say that I never saw "The White Lady" walking down the road. But I had to tell the story.

Graduate School and Community Work

If somebody had told me before I got to the Philippines that I would begin to work on my Master's degree, I would not have believed them. Or if somebody had told me that when I got to the Philippines, I would start my lifelong effort to volunteer my time in the community, I would not have believed them. Well, that is exactly what happened.

I will address the graduate school situation first. As I said earlier, Subic Bay was like its own city within the city of Olongapo. Accordingly, there was a campus of the University of Southern California located at Subic. After going up to Manila to take the GRE, I enrolled and started to take graduate classes towards a degree in Information Systems Management. I worked the same work schedule in the Philippines that I had worked in Morocco. Like Morocco, the duty in the Philippines was almost like a vacation for most. So the Navy was very flexible on its approval of work schedules. I worked for two days, got one day off, and then worked for two nights and got four days off. That gave me a lot of time to study, and to enjoy my time there as well. The instructors for USC were sent from southern California to teach the classes. They were all smiles during the semesters that they were there. They had a pretty easy load because they taught whatever class they were there to teach, and the rest of the time was free time for them to experience the Philippines.

Most classes met two times per week, so with the work schedule I had, it was rare for me to have a conflict. Attending graduate school worked out very well for me because I was able to complete thirty units. I could not finish my masters while in the Philippines. It gave me a good start that would allow me to complete it when I got to San Francisco. But the important thing is that I was able to take advantage of working towards my master's while still on active duty and, at the same time, enjoy the Philippines.

Dealing with International Jim Crow - Overseas

One of the book's primary objectives is to discuss how Jim Crow has impacted me, my decisions, my life, and how I have dealt with it. When we think of Jim Crow, we generally think of its impact on African American citizens in the United States. Whether the proper thing to do or not, we usually tend to further confine Jim Crow to a specific section of the country. But what about its impact on African Americans outside of the United States? Are there examples of Jim Crow on African Americans overseas either by the institution they might be associated with or the host country? The answer to the first question is yes. Jim Crow can have an impact on African Americans overseas and out of the United States. I also think that the answer to the second question is yes. I believe some specific examples can be cited of the impact of Jim Crow on African Americans overseas by institutions or the host country. But I think this is mostly Jim Crow practices that have been conveniently exported to other countries.

During my two-year experience in Morocco, there was never a time when, in any way was I reminded of Jim Crow. That is

Weak Start Unapologetic Present

an experience I have not had since. That is saying a lot since we are talking about the Navy and a foreign country. Jim Crow was not just a group of laws and practices, but it was also an attitude. So it wouldn't matter where you are located. If you are a member of an organization that accepts and promotes a Jim Crow attitude, Jim Crow will have caught a free ride overseas. On the other hand, if Jim Crow practices are normally part of the organization's practice and, in this case, the Navy, but not present in sailors, then Jim Crow would not be present overseas. In my situation, I believe that was the case for my stay in Morocco. But taking this scenario a step further. If it was not present within the institution that was responsible for me being in Morocco, could it have been present in the country of Morocco itself? I believe it could be, but in my case, I don't think that it was. Or at least I cannot cite any of my experiences in Morocco that would cause me to believe that there were traces of the Jim Crow attitude around. My experience was just the opposite.

I am posing these questions to make this point. One day, I was off work and was at one of my friend's house in the Philippines, who was married to a Filipino. His Filipino wife asked about a movie that was being played on television. She wanted to  know why the African Americans on television in the movie they were watching behaved the way they did. I glimpsed at the movie, and it was a movie with Stephen Fletcher. I don't recall the movie's name, but Stephen Fletcher was one of the movie's main characters. I realized that the person had a conflict separating the people's behaviors in that movie and the African Americans she knew. They saw enough of these movies that they had concluded that we were just different, but the people on television portrayed who African Americans are. I thought about that a lot and concluded that what I was seeing was the impact of Jim Crow on an international basis. The Jim Crow message from this movie was being received loud and clear. These people were being brainwashed to think that it was the norm for us to behave as inferior. The more they saw African Americans on television acting as if they were inferior, the more likely they were to think of African Americans as inferior, shiftless, lazy, dumb people who needed a White person to hold their hand to live and survive. This was international Jim Crow at work.

Linda and I had met several young African American couples at Subic Bay. Together we formed an organization called "African Americans United for Success." The organization initially came together to address some concerns of African American Navy wives. Many African American wives were there, but the Navy Exchange had not taken the initiative to get the female products and services they needed. For example, there was nobody on

Weak Start Unapologetic Present

Subic Bay who could dress African American women's hair. They didn't have products like hosieries, makeup, etc., for African American women. When we organized and approached the right people about these concerns, they were addressed. They even sent Filipinos to the United States to learn how to work with African American women's hair, and brought in a specialist in African American hair.

[Newspaper clipping: "Africans in the making of America" by RM2 Lester Patrick, SUBIC BAY NEWS]

But one of the other goals that we set out to accomplish was to change the negative stereotypes that some Filipinos had of African American people in general. So we put together some activities to help address this problem. These activities were designed to counteract the international Jim Crow influence. One of the things that we did was fundraising for a local orphanage. We did the fundraising on base at a community center and then delivered the donated items to the orphanage. We had television coverage that came from Manila to give coverage not just in the local area but also in other areas away from the Navy base. I am sure this had an impact on our image overseas.

Have you ever seen thousands of sailors come into port after having been at sea for sixty to seventy days? The first thing they are looking for is the closest bar with all the beer they can drink. Believe it or not, we were able to convince some sailors who had just come in from the sea to work on the roof of an orphanage. That helped to prevent the kids from getting rained on during the rainy season.

I wrote several articles for a local newspaper. It had a pretty wide distribution because it was also distributed to the ships in addition to all the bases in that area.

With all the Filipinos working on these bases, it reached one of the major audiences I intended for it to reach. This of course, was another attempt to counteract the international Jim Crow influence spread to the Philippines. An example of one of those articles is posted here. All these things working together did present a more positive image of African Americans in the Philippines.

Eating Nontraditional Filipino Foods

My first Easter in the Philippines shocked me like nothing else had shocked me since being there. I was still learning things about the culture. But this event surprised me even beyond the experience I had one day riding the bus between San Miguel and Olongapo. I had already boarded the bus, and then a man got on after me holding a sack in one hand. What caught my attention at first was that the something he had in the sack was moving. Then I heard a wimping sound coming from the sack. It was a small dog because it started to bark. I asked the person sitting next to me, do you hear the dog crying in the sack?

"Yea," he said.

"Why would you have a dog tied up in the sack that way?" I replied. Would he smother the dog? I thought to myself.

"That dog is not a pet," the man said. "It is for him to eat once he get home. He will barbecue it and serve it for dinner." I was not sure that I had heard him correctly. I had heard rumors that a certain species of dogs were eaten there, but I had not up until that time seen any. I had also listened to a lot of sailors talking about them having eaten monkey on a stick. I never saw any being sold, but who knows. At least I don't think I had.

Some months later I was over one of my friend's house, and we were playing games. Meanwhile, his Filipino wife prepared us a snack. It was a Filipino dish with vegetables and small pieces of meat over rice. One person asked, "What happened to that little puppy you had the other day." My friend's response almost knocked me off my feet or out of my seat.

"You are eating it," he said.

"I thought so," the person responded nonchalantly. That other person had been in the Philippines for a long time. As for me, I didn't quite know how to respond, because I was eating it, too, and it was very good. So I finished up my snack. But from that day on, even though my snack was very tasty, I decided, in the future, I would inquire as to what I was eating before I accepted anything to eat.

In every culture, some popular foods might be a little bit out of the general public's norm. For some African Americans, that food might be chitlins. I grew up eating them regularly and thought they were great. I haven't eaten them since growing up because it has been about forty-five years since I have eaten any type of meat other than seafood, chicken, or turkey. But during that stage of my life, I couldn't even begin to comprehend why some people had such a negative view about eating chitlins.

A very popular delicacy served in the Philippines is a snack or street food called *balut*. It is a fertilized bird egg. It's usually a duck's egg, buried or incubated for up to twenty-one days. Once the process is complete, the eggs have a developed embryo, but still soft enough to chew and swallow whole. *Balut* is eaten right out of the eggshell. In the Philippines, it can be bought in stores and the market. Most people who eat it love it and say it's delicious. Like chitterlings, you have to first get past the smell.

Those are a couple of examples of nontraditional Filipino foods. And by nontraditional, I do mean from the American perspective. But there were so many other good Filipino foods that we loved to eat. They are too numerous to mention here. Linda and I used to have a Filipino lady cook Filipino food for us at our house. We loved her *lapu-lapu (fish)*, chicken or seafood adobo, *pancit lomi* (noodles) with chicken, and red snapper dishes. Filipinos are also very big on pork. So if you were a pork eater, you would love suckling pig. And don't forget the rice, because steamed rice was served with just about all dishes.

Easter Crucifixion in the Philippines

I found Filipinos to be very religious people. They are mostly Catholic. The exception is the people who live on the island of Mindanao. Many of the people who live in that part of the Philippines are Muslims. They make up about 5% of the entire population of the country. This brings up an interesting point when mentioning this part of the country. The Philippines consists of seven thousand islands, with the largest one being Luzon where we lived. The southern part of the Philippines was not totally controlled or governed by the president or the government. The Moro National Liberation Front has a solid presence in southern Philippines. It is a political organization consisting of Muslims that evolved from the "Muslim Independent

Movement." They are a separatist group that first became active in the seventies. Muslim insurgence in this part of the world has been going on for hundreds of years. This group of people have resisted invasions by all foreign countries and still operate independently. Belief-wise, they are associated with the Moors of North Africa. I find their story to be fascinating—especially that connection between the two countries or two continents. I should also add that the original Filipinos are a group of people called *Negrito*. They are very short dark-skinned people who physically look very much like the pygmies of central Africa or Congo.

All of that was necessary before addressing Easter in the Philippines.

The overwhelming portion of the population of the Philippines is Christian. They practice Catholicism. I was amazed to see Easter celebrated across the country in such an unusual way. It did not disrespect God, but it was very new to me, and I didn't understand it at all. But nevertheless, it was exciting to observe.

The week started with makeshift altars being placed at different locations throughout the *barrios*. They were made of bamboo and coconut leaves and were placed along the roadsides and on street corners. In some areas, the story of Jesus' life was read aloud by senior people to those who gather to hear it. Then there were the flagellations." Throughout the *barrios*, flagellants reenacted a simulation of the bodily suffering that Jesus experienced on his way to the Calvary on Good Friday. They did this by placing hoods over their faces, walking and crawling barefoot through the streets, while wearing a crown with twigs and leaves. They used long split bamboo tapered with bits of iron and whipped and lashed their backs until they drew blood as they crawled through the streets. Blood

Lester Patrick

sometimes splattered as they beat themselves with the split bamboo strips.

panga, one is actually nailed to the cross.

He is Juanito Piring, a 37-year-old farmer, who has been "crucified" annually on Good Friday for the past eight years. Followed by a procession of flagellants, he carries a cross to the the crucifixion site, where he is nailed to the cross for about two minutes. He is then taken down, the spikes are removed and his hands bandaged. Piring's annual crucifixions are part of a vow he made reportedly when his mother recovered from an illness.

MORIONES FESTIVAL

In a colorful pageant held on the island of Marinduque, the whole town is transformed into a Roman village.

The men dress up like

The cross on which Juanito Piring is nailed is raised above the crowd. Piring has been "crucified" every year on Good Friday for the past eight years.

*An electronics technician formerly assigned to Naval Communications Station Philippines, San Miguel, Allen worked as photography instructor at Los Angeles Community College, Subic Bay.

A procession of flagellants attracts big crowd in this Philippine barrio.

Weak Start Unapologetic Present

There were times when others would assist them by also striking them across their backs as they attempted to re-enact Jesus' trip to Calvary. The people standing along the streets watching this happen also played a role. They taunted the flagellants just as if they were the people during Jesus' time who taunted him as he carried his cross. At the end of the day, the flagellants dipped themselves into the river for healing. They claimed to have received healing of their wounds they created by striking themselves all-day long on their backs. It was an astounding thing to watch.

But that was not the most unbelievable part of the Easter celebration. When I was there, a man named "Juanito Piring" who was 37 years old then, would offer himself to be crucified by being nailed to the cross. This was a big event. He was actually nailed through his hands to the cross! It was around sundown when he was nailed to the cross for two or three minutes and then taken down. People who participate in these events then usually gathered at their local churches and held services. Again, this was undoubtedly an unusual celebration of Easter on Good Friday. It is an Easter crucifixion and celebration that can only be experienced in the Philippines.

Returning to the United States

After two years in the Philippines, it was time to leave for a new duty station. My first choice was California. I did get my first choice of duty stations at Naval Communications Station Stockton, CA. I didn't know anything about Stockton, but the name of the facility at that time was Naval Communication Station San Francisco. I learned after I received orders, the base was in Stockton.

We had experienced life living in the Philippines, been exposed to its culture, visited some of the islands other than Luzon, met and shared life with people from different parts of the world, and now it was time to go home. So we did. We left the Philippines but took a three-day break in Japan. One night while there, we went out to dinner, and I lost my military ID. Having a military ID in addition to my passport was a requirement for getting on the airplane. So I had to get on the train in Tokyo, travel to an airforce base, and have a new ID made. That was not an easy task. It was not as easy as I thought it would be to find somebody on the train who spoke English and tell me when I needed to get off the train. One gentleman heard me attempting to communicate and came to my aid. He wrote down the name of the stop and the base name on a piece of paper in Japanese so I would have something to show if I got lost. I was very thankful for that. And I did get lost. So that was a great help. Eventually, I got to the base and took a picture for my new ID. I waited while they prepared it. They also gave me very detailed instructions on how to get back to my original location. I was able to get back safely with no major problems. The next day, Linda and I left Japan for San Francisco. Once there, we took a flight to Stockton and stayed there for two days before leaving for Raleigh, North Carolina for a thirty-day vacation at home. We were back home!

Returning Home to Winterville

Aunt Nellie and Uncle Winser picked us up at the airport in Raleigh, North Carolina. They were as happy to see us as we were to see them. Things had changed a lot, though. First of all, Aunt Nellie had a heart attack while I was in the Philippines. She had tried to keep it hidden from us by not telling us while we were away. But one of Linda's aunts had called us in the Philippines to make us aware. I was told she was much better than she had been, but she was not the same as before I left. But now we were back, and whatever happened, we would be just across country. Things had also changed with Jackie and Butch. They had grown up over the four years I had been gone. Over the previous four years, I had only lived in the United States for about sixty days. Jackie had gotten married and had a boy by the name of Ramon. Her husband's name was Samuel, who we called Sammy for short. I don't know if Butch was married or not, but he had a daughter named KeKe. She was living with Aunt Nellie. He had completed his mortuary school, was working, was very busy, and seemed happy.

Those were just some personal changes that had taken place since we had been gone. It was tough to put my finger on, but Black people's attitudes about life, and each other, had changed. People didn't seem to care as much about each other anymore. I started to notice this when I would inquire about a person I may have grown up with. I would get a response like, "Oh, I haven't seen him in two years." Well, that's about how long it had been since I had seen the person also. But I had been out of the country. I guess what I am saying is that the time when people would make a special effort to inquire about the people they knew growing up was behind us. In the Black community, we used to make a special effort to do that. Something about us as a group of people had gotten lost. And as I got readjusted to being home again, I assessed that the deterioration in relationships, if I can call it, was ongoing.

One of the reasons this was so evident to me was that I had only spent about sixty days in the United States over a little more than four years. Even though four years doesn't sound like a lot, it really was. But it reminded me of a conversation I had several months before, with a sailor I met in the Philippines. Some of the ships docked away from the primary dock at Subic Bay because they were smaller ships. As a result, there were not as many taxis just waiting to give them a ride as if they were on one of the larger ships docked near the main gate. Often, sailors would walk to the main gate, which was about three miles. I lived over in that area, so if I saw a sailor walking to the gate, I would stop and give him a ride. One day this brother sailor was walking to the gate, and I stopped to give him a ride. We had a quick conversation. I learned he was from Chicago.

I had just read an article in *Ebony* magazine about Black people and some of the challenges we were having then in the United States. I expressed to him my concern about what I had read in the article. I was excited to share my concern with an African American who had just come from the United States and get his perspective. You see we had only limited access to American television, etc. so magazines were about it. But I will never forget his response. I remember he said, "Brother, you are living in the Philippines. If I were you, I would just enjoy myself because Black people in the United States don't care anything about you." Now being home, I realized, this brief conversation with him was actually a reflection of the evolving attitude among African Americans in the United States. What I was now seeing firsthand was the result of the attitude even at home in small-town Winterville. That attitude was that Black people, in general, no longer made a special effort to care for each other as they once did. I will assume that it had been happening for a long time, but me being out of the country for four years had given me a clearer view of it.

I had to make some adjustments, but I became accustomed to the new attitude even though I didn't like it. I didn't see how we could become a more successful group of people with that attitude. But there were some other very necessary changes Linda and I had to make. The way we were dressing now coming from the Philippines was way out of touch with the way people in the United States were dressing. So we had to make that change quickly. We had clothes tailored based on what we thought people were wearing at home. We didn't realize that by the time we had access to the resources we were using to have these clothes tailored, they were already very outdated. That became a little amusing, but we got through it. After thirty days of being home enjoying my family, Aunt Nellie's cooking, and seeing friends, it was time to relocate to Stockton, California. I purchased a new van and drove across the country to Stockton.

Arriving in Stockton

As I pointed out earlier, we made a quick stop in Stockton on our way from the Philippines. But we were only there a couple of days, so we didn't get to see a lot. But now that I was returning, I was able to see much more. Some things about both the Navy in general and about Stockton did surprise me.

Weak Start Unapologetic Present

We drove across the country in our new van. That was a good experience. I had never driven across country before and have not done so since. We arrived in Stockton and checked into a hotel that the Navy had sent me in the mail as a place to stay while I looked for a permanent residence. We got here over the weekend, so I drove over to the base the following day to check in. I attempted to check in with the senior chief. He took one look at me and said, "Sailor, I am going to give you the rest of the day off so you can get yourself a Navy belt, your shirt stenciled over the left pocket, and get a haircut." I left his office to take care of those things.

Except the time I had been in boot camp and training, I realized I had spent all of my Navy time overseas. I couldn't even wear Navy clothes in Morocco except at work, and then only about three people saw me. So it didn't matter how I looked. In the Philippines, it had not been much different. I worked up on the hill at Cubi Point. I was the only person up there and the only person on my shift. When I got a trouble call that required me to run down the hill to take care of, nobody was concerned about how I looked. I never wore a hat. I don't even know if I even had a Navy belt. And as far as my hair was concerned, I was sporting a nice Afro even though I was in the Navy. Almost all of my time up to that point, I had not been in a location where my military appearance was important, or should I say the Navy was very relaxed on its attitude about appearance where I was. But I was quickly made aware by the senior chief that I was in the United States now, and *in* the Navy!

Getting prepared with the proper belt and getting my shirt stenciled was not a problem, but I had no idea of where to get a haircut. I saw an African American civilian walking on base, and he told me about Gain's Barbershop and how to get there. So I drove over to Gain's and got a haircut. Mr. Gain was at the barbershop cleaning up, but it was Monday, so the shop was not open. After he learned I was just arriving in town, he stopped what he was doing and cut my hair. With that taken care of, I was all ready to check in the following day. I checked in the next morning and was introduced to the people I would work with. The facility was supported by Navy and civilian employees. I noticed at the very beginning that there were only about eight African American sailors there. All the rest were White. I would guess that there were probably about forty sailors working at the communications station and probably about twenty civilians.

The first day I was there, I met one of the African American federal civilian workers who asked me where I was living temporarily. I told him I was living on Charter Way in a hotel. He said, "I thought so because that is where they usually send African Americans rather than sending them out north." I didn't know what he meant by that. I didn't even know about north Stockton. But I would learn later that what he said was correct. That Jim Crow attitude was not only part of the Navy here in Stockton, but it was an integral part of the Stockton community's attitude in general.

Jim Crow Behavior in Stockton

As I pointed out early in this book, Jim Crow doesn't just involve laws that govern and curtail African Americans' rights. But it also dictates a specific behavior by people who keep it in place and of the victims of it. My first introduction to the Jim Crow policies here in Stockton immediately started after I was here and before being settled. As a newly arriving sailor, naturally, I was looking for an apartment. Some White sailors I worked with told me where they lived. Because they said, there were plenty of vacancies in the apartment complexes they lived

Weak Start Unapologetic Present

in. After making visits to at least two of those locations and being told that there were no vacancies, I was about to believe that I would only find a place in south Stockton. At one of the locations I applied, a property manager did assure me that there were some south Stockton vacancies. And for a couple of days, I just quit looking. I had visited so many places and couldn't find a place.

One day, Linda was reading the newspaper, and she said there is a grand opening on Saturday at this location. We were excited because we knew there were vacancies since it was a grand opening, and we knew we were going to be first in line even if we had to sleep there that night in our van. We didn't sleep there that night, but we were there at least an hour and a half before the first person came to open the door. We were sitting in the van when the property management person opened the door. We got out of the van to make sure we were first in line. At that time, we were the only ones there. As I approached the door, the person turned and looked at us. I smiled and said, "We wanted to make sure we were first in line to get an apartment."

She smiled also. "I am so sorry you came out here, but all the apartments are already rented," she replied.

"But the newspaper ad says it's a grand opening, and this is the first day!"

"I know, but they have all been rented," she said. "But, if you like, I can still take an application and keep it on file if you would like."

"No, thank you," I answered back. Linda was disappointed to say the least. We both knew they had probably a hundred vacant appointments but would not rent one to us because we were African American. As we left the premises, I could see all the big signs reading "Grand Opening!" I could also see in my rearview mirror the ribbons flapping in the wind as we exited the driveway. I had to work later that day, and one of the White sailors asked me where I had found a place. I was embarrassed to tell him that I could not find anybody in north Stockton who would rent to me. I was not just a victim of Jim Crow policies, but I was also beginning to act it out. I participated in it by not being so angry that I didn't take the time to file a federal complaint. But there was still something inside me to remind me that I could not give in to it. I had been there before while at N.C. A&T when I simply could not give in to the Jim Crow ways of the Greensboro police and the North Carolina National Guard. And I couldn't give in now. So we kept searching. About two days later, we saw an ad in the paper for a duplex apartment availability. We applied and were given the apartment. So now that was behind us right, and I could just focus on my job. But I would learn later that wasn't quite the case.

The woman who denied us access to this apartment complex practiced behavior carried over into the seventies that went back to the thirties. Her behavior was in following past practices of not renting to African Americans. This practice was first established by the Federal Housing Administration and later practiced by the Veterans Housing Administration and banks by rewarding builders of houses and apartments who discriminated against African Americans. The federal government made not renting or selling to African Americans a requirement to receive the funds necessary to build all construction projects. So property managers were practicing the policies that the federal government had established to follow. I believe the people who worked in positions like the one this woman was working in were simply following instructions given them not to rent to African Americans. This practice is much more common than most care to admit. This was 1978, and laws such as the

Housing Rights Act of 1968 prohibiting that practice, but people still continued to practice it.

There are even real estate applications in use today here in California that states on the applications that this property cannot be sold to any person of the Negro race. I know, the same question comes to my mind also. If it is illegal, why hasn't the state had the statement removed from the application? My personal opinion is that there are enough people who would like to see it remain because it reminds them of the time when it was legal. Our president and his supporters would refer to it as "Make America Great Again."

Whatever the case is, I learned early on when moving to Stockton that Jim Crow was alive and well. This was only the beginning. I would continue to experience its impact as I continued to live in Stockton. And that is one of the primary reasons for writing this book.

Working at Navy Communications Station Stockton (NAVCOMSTA Stockton)

I mentioned earlier in the book that God has always placed me in the right place at the right time when it came to my career. I could not have arrived in Stockton at a better time. I have talked about some of the components of the Navy communication system. It includes message centers, fleet centers, crypto centers, torn tape relay centers, radio transmitting, receiver sites, and other elements. I have also emphasized that much of the work being done inside the message centers then, as far as transmission and the receiving of messages, required human interaction. But the Navy had designed a new communication system called NAVCOMPARS. The acronym stood for Naval Communication Processing Automatic Routing System.

There were five major processing centers in the world. They supported worldwide communication for all Department of Defense agencies, NATO, the White House, agencies like the CIA, and a host of individuals and spies stationed in foreign locations. One of the centers was located in Hawaii. The Navy had plans of upgrading the then-current communications system with new Univax mainframes. These mainframes were all scheduled to be shipped to Hawaii when a typhoon hit Honolulu and did so much damage that the Navy had to make last-minute changes. This was a major decision.

Additionally, the Navy had also developed a satellite system that would replace the message interface used to communicate ship to shore and communications with submarines. This system was called CUDIXS. The acronym stood for Common User Digital Exchange System. CUDIXS was a store and forward system that interfaced with a communications satellite to send and receive messages to and from ships and Navy shore stations. It replaced the then high-frequency ship-shore-ship communication that was being supported using high-frequency radio frequency transmitters. The CUDIXS system was also interconnected to the ATODIN network. The ATODIN acronym stands for Automatic Digital Network. It was the first completely automated message switching system that the Department of Defense implemented.

So the timing was perfect for me to arrive in Stockton. As a result of the typhoon that devastated the communications station in Hawaii, Washington's decision was made to transfer everything to Stockton. The Navy rerouted the Univax mainframes that would be used to run NAVCOMPARS to Stockton rather than to Hawaii. They also made the decision at the same time that employees from Honolulu would not be transferred to Stockton to support the system. This meant that Navy and federal civilian employees had to quickly be trained on the new, state of the art communication systems. I was selected along with four other sailors to go to San Diego to be trained on the CUDIXS satellite system, and to come back and teach it to other sailors. The other four sailors were White. I was also given training on the operations of the NAVCOMPARS Univax mainframe. For this period in information technology, getting exposure to this quality of technology was unusual. These systems were located in the same building, and I got to work with all of them. This is what I mean when I say that God placed me in the right places at the right time. This was 1978, and DARPA scientists had just developed TCP, the transmission control protocol.

Later in the implementation of NAVCOMPARS, we started to support TCP and TCP/IP when IP was integrated with TCP.

Other technological things that were taking place at the same time in 1978 included bulletin board software being introduced and the Internet Protocol (IP) added to the Transmission Control Protocol (TCP) to form TCP/IP. This greatly improved the transmission capabilities of the ARPANET, which evolved into the modern-day Internet. TCP/IP is still the predominant communications protocol today on the internet and also on internal networks.

The Walker Spy Ring

Additionally, one of my responsibilities as a radioman was to inventory the crypto materials and articles in the crypto room. This was an exciting task, and I did this for whatever shift I was on. I had received a "special category top-secret clearance." Attached to the computer room was a room called the crypto room. The crypto room was where all of the crypto keys, crypto blocks, literature, diagrams, schematics, and other support documents were located. The keys were sheets of paper that listed the combinations of how to set up the crypto blocks. All Department of Defense networks worldwide, including other systems that interface these networks like NATO, were taken down at the same time every day, so the new crypto blocks could be installed. Ships in the ocean and submarines also participated in the same procedure at the same time each day. When the systems were taken down and replaced with the updated, configured blocks, all systems worldwide could communicate again with each other. This assumed that everything came back up error-free. The newly installed blocks had to be manually set up with appropriate encryption configuration based on the current key configuration. All messages transmitted and received over the networks were encrypted. The entire year's key configuration could be found in the crypto room along with the encryption blocks.

It is important to point out that if the encryption blocks or encryption keys got into Russia's hand or any of our enemies, it would be of grave security concern to the United States government. If this happened, they would be able to decipher all communications between any Department of Defense entities. That would be true whether the Navy communicated with its ships, submarines, communication between other DOD agencies, or the White House. It would create a significant security problem for the country. Only about eight people on the base had access to the crypto room. I was one of those who had that access because it was part of my job as a radioman to inventory the room's articles.

Another person who I thought at one time had access to the room was a Navy chief by the name of Whitworth. He was stationed at the Navy Communications Station in Stockton for a very short period of time while I was there. At another facility in the Bay Area where Chief Whitworth was stationed he was taking pictures of and copying top-secret material that he supplied to a friend of his by the name of John Walker. Chief John Walker was the leader of a spy ring that supplied top-secret crypto keys and other very sensitive materials to the Russians for about fifteen years before he was caught. In addition to Whitworth working with Walker, the brother and son of Walker were also in the Navy and were part of the spy ring.

In January of 1968, the North Koreans had captured an American spy ship USS Pueblo in international waters. Aboard the spy ship was a KW7 device along with manuals and other documents. Within two days of the USS Pueblo's capture, the North Koreans flew this equipment to Moscow and turned it over to Soviet intelligence. What this meant was that they now had the encryption hardware taken from the USS Pueblo. And now, they also had the encryption key lists that the Walker spy ring was supplying to them. This gave them access to all Department Of Defense communications worldwide. This continued as long as the Walker spy ring was active and until the communication system was redesigned.

According to some sources, the Walker spy ring created the most damaging security breach of the Cold War. Director of Naval Intelligence Rear Admiral Williams O. Studeman declared that no sentence a court could impose would atone for its "unprecedented damage and treachery." Secretary of the Navy John H. Lehman tried to overturn John Walker's plea agreement, but Secretary Weinberger restrained it. The KGB officer, Oleg Kalugin, who managed Walker for the Russians, wrote that this was "by far the most spectacular spy case I handled in the United States." So as you can see, this spying activity had a grave impact on the United States' security.

They all were captured and sentenced in 1986. Walker made a deal that included discussing his espionage in detail and pleaded guilty. His son, Michael, also was allowed to plea. But Chief Whitworth was sentenced to 365 years for his role in the spy ring.

Over the years I have wondered whether any of the materials supplied to the Russians came from the crypto room at the Navy Communications Station where I had the daily responsibility of inventorying the materials in the crypto room. I also had other questions that seem not to have ever been answered in any of the readings I have done of the Walker spy case. Consequently, when I started to write this section of the book, I contacted Chief Wintworth in federal prison in an attempt to get answers to these questions. I was able to establish communications with him. We corresponded two or three times. In my second communication with him I presented him with a list of questions. Recently he informed me that he would not be answering my questions. He reminded me that several books have been written about the spy case. But he also informed me that his story has not been told. He did not testify at the trial. But most importantly, he relayed to me that he is in the process of writing his memoir. So I am looking forward to reading it.

Settling in to Stockton

Everything was going great. I had been sent to San Diego for training on the CUDIX satellite system, had received training in Alameda on NAVCOMPARS, and was loving my job. I was also taking computer classes at Delta College. I wasn't working toward any degree or anything at Delta College. I was just making sure I understood at the greatest depth what I was doing at work. This was especially true for NAVCOMPARS and the Univac mainframe that I worked with. The Navy was very generous in letting me off work to attend classes when class conflicted with my work schedule. This was an opportunity that the Navy gave to anybody who would take the initiative to attend classes. But only a couple of us took advantage of it. I had started working on my Master's in Information Systems Management while I was in the Philippines with the University of Southern California. I had to leave before I could complete it, but I had accumulated a lot of units.

Meanwhile, I learned that Pepperdine University had a campus on Treasure Island, just across the bridge from San Francisco. I inquired about it, applied, and was accepted into the program. It was a very rigorous program. I attended class on Thursdays from six to nine, Fridays from six to nine, Saturdays from eight to five, and Sundays from eight to five.

And of course, I lived in Stockton, so I had to drive to Treasure Island and back each day. This usually was a two-hour drive in one direction, depending on the traffic. Just as the Navy was being very flexible with me for my computer classes I was taking at Delta College, they also extended the same amount of flexibility to get off work to drive to Treasure Island for graduate classes. Everything was going great! But it got even better because we were also expecting our first child in the middle of all this. And Linda was also working on base in the accounting office, we were utterly settled into Stockton.

Fighting the Navy from Within

One day one of the other African American sailors said to me, "Man, I wish I could have received the training that you've received." He expressed that he would be discharged from the Navy within three months of that conversation. He felt that the Navy had not kept its recruitment promise to him that they had made. They had promised him he would come in, get training, and would be able to walk out of the Navy prepared to walk into a civilian job. As I talked to him, I also learned that some other African Americans felt the same way. Now the reality is that they were getting on-the-job training. But what he meant was that he wanted formal training. He wanted some certificates stating that he had formally completed specific training on the technology he had exposure to. Another reality is that he would have to market himself once he was out of the Navy. That skill definitely would have aided him in getting an excellent job considering the exposure he had working with the technology he was dealing with. But that was another story.

I thought about what he was saying, and I felt awful about it. In my case, I already had a degree, was working on a master's, was taking computer courses, and had been given the formal training on the systems I was working with. And even I admit, the Navy had given me some opportunities others simply had not received. I would be getting out in about a year from then and felt I would be just fine as long as the job market was OK. But I felt bad about their situations. So I approached one of the chiefs on their behalf and asked if they could get formal training.

I was shocked at how they responded. I was asked if I felt that I had been given more opportunities than most other sailors. And I admitted that I had. But I explained to him how the Navy had not kept its promise to these African American sailors. This was a very sensitive issue. This complaint had come up at other locations throughout the country. The Navy was recruiting African Americans for eighteen month tours of active duty, with the rest serving in the reserve, but not really giving them the promised formal training. So when I brought it up they were very sensitive to the issue. They responded in ways I never would have expected. Before then, I was an exceptional sailor, but after bringing up that issue, I instantly became dirt.

One day I was called into the office and was confronted with the perceived complaint. I will not go into the details of what was said, but the chief tried to provoke me. I learned later that there were a couple of other people on the phone in another room listening to the conversation to be witnesses. But after he couldn't provoke me to respond in a way he had hoped I would, he reached down on his desk and handed me a form to formally make me aware that I was now on the report. He had charged me with about five very serious accounts. Any of these accounts could have resulted in me being discharged from the Navy with a bad conduct discharge. This process was all designed to make an example of me to the other African American sailors who would ever think of the possibility of complaining. Part of their plan was to send me to captain's mast and destroy my prospects of getting a good job once I was out of the Navy.

There were not many sailors even assigned to the base and only about eight African American sailors working in the fleet center. The rumors spread to other departments about what had happened. There were two African American Navy chiefs on base working in other departments. One of them approached me to find out what had taken place. I will call him Chief Smith. I explained to him what had happened. His response was, "If he wrote you up for no reason, why don't you write him up?"

"What? Write up a senior chief?" I said.

"Yes," he replied. I proceeded to ask more about the process. He gave me his contact information and home address, then told me to be at his house that Sunday morning at ten, and he would walk me through the process. I met Chief Smith that Sunday morning at his home. He showed me the regulations that governed the procedure for writing up the senior chief from the Uniform Code of Military Justice. Chief Smith had been in the Navy for over twenty years already. He had seen these kinds of things happen to African American sailors throughout his entire career. He reinforced for me what their goal was. Even with his input with their intentions, it was still hard to believe that they would be so mean. And that they were willing to take such drastic actions against me when I hadn't done anything at all wrong. But that was exactly what I was facing. He proceeded to walk me through placing the senior chief on the report and the proper process for serving him. The next morning, I served him in accordance with the procedures. He was shocked that I had done this. This was one of those procedures that existed in writing but that nobody ever did. But I guess if you had been an African American chief like Chief Smith, you had always to be prepared to protect yourself. So he knew tactics that were legal but rarely used.

Shortly after I had served the senior chief, I learned that it was time for me to take Linda to the doctor to give birth to our first child. The first almost twenty-four hours she was in the hospital, she had not given birth. But the baby was born about two in the morning on July 18, 1979. It was a boy, and we named him Nigel. I gave him the middle name Winser, but somehow it never got recorded on this birth certificate. We brought him home the following day. It was a real experience having a newborn. Suddenly, I felt the reality that should have been obvious already, that I was now a father. And that I now had the responsibility of a newborn person. When we first got home, all I could think about was what do I do now? Could I keep up the fight that I had started with the Navy, continue with school, perform my job, stay focused on all these things, and also be a husband and father? Chief Smith had already warned me that it was not going to be easy fighting the Navy and that I would always have to avoide making any mistakes or slipups because they would be looking for that to happen. Those thoughts then dominated my mind, and I didn't know how I would be able to get through it all. But I didn't make any decisions that day. I had to keep my mind focused on Nigel and Linda.

Meanwhile the African American sailors I was complaining on behalf of, were given some sort of special treatment at work. As insignificant the gesture was, they were being released from work early on weekend nights to go to the disco and party.

Believe it or not, they forgot all about formal training. So there I was in the fight of my life with the Navy on their behalf, and they were bought off so cheaply by simply being let off work a couple of hours early.

Things were about to become very intense. Chief Smith recommended that I seek the assistance of a lawyer. He gave me the name of the president of the NAACP. His name was Mr. Percy Barrows. I contacted Mr. Barrows, and set up a meeting with him. I explained to him what I was experiencing on base with the Navy. He was not surprised because he had heard rumors about African American sailors' treatment on the Navy base in the past. During the meeting, he gave me a name and contact number for Attorney Nathaniel Corley in Sacramento. I contacted him and was able to set up an appointment. At the meeting, I started to explain what had happened and how we had reached this point. Generally, in cases like this, there is some burden to convince your lawyer that you are telling the truth to get his full support. But in this case, about halfway through the story, I was stopped because he was very aware of the Navy's situation.

Some time ago, there had been a race relations problem on a Navy carrier so severe that there was a riot between African American sailors and White sailors. Because of this riot, the carrier had to be stopped in the middle of the Indian Ocean. When a carrier has to make an unscheduled stop in the ocean, it poses a problem as far as readiness is concerned. So this was a major negative for the Navy. Attorney Corley was one of the people who were flown out to the carrier to help resolve the conflict between the sailors. So he was very aware of race relations in the Navy. He was also on the National Board of Directors for the NAACP. He contacted the only private African American lawyer in Stockton about me and set up a meeting for us to meet. His name was Attorney Brown. He was then representing the NAACP in Stockton.

I met with Attorney Brown and gave him the details of the story. During the time that elapsed between meeting with Attorney Corley and Attorney Brown, I learned from another sailor that he knew a sailor at work that heard the conversation the day Senior Chief Jones wrote me up. It appears that the door was open, and the sailor was working just outside the senior chief's office, and he heard the whole conversation. He could validate that none of the charges the chief had charged me with were valid. I went to that sailor, who was a Hispanic and got a signed written statement from him to take to my meeting with Attorney

Brown. So now, I had a witness to validate that all the charges were false.

Based on other advice from Chief Smith, I also drafted and mailed a letter to the Chief of Naval Operation, the Commander of the Sixth Fleet, Admiral Gravely, and to the national Board of Directors for the NAACP. I also sent a copy to Attorney Corley in Sacramento. In the letter, I explained the whole situation—how it started, why, and all the essential details. This letter got some attention and prompted some phone calls. Meanwhile, I was referred to Rev. Henry, a pastor at the Church of All Nations in Stockton. I met with him and explained to him what was going on. He listened and vowed to give me his support. So at this point, I had secured the service of attorneys and assistance from the NAACP. I had also contacted senior leadership in the Navy. I was doing everything in my power to prevent the Navy from getting away with destroying my life without a serious fight.

Meanwhile, Linda was recovering from the delivery. I was still adjusting to being a father. I was still continuing my graduate school routine, school at Delta College, performing my job for the Navy, and being very cautious not to get in any trouble. Linda was ready to go back to work. So we had to find a baby sitter for Nigel. We found an older Black lady by the name of Mrs. Jackson. She took good care of Nigel when he was a baby. Things were looking almost like they were going back to normal. The actual interaction I was having with the chief I had written up and who had written me up, I think I would best describe as a sane one. Writing him up had established a sense of respect that didn't exist before then. But I was still very cautious in my dealings with him.

Request for a Court-Martial

I got a notice one day while at work that I was being scheduled for a captain's mast. I notified Chief Smith. Our hope and expectation that after writing the letters and writing up the senior chief, they would then drop the charges. But they seemed to have been ignoring the request to drop the charges. Because they were sending me to captain's mast, I went over to Chief Smith's house for us to discuss the situation. He reminded me that their plan was to send me to captain's mast and destroy my future and my ability to support my family. That was becoming even clearer and more important to me now that Nigel had been born. If found guilty, any one of the charges would have resulted in me getting a bad conduct discharge. A bad conduct discharge was not uncommon for the Navy to give to African Americans sailors. Chief Smith said to me, "You can always request a court-martial. That way they can't send you to captain's mast. Then you will have time to figure out how to deal with it." It sounded like a good strategy.

On the day the captain's mast was convened, I stood in front of an altar facing the commanding officer, who stood on an elevated platform that required me to look up at him. On both sides were Navy officers standing on either side of me dressed in Navy whites. Everybody was White. I didn't even know most of them because they were not in the same department I was in. There was only one person there I knew. The lights were very dim and candles were burning directly in front of the commanding officer. He read the charges and asked how I pleaded. I then respectfully requested a court-martial. He stopped the proceeding and asked me to step behind the curtains. I did. And he asked, "Do you know what you are asking?"

"I do," I replied.

"Do you realize you are going to jail if you go to a court-martial with these charges?"

"I do."

"Who will take care of your family while you are in jail?" he went on.

"We will be OK," I said. He knew Linda because she worked in the same building just a few doors down the hall from his office. So he knew that we had just had our first baby. Anyway, we returned to the ceremony, he granted the court-martial and dismissed the captain's mast. This bought me time, but it created a major problem for the senior chief. It created a much more significant problem for him than I could have imagined when I wrote him up. He had received his orders already for his next duty station. But because he had been written up, he could not relocate because, technically, he was placed on legal hold.

Being Arraigned for Court-Martial

I had the support of the local community from the NAACP and Rev. Henry. I had also been assigned an attorney by the NAACP, and I had avoided allowing the Navy to prosecute me at captain's mast by requesting a court-martial. And I had also been assigned a Navy attorney, but I had submitted a formal request to make my civilian attorney the lead attorney.

Now the day had come when I would be arraigned in San Francisco on Treasure Island. The court was to convene at 10:00 a.m. I picked Chief Smith up from his house at about 6:45 that morning to make sure we were there on time. I was unsure of what to expect because I had never been involved in any proceeding that would require me to be arraigned. During our trip there, we went over the issues affecting my case as we talked about them over the last couple of months in preparation for that day. The day before, we talked to my Stockton NAACP lawyer about how the day should proceed, but there were no guarantees.

We arrived at the courtroom at Treasure Island with plenty of time and sat down in a small military courtroom. It was extremely quiet. As I sat there, the question the commanding officer had posed to me when he called me behind the curtains at captain's mast kept playing in my mind. Are you sure you know what you are doing? What will happen to your family if you go to jail? Just as he had said, the charges that I was facing were serious. And going before a military court-martial on these charges would most certainly result in me being sentenced. Being convicted on either of the five charges against me would result in me receiving a bad conduct discharge. This was what this was all about. You see, this was just one more example of a Jim Crow practice playing out. In this case it was being practiced by members of the United States Navy.

Their objective here was to tear down an "uppity" thinking African American man. They looked at my situation and saw an African American sailor with a hopeful future. They saw an African American sailor with an undergraduate degree working on a master's degree, taking computer classes at the local college, having a "special category top- secret clearance," and having received quality technical experience. But I had the audacity to complain, not about how I was being treated, but how other African American sailors were treated. They knew I had the potential to have a very good future, and because by their assessment, I had complained, their plan was to prevent me from realizing any success after the Navy. They intended to send the message to all the other African American sailors—stay in your place, take what we give you, be happy, and shut up.

At about 9:30 a.m. we had assembled in the courtroom. Attorney Brown called to inform the court that he was on his way but had run into a minor problem with his car. He relayed to the court that his car had stalled along the freeway, and he would be there as soon as he possibly could. So he asked for a delay until he could get there. It was clear that he could not get there by 10:00 a.m. when the case was scheduled to begin. The judge advocate rescheduled the case to begin at 11:30. But after my attorney had not arrived by that time, he dismissed the court for lunch to resume at 1:00 p.m.

Chief Smith and I went to lunch and returned to court, expecting to begin at 1:00 p.m.. When we returned, we learned that Attorney Brown had not arrived. Shortly afterward, he called the court to request that the case be continued because he simply could not get there. The court granted his request. So I was spared being arraigned that day.

Meanwhile, we were starting to see some results from the letters I had written. For example, suddenly, the Navy approached my attorney about convincing me to drop my motion for a court-martial. But they were only interested in me dropping my request so they could resolve the situation at captain's mast. Of course, this still could result in the same thing happening that had caused me to request the court-martial in the first place. So we continued to reject that request.

Additionally, we knew that Senior Chief Jones was by now several months past the time he was supposed to have reported to his next duty station. Needless to say, this didn't look good for him. He was being delayed because he had been placed on report from the charges I had submitted and could not leave. So the urgency to get this case resolved increased with every day that passed.

Admiral Gravely Unannounced Visit

I need to take the time here just to highlight how God sometimes works. At the time, there was an African American man in the Navy by the name of Samuel Gravely, who had risen through the ranks to become a vice-admiral in the United States Navy. He was the first African American sailor to command a warship and the first African American to make many other achievements in the Navy. But most importantly, for this time, he had become the very first African American to have been promoted to the rank of admiral! At that time, one of the things he was responsible for was the Defense Communications Agency. All Department of Defense agencies' communications was and still is part of the Defense Communications Agency.

I got to work one day and was told that I was not to report the following day at my regular time of 7:00 a.m. But my schedule was being modified for one day, and that I should report the next afternoon at 3:00 p.m. instead. I knew that was very unusual, especially with such short notice. I wondered if it could have anything to do with my case. But of course, I didn't have the answer to that.

The following day while I was home, I got a call from Rev. Henry. He asked how I was doing and then proceeded to ask me If I knew Admiral Gravely. My response was, "Of course, like everybody else in the Navy or the nation, I know who he is. But I don't know him personally." He laughed, then said, "Admiral Gravely is a very good friend of mine. And he is making an unannounced visit to Stockton tomorrow. He will be at my church to speak at 6:00 p.m., and I would like to allow you to meet him and tell him face to face about your situation."

I could not believe what I was hearing. He was also going to be making a stop at the Navy station. His base visit had not been announced either. The only problem was that the Navy had changed my schedule for that one day. Now it was obvious why they had done so. They wanted to make sure that I was not there when Admiral Gravely came through, so I couldn't talk to him. I informed him of my schedule change. He understood and assured me he would make sure that he told Admiral Gravely what was happening with my situation.

I didn't understand what was happening with things shaping up so that I would not be there, but still, this could only be God working this out. Only God could have pulled this together. We could not have planned it, even if we tried. It was God who had put me in contact with Rev. Henry, who was a close friend to Admiral Gravely. It was God who had put me in touch with Attorney Nathaniel Corley. Attorney Corley had been sent by the Navy Secretary to resolve the racial conflict aboard an aircraft carrier stopped in the middle of the Indian Ocean due to a race riot. It was also God who had sent me in the first place to meet Mr. Percy Barrows, president of the NAACP. Only God could have orchestrated all of this and for it to happen exactly when it did.

I resumed my regular schedule the following day. Some people relayed to me how friendly he was. He had stopped to hold short conversations with sailors, asking about what they thought about the base, etc. They were afraid for me to be there to give him a good reflection of what was going on, but still he got that through Rev. Henry. And it did make a difference. Because in just a few weeks from then the commanding officer was again practically begging us to drop the court-martial request and come to captain's mast to resolve the issues.

Shortly after this time, the commanding officer of the base was unexpectedly transferred back to Washington, D.C. Then Attorney Brown negotiated an agreement with the Navy for me to drop my request to have a court-martial and go to captain's mast. The Navy would drop all the false charges Senior Chief Jones had charged me with. And lastly, there would be no record of my ever having gone to captain's mast in my record. The deal to drop any record of captain's mast was a major thing. So we all agreed to those terms. I went to captain's mast and they dropped the charges.

That afternoon, Chief Smith called to congratulate me. In his words, "You have beat the Navy. You had better watch your back because they are going to be looking at ways to get you!" I took his advice very seriously. I stayed focused on everything I was currently involved with, especially on my Navy responsibilities. My son was growing fast and crawling all over the place. And in just a little while, he was walking. I think he walked so early because he was around a couple of other boys several months older than him during the day at Miss Jackson's house. He tried his best to keep up with them.

Honorable Discharge or Not!

As far as the Navy was concerned, I did everything I was supposed, and some more and stayed out of trouble. It was just days away from the time for me to be discharged. Then on my discharge day, I had to drive up to Oakland where a person would simply type up my discharge, give it to me, and I would be officially discharged.

I drove to Oakland and located the office where I was to deliver my records. I had been given my records in a sealed envelope. They were to be handed to the person who would type my discharge. I hand delivered it to an African-American lady who processes discharges. She opened the envelope and asked me to please have a seat because she needed to make a phone call. So I did. After about an hour, she called me again and told me I should go and have lunch, and she was sure she would have it ready by the time I got back. I went to lunch, but when I got back, she still did not have my discharge ready. Now it was getting to be around three in the afternoon. I was starting to be concerned. Because I knew I had to be discharged that day since my enlistment was up at midnight. So everything had to be completed by close of business.

Finally, right around four o'clock that afternoon, she called me back into her office just before the office closed. She proceeded to explain to me why what should have taken about half an hour had taken all day long. She told me that when she opened my record, the paperwork filled out was issuing me a bad conduct discharge. She then went on to say that she looked through my entire personnel folder and could not find anything to support issuing me a bad conduct discharge. So she called the Navy base in Stockton and told them that, either they had to fax over something that would justify issuing me a bad conduct discharge, or she would simply have to give me what my records indicated I should get. My records had already been sealed and closed out. So, to then fax her something over to support the bad conduct discharge would not happen. I don't think anybody in that office was that dumb.

This African American civilian lady told me she was not about to issue a young African American man a bad conduct discharge without justification. If there had been some other person that day who would have processed my discharge, it is very likely they simply would have issued me the discharge they had been instructed to issue, with no questions asked. Here was God at work again!

PART IV

Entering Civilian Life

She handed me the discharge, and just like that I was instantly a civilian. I looked at the discharge. It said, "Honorable Discharge." It listed my accomplishments such as the specialized schools I had attended, etc. With this piece of paper, I now had access to educational benefits, VA housing loans, dental care for some time, and some other benefits. This was what they were trying to keep me from. These people had not been able to uphold the Jim Crow tradition of putting what they considered an "uppity" Black man in his place. And just remember, I had not done anything wrong. I hadn't even complained. I had simply requested that the other African American sailors be given an opportunity to receive formal training in the areas they worked in.

I had learned a critical lesson from this experience. I had a choice to make. I could take that experience and feed hate and anger against the Navy and White people. Or I could properly assess the situation by evaluating everybody's role, including my own, and then draw a conclusion. But lastly, it was essential for me to be as honest as I could be about it if it would make a valuable contribution to me as an individual. I think I was able to do that. I was able to conclude that this was not about the U.S. Navy.

Now that is not to say that there was no institutionalized racism in the Navy. But in this case, it was about the Jim Crow attitudes of several people. It was about the fact that the Navy base happened to be in a location of the country where the individuals I was dealing with felt very comfortable behaving as they did. If we had been in some other parts of the country, it wouldn't have been an issue if I had brought up the same request.

One of the things I had learned from having been stationed on two other Navy bases was that the location, and how people responded to things, had a lot to do with where you were located. For example, in the Philippines, our group "The African American Cultural Workshop," had asked the commanding officer there to address the problems that we had with our African American wives not having access to the personal items and services they needed. His response was overwhelmingly positive. They did everything in their power to make it happen. If some of us had made that same request in Stockton, we would have gotten the same response when I requested that other African American sailors receive formal training.

The bottom line was this: when people looking to act out Jim Crow ways are surrounded by an environment that promotes a Jim Crow attitude, they feel empowered to engage in Jim Crow practices themselves. So my conclusion was that I needed to understand that I could not and should not develop hatred from the Navy institution. This was not the attitude of the Navy that I had experienced to this point. And I also could not develop an attitude that this is the attitude of all White people, because that was not true, either. But it was the attitude of this group of White people I was dealing with then.

Now here is the downside of my conclusion: for this aspect of the situation, I concluded that even though I could not hate White people, I also could not trust them. In other words, I felt that at that stage of my life, I had to second-guess everything and every situation that caused me to have to deal with White people. This is extremely important because I was just beginning to enter into the civilian workforce. And I would learn later

Weak Start Unapologetic Present

that I would have to go back to the drawing board on this particular issue. I would learn that I could not put all White people into the same group with the attitude that no White people could be trusted.

So looking at that discharge empowered me because it represented victory. Sure I deserved it because I had performed outstanding work for eight years for the Navy and had not gotten into any trouble. But the fact that some people had tried to take it away from me for Jim Crow reasons but were unable to do so was indeed a victory. So when I held that discharge in my hand, I could not help thinking about how my life would be and what my future would have been had I gotten a dishonorable discharge." I would have spent the rest of my life trying to overcome it just as a lot of African American veterans have had to do.

In many cases, they are dealing with this situation simply because some White people in the branch of the military they served in didn't want to see them get out of the military and receive the same veteran benefits they themselves would receive. Again, this reflected the Jim Crow attitude—"I am better than you, and we cannot equally share the same veteran benefits even though you have earned them." Just one more example of how God had influenced the situation for me.

I was driving a Navy vehicle that day. So once I had received my discharge, I had to drive back to Stockton and return the car to the base. I returned the car, said goodbye and went to be with Linda and Nigel. It was a different feeling. I was coming home from work, but it was my last day. We had been married now for about eight years. We had our first child, and I was unemployed.

Lester Patrick

The Job Search

I got out of the Navy in the summer of 1980. The economy was in the middle of a recession. I had some sailors to question my judgment about getting out during a recession, especially since Linda had just had a baby that was not quite a year old. I even had one sailor to tell me that he got out of the Navy once during a recession and ended up in the soup line. He assured me that with the economy being the way it was, he would be seeing me come back in soon. I didn't listen to that negativity. I had decided to get out, and I was going to realize success even if there was a deep recession.

I immediately started to apply for jobs. I focused my attention, for the most part, on federal jobs. I didn't want to relocate at the time, simply because Linda was working, and it had been not quite a year since Nigel was born. Moving to another location during the recession, Linda finding another job, finding a babysitter, a place to live and all those things just seemed like too much to take on right then. So I tried to confine my job search to this area of California initially.

But later, I filled out applications for jobs across the country. For example, I received a call for an air traffic control position, but I had to relocate to Oklahoma for an extended period for

Weak Start Unapologetic Present

training. I also got called for the Jet Propulsion Laboratory in Southern California. But because Linda would be in Stockton alone, I turned them down. And there were some others. After a few weeks, I ended up working for a government contractor that had contracted with the Navy to support their radio transmitting facilities. They managed one in Dixson, CA. So I commuted there for probably three months while I looked for other jobs. The nice thing about the job was that it was not very busy. So after I got there on a shift and performed the routine tasks, I could study. I spent most of my time studying to take my comprehensive examination to complete my Master's in Human Resources Management from Pepperdine University.

That turned out very well because, unlike most all other students who took the exam in two sittings, I prepared for the entire exam and successfully completed it in one sitting. That was a major advantage because while I was in the Navy, I could get off work to attend classes, but they were not as flexible in that area in the civilian work environment. When I first got out of the Navy, I also applied to the Post Office. At the time, it had been years since the Post Office had an open register. Because in addition to the recession, there was also a freeze on hiring for federal jobs. So it wasn't easy finding a job. But then I got a call from the Post Office in Sacramento for an MPLSM operator. I had scored about a hundred on the test. The Post Office added my five veteran points, and I leaped to the top of the list. They called me in for an interview, and I accepted the job.

I thought I was getting my foot in the door, and then I would be able to apply for professional jobs. There was a training period in which I had to qualify on a computer for the position. For the first few weeks, I worked as a manual postal worker and went into the training room for a couple of hours each day to work towards qualifying for the position. I eventually qualified for the job and was placed on the MPLSM machine. Working on the actual machine was a lot different from qualifying on the computer. Working on the machine required almost perfect dexterity and synchronization between eyes, fingers, and your ability to key in the appropriate code for the mail to be routed to the correct carrier. The bottom line is that even though I had qualified on the computer, I didn't have the dexterity necessary to adequately perform on the machine. I realized that the very first night I was on the machine. But it was an entry-level job into the Post Office, and I was just looking for an opportunity to apply for professional jobs. The only problem was that the union had negotiated a fifteen-month lock-in period on the machine with management before a new employee was eligible to apply for other jobs in the Post Office.

So anyway, I qualified and was placed on the machine. I came home that night and told Linda that I had qualified. Her response was, "That's great! Tomorrow we can go house shopping." So we did, we went house hunting and found a house we liked and purchased it. We were very excited. We had a new baby, I had a new job, Linda was working, and now we had a new house. Things were looking pretty good. But there was just one problem. I was working on that machine, and I was so bad at it that I didn't know from one day to the next if I would even have a job to go to because I simply could not key the mail with any degree of accuracy. The union had an agreement in its contract with management that every employee on the machine had to maintain an accuracy rate of 95 percent or better. I rarely had a 95 percent accuracy rate. Additionally, throughout the contract, each MPLSM employee received a possible 250 pieces of mail at random intervals by which they were audited. These audits could be in increments of twenty-five pieces or fifty pieces. So if you were not good at keying the mail and you

Weak Start Unapologetic Present

got two audits within two weeks of fifty pieces each, and you didn't do well, then you only had 150 pieces of mail left to bring your average up to 95 percent. That was not a problem for most employees on the machine. But for me, it was a significant challenge because I simply could not key mail well enough to keep my average up. So I spent most of my time on the machine wondering if this would be the day that I would get fired. So I had to devise a plan that would change that.

During this same period or just before, I received my Master's Degree in Human Resource Management. I was just trying to play it out to get off of the machine into a professional job. I created a flowchart diagramming my career goals within the Postal Service, complete with specific job titles and grades. I made copies of my Navy discharge, my master's degree, and my bachelor's degree. During every break and every lunch, I spent that time approaching managers introducing myself, giving them a folder of my credentials, and asking them for their assistance in helping me reach my career goals. Ninety-nine percent of them would look at me as if I was completely crazy. Because I am sure that as bad as I was on the MPLSM machine in keying mail, there is no doubt that they all knew my very low accuracy rate. So they took the folder, but all of them looked at me as if I was completely crazy.

One night, I approached this Japanese man who was a manager on one of the MPLSM machines. I walked up to him and introduced myself. Then I said, "I have a folder with my career goals, copies of my degrees, along with transcripts, and a copy of my Navy discharge I would like for you to review at your convenience. I believe I could be much more valuable to the Postal Service in a different position than I am currently in. Can I count on your support in helping to achieve that?"

"Yes. I will help you," he said.

Lester Patrick

"Thank you so much," I replied. Lunchtime was about over, so I went back to work.

Meanwhile, I applied and was accepted into the telecommunication management master's program at Golden Gate University. The master's program was on the main campus in San Francisco. We attended classes on Tuesdays and Thursdays from six until nine o'clock. At that time, I was working the graveyard shift. That allowed me to go to school and also to work. There was not a lot of time for sleeping and resting. On Mondays, I would work on a regular midnight shift and get off at seven in the morning. I would then drive thirty-two miles to Stockton, get a little sleep, and study. About four in the afternoon, I would drive about ninety miles to San Francisco to attend class.

Once class was over, I would have just enough time to grab a quick sandwich while driving 110 miles to Sacramento to make it in time to check in for the graveyard shift. I would then work all night until seven in the morning and drive home to Stockton. I would get a few hours of sleep and then get up and do homework and study until time to go back to work. Then I would work that night again until seven in the morning, follow the same routine by getting a few hours of sleep and getting up to study. At about four o'clock, I would leave Stockton for San Francisco for class. After class, I would then drive the 110 miles from San Francisco to Sacramento to the Post Office in time to check in for work at eleven o'clock. I kept up this routine for over a year until I completed my master's degree in telecommunications management.

It had been about a week since I got the positive response from the Japanese manager. I was working on my machine, when, suddenly, someone interrupted my work. I could see a hand holding the mail back, but I didn't know who it was. I was

Weak Start Unapologetic Present

very familiar with this situation because this was what happened when you had been audited. My thought was, here we go, this is it because I only had about fifty pieces of mail left on which to be audited. There was no way I could mathematically raise my overall average to 95 percent. So I was prepared to be told that I had been audited and would be fired. But when I could see who had interrupted my machine, I was surprised. It was the Japanese manager who said he would help me. He leaned over and whispered, "There is a job coming open this week. Apply for it." I whispered back, "Yes, I will." He left, and I went back to work, miskeying mail as always.

I applied for the job, went through the interview process, and was selected for the job. It was a relief job working in the time and attendance office inside the Post Office but off the floor. Being in a relief position technically meant you would be on call if they needed a person for backup, but your primary job would still be on the MPLSM machine. That prevented a lot of people who had a major seniority over me from applying for the position. But even if they had applied, the ones I know who were upset about me getting the job would not have done well in the interview process because the interview required a face-to-face interaction before a review board of four people. Many people freeze up in that situation when required to respond under pressure to questions being asked under those conditions. I had plenty of experience doing that and felt very comfortable in that situation. These people had no experience of this type. But it didn't stop a lot of them from filing union complaints about me getting the position. The exciting thing was that I started to work in the position the following week, and I never worked again on the machine.

When the Japanese manager told me to apply for the position, he knew that the person I was filling in for would not be returning to work, because he was terminally ill. So I never had to go back on the floor unless I was required to talk or warn some employees concerning the way they were checking in, or something related to their check or leave, etc. Even though I was technically still attached to the MPLSM, as soon as the person I was filling in for passed away, they reannounced the job and permanently placed me in the position. That was a significant step forward.

One of the major advantages of being in that position was that I was then required to interface on the phone with people at the Postal Data Center in San Bruno. Now I had my first glimpse of how the Postal Service was organized as it related to information technology. That was a tremendous advantage because that was the next step on my career ladder—to acquire a position at the Postal Data Center. But I was faced with the disadvantage of not having a contact to make that happen. People were reluctant to give out the contact information of managers. One afternoon as I was discussing with a person over the phone about trying to get a contact there, he gave me the name of the Network Control Center manager. That was great. The only problem was that he would never answer his phone. So I had to come up with a better plan than just calling him on the phone.

I had weekdays off, so I decided that I would drive up to San Bruno and call the Network Control manager and ask if I could come by and talk to him on my days off. I did that several times, and finally, one day, when I contacted him, the person who answered the phone said, "Hold on, he is standing here at my desk." The person gave him the phone, and I asked if I could come by and talk to him for a few minutes about how I could help him at the data center. He said, "Sure. Give me a call sometime and we can talk about it."

"I only need just a few minutes," I interrupted before he could hang up. "It doesn't have to be formal. I can just drop by. I can actually be there in ten minutes."

"OK. But I can only give you fifteen minutes," he said. I rushed over to the building. I was calling him from the payphone about a block away. I got my things set up in the break room. I had my resume, copies of my degrees, transcripts, and a couple of textbooks for a class I was currently taking at Golden Gate University. He came out, introduced himself, sat down, and said, "I can only give you fifteen minutes." I started to talk and showed him a description of the class I was currently enrolled in at Golden Gate, and began to tell him about it. About five minutes into our conversation, he stopped me, stood up, and said, "I will be announcing a job within the next couple of weeks. I would like to have you apply for it." I stood up, shook his hand, and he went back into the Network Control Center.

Promoted to the Postal Data Center

I did apply for the job and was hired to fill a telecommunications specialist/computer specialist position. This was another time when God had put me in a place at the right time to get exposure to state of the art technology for that time. I came on board just about three weeks after the meeting in San Bruno. The Postal Data Center was in the process of relocating to San Mateo. The Post Office had purchased a building on San Mateo Drive and was moving in. It was an imposing building and an exceptional location to work. The rooftop dining area provided a view of the bay and skyline of San Francisco on a clear day. Now the commute was a different thing because I had to travel over the San Mateo Bridge to work. San Mateo was about one hundred miles from Stockton. So the commute was considerable.

Lester Patrick

The Postal Data Center was one of six data centers that the post office operated across the country. There was a data center in: New York; Washington, DC; Saint Louis; Minneapolis; Raleigh; and San Mateo. Each of them fulfilled different roles, but my primary concern was with each site's networking aspect and how it interacted with the Data Center in San Mateo. My job was to work on trouble tickets transferred from customer support reported to them by customers. Customer service did first level troubleshooting, and then passed any calls they were unable to correct over to the Network Control Center (NCC). Some calls received were ones that individual customers were experiencing, but others were calls that impacted thousands of users. Those were the ones that took priority.

The technology and network configuration I was working with there was quite different from what I had worked with in the Navy. I had primarily worked with radio frequency and satellite communications in the Navy, supporting communications to ships, submarines, and other Navy facilities. The actual applications I supported were primarily messages between these entities. We supported broadcasts to ships, and we received and relayed messages between ships and other facilities. But all of the communications were transferred via radio frequency or satellite.

In the environment at the Postal Data Center, I was supporting communications over dedicated communications links. At the time, the post office had about 50,000 buildings, some large and some small. There was a requirement to have connectivity to each of these facilities. Let's take, for example Denver or any of the major metropolitan areas. In the Denver area, there were a lot of post offices. Those post offices had dedicated connections by way of landline connection through the local phone carrier to one large centralized or main post office in Denver. That large post office then had a direct link to the San Mateo Postal Data Center. A customer in the local Denver area with a direct connection to the main post office in Denver might need to use his computer to send a report to Washington, D.C. The report would be transmitted to the Denver main post office, and then routed through the San Mateo Postal Data Center over to Washington, D.C. So the technology and the network configurations were different between the two agencies. And the applications were grossly different. As I pointed out already, in the Navy, the primary application was that of transmitting emails. But in the Post Office, the applications were numerous. The applications ranged from personnel information, time, leave, attendance data, express mail transactions, mail volume data, and data generated from all of the many applications and work-related activities you would find at any post office across the country.

Additionally, at the San Mateo Postal Data Center, I was now working with an IBM architecture called SNA. This acronym stands for System Network Architecture. It had only been introduced a few years earlier by IBM, and was then the predominant architecture of the networking environment. Most other architectures in use were modeled after SNA. It even influenced the seven layer OSI model, which is the international network model. SNA's protocol was the Synchronous Data Link Control (SDLC) protocol. It preceded TCP/IP. At one time, TCP/IP and SDLC competed to be the dominating protocol running over network backbones. It is pretty easy to conclude that TCP/IP won that battle. It won for several reasons that I will not go into, but I do want to mention its openness. TCP/IP is an open protocol and can be implemented anywhere in the world as opposed to SDLC being a proprietary protocol, which means that to communicate with it, a device also has to implement a version of SDLC. In this networking environment, I was introduced to front end processors, cluster controllers, and the semi-smart devices connected to them. These devices were usually terminals with all of the intelligence residing in the cluster controllers. By comparison, the intelligence resides in the desktop PC or laptop today.

This environment was extremely broad. This period of working in the networking arena was so much different than today. In a sense, networking was still in its infancy stages because, up to that period, only the Department of Defense and other federal agencies had the apparent need for that level of networking. But after the proliferation of the PC, that changed and is still even evolving today as more and more people own personal computers and other networking devices. Because the networking environment was changing so rapidly, it meant that there were not many people available with the skills necessary to support the networks. This was true for both small and large networks. And it was a real plus for people like me. Suppose you were in the industry during the period. The rate and amount of different kinds of technology you were exposed, to some degree was based on your initiative. For example, as a telecommunications specialist at the Postal Data Center, I was able to do everything from network troubleshooting to the programming of job control language (JCLs) to update the front end processors' software.

I got exposure to multiplexers, diagnostic equipment, oscilloscopes, data analyzers, protocol analyzers, and other equipment necessary to monitor, analyze and troubleshoot data traffic in this environment. Needless to say, I was glad to be there. I was one of seven other telecommunications specialists when I got there. But after I was there for about nine months, I was promoted to be the lead telecommunication specialist. I got the opportunity to do quite a bit of traveling to the other data centers' cities. And there were many times when users required a person to be physically on-site to assist them with setting up their networks, troubleshooting, etc. I was usually the one who was chosen to travel to those states to give that support.

Tragedy Strikes

I had been at the San Mateo Postal Data Center for about three years. I had been promoted to a senior telecommunications specialist position and was developing my expertise to a level that was above average for the amount of time I had been exposed to this technology. We had purchased a house and were very comfortable in it. But another major event that had taken place in our lives was that we had had our second child. It was a girl, and we named her Kenitra. She was named after the town where we lived in Morocco. I had always said that if I had a girl, I would name her Kenitra. And we got the opportunity to do so. Things were not perfect, but they were looking very good. This was true even though we were both very busy. Even our babysitting situation was resolved. We were really stressed out about finding a babysitter by the time Linda went back to work. Linda happened to be talking to a neighbor across the street one day, and she offered to babysit Kenitra. She was a Mexican lady just a few years older than us. That worked out great, because then as far as Kenitra was concerned, all Linda had to do in the morning was get Kenitra ready for the babysitter and then take her across the street. And then pick her up after work. Nigel at the time was picked up by an afterschool program called Kindercare. Linda picked him up from there on her way home. Later when he was older he walked home from school and stayed at our neighbor's house until Linda got home. My commute was rough. Usually, I had to be at work by about eight o'clock, but I usually worked late until the bridge's traffic was lighter.

One night just as we were preparing for bed. I was all ready to get into bed. Nigel was in his room and was supposed to be in bed, but wasn't. Linda was taking Kenitra out of the bathtub and drying her off. Everything looked very typical until Nigel screamed, "The house is on fire!" I ran to his room across the hallway to see that his room was on fire. I called the fire department while Linda gathered the children to get them out of the house. My neighbor saw it burning and took his water hose to try to fight it, but it did little, if anything at all. Then the fire department arrived and worked immediately to put out the fire. But by that time, the whole house was in flames. They were able to put it out, but not before major damage had been done. Juanita, the Mexican lady from across the street, came over and took Kenitra and Nigel.

About forty-five minutes later, I remember Linda and I were sitting in front of the house on the side of the street, stunned. The remaining firemen were boarding up the house. And they were also pulling particles from the house to make sure the fire didn't reignite. We were just sitting there on the street in front of the house in the dark in silence. What just happened? Neither one of us had a good explanation at that time for what had happened. Forty-five minutes before, we were so happy. The children were doing their thing, getting ready for bed, etc. We really didn't have any real issues to speak of or to complain about life in general. But less than an hour later, we had become homeless! Linda contacted one of her coworkers to tell her what had happened. She asked us to come over her place and get some sleep so we could be prepared to deal with it the next morning. We were still in shock. So we didn't go directly to her house. We first went to an all-night restaurant to have a cup of coffee and just talked and tried to collect ourselves.

Finally, after about two hours, we went to Shirley and Woody's house to spend the night. By then, it was very late. I could not believe how responsive our insurer Allstate was the next morning. They put us up in a hotel the next day, approved for me to replace suits, shirts, ties, shoes, and other things I needed to go back to work, etc. I cannot complain at all about how they handled the situation. They made the process a lot less stressful than it could have been. Linda and the children recovered well with no major problems. Unfortunately, we were out of our house for six or seven months.

Special Projects

I was reassigned from the Network Control Center to another area called Systems Software Support. Its focus was on telecommunications software. I was still a telecommunications specialist, but my new duties were to serve as an escalation point for telecommunications specialists in the Network Control Center. That meant that I only got involved with a network problem unless they could not get it resolved within a certain amount of time. If they couldn't, they escalated it to me, and I had a certain amount of time to get it resolved before I notified the manager of that department of the details of the problem. That was one of my responsibilities. But my other responsibility was to work with new technology and to evaluate it to see how it could improve the Postal Service's ability to meet its mission and improve its service to the public in general. This job required me to keep up with new and evolving trends and technology. I was able to do that by attending network conferences across the country, reading network magazines, attending seminars, and inviting vendors to come into the data center to present their products.

One process that I loved was bringing vendor's products in house and evaluating them for thirty to sixty days. I was able to learn a lot of different technologies in a short time frame. The reason is that I would develop a test plan, and the vendors would leave their product, and I tested it against what the Postal Data Center's requirements were—and then documenting the findings by writing a white paper and making a recommendation.

We were also assigned projects from Washington, D.C. that they may have needed to implement nationally. For example, I conducted an extensive and vital modem evaluation for the Postal Service. There were about twenty modem vendors who responded to the request for proposal. I performed the evaluation over about three months and documented the results. I then made a recommendation as part of the final report. The modems selected were used to support the express mail IRTs deployed at every post office in the United States. This was a very large national contract and of course, an extremely important project. There were others that I was assigned while at the data center, but I don't want to go into detail about them here. But I will point out that I evaluated video conference technology back in the early eighties. This project resulted in the implementation of video conference rooms at each of the Postal Data Centers nationally and at many of the large post offices across the country.

Additionally, after the divestiture of AT&T, the Post Office was one of the first, if not the first, organizations to implement a national private backbone that would integrate voice, data, and video over the same network. There were extraordinary advantages in both cost and efficiency to implementing this configuration. I was selected to implement the nodes on the West Coast in Seattle and San Mateo. There are many other projects I was involved with and could talk about, but this book is not meant to be a technical manual. So I won't.

Jack and Jill of America

Linda was a member of Jack and Jill of America until both Kenitra and Nigel graduated from high school. One of the needs for an organization like Jack and Jill was due to so many middle-class African American families living in areas where their children simply didn't have contact with many other African American children.

That was the situation when we first moved to Stockton. For several years, we had Nigel in a private school until we realized that some school staff members were mistreating him. Additionally, he was the only African American student in the entire school. We took him out of private school and put him in a public school where he could interact with other African American students. Still, there were only one or two other African American students at the most in his class.

We followed the same trend for Kenitra and came to the same conclusion eventually for her. Kenitra was in private school up until the sixth grade. It was then when we decided that she needed to have more interaction with African American kids. There was only one other African American student in her class and only six others in the school. That situation was not healthy for her development. So we took her out of private school and transferred her to public school. The mothers of Jack and Jill did weekly activities with the children so that African American children could have interaction with other African American children. There was also a teenager group that involved the teens in activities together.

Additionally, there were numerous activities that involved both parents and children. Most of these activities were held at members' homes. Then there were the regional and national conferences that took place during the summer. At these events, Jack and Jill children and their parents came from all over the country and region usually for three or four days. Jack and Jill always held its teen conferences on college campuses. Annually, there was a graduation at the summer conference for graduating seniors. Most Jack and Jill children had been part of Jack and Jill all their lives, so they looked forward to graduating from the organization. Both Nigel and Kenitra are Jack and Jill graduates. It was like no other graduation they would ever participate in. Jack and Jill of America played a critical role in both their lives.

I have already talked about Nigel, how he got a slow start in high school, ended up making a perfect score on his advanced program test and then graduated and went on to Saint Augustine College in Raleigh, North Carolina. He now works at a hospital in the bay area.

Kenitra was a mediocre student up until about the tenth grade. When she was in the tenth grade, she was also a member of the city's teen advisory board. The board was managed by a lady by the name of Penny Ruffins. Every year some representatives from the group participated in a debate at the capitol in Sacramento sponsored by the California Black state legislators. Kenitra was asked to participate.

She reluctantly agreed to participate. Tama Brisbane was acquired by the city as the coach. She coached Kenitra and the team daily until the weekend of the debate. When they got to the debate, they were split up and placed on newly created teams with students they didn't know. Kenitra and her team moved through all levels of the debate until the finals. They were placed again in newly created teams for the final debate. Kenitra and her team won the state championship. This had a major impact on her life and her outlook about college, etc. She graduated from high school, spent a year at Delta College, and then transferred to Bennett College in Greensboro, North Carolina.

Unfortunately, she did not like the atmosphere. She had been raised in California in a very diverse environment. She didn't like attending an all girl's college. Her preference was a more diverse environment like California. After her first year, she transferred to Sacramento State, then finished her Master's in Marriage and Family Theraphy at the University of San Francisco. For about ten years, she has worked as a mental health therapist. But recently, she has taken a temporary leave from working due to a health issue.

A Second Tragedy–Is God Listening?

Things were going well. I was involved with some exciting and successful projects at work. I had completed a second master's degree since I had been at the Postal Data Center. This one was a Master's Degree in Telecommunications Management from Golden Gate University. It was an excellent program that covered subject matter I never thought I would be involved with, such as network design. Several of the instructors had been called to testify before Judge Greene during the divestiture of AT&T. We were getting real time instructions in some cases by instructors about the divestiture, before it was even formally published. It was exciting having a first hand introduction of how things were unfolding before it was even reported on by the media. There was a lot going on.

Then one morning I was on my way to work, driving down business ninety-two through Hayward. I was on my way to the San Mateo Bridge that I needed to cross to get to work. As I drove in the middle lane towards the bridge, suddenly a toddler walked from the curb directly in front of my car. I instantly hit my breaks, but I still hit the little boy. His body went airborne and landed onto the highway, about twenty-five feet in front of my car. I remember seeing him slowly move through the air and then hit the ground. I screamed as he floated through the air.

Traffic next to me in both lanes suddenly stopped. I jumped out of my car and rushed to see his condition, but I could not tell because he seemed not to be moving or breathing. He had landed facedown and was still lying on his stomach. I was extremely nervous. It felt like it was taking forever for the emergency crew to get there. But actually, not more than three or four minutes had passed. Finally, they came, just about the same time the police arrived. Three or four other drivers who were driving close to me also stopped and gave the police statements. I don't think there was any doubt that I could not have avoided the collision. But still, I had hit a little child, and I didn't know if I had killed him or not. I felt terrible. There were so many unanswered questions. Where did the child come from, and why was a two-year-old child alone crossing the street? The police asked me those questions. I didn't know the answer to the questions. But after giving my statement, I got in my car and continued my commute to work. With no traffic, I was only about fifteen minutes away from the building. My mind was completely immersed in what had just happened. As I got out of the car, I could see blood stains from where I had contacted the child. I called Linda at work to let her know and asked her to pray for the little boy. And I told my manager.

I could not focus my attention on work, so I just had to leave and go home. On my way back to Stockton, I found myself saying, "God, please don't let him die!" When I got to Stockton, I stopped by the car wash to wash the bloodstains from the car. I continued my prayer, "God, please don't let him die!" This was all I knew to say.

I had been raised in the church since I was about five years old. Aunt Nellie had made sure I was in church and Sunday school every Sunday as long as she could. But when I went off to college, my attitude had changed about God and religion. I had so many questions and no answers. When I would come home from college, Aunt Nellie would ask me to come to church, but I never did. One Sunday morning when I was home, she came to my bedroom and asked me to come to church. I said OK, I will be there. But I didn't go. When she got back, I told her I didn't realize at the time, but my suit was not clean. When I grew up, we wore suits to church, as if that was a requirement by God. So she asked me again the next weekend. But this time, she told me, she had put my suit in the laundry, and it was already hanging in the closet. So I assured her I would be there. That afternoon she returned home after attending Sunday school and church and then staying for a luncheon or some event they had at the church.

"I noticed you didn't come to church," she said entering my room.

"Oh. I guess I must have overslept," I reasoned. It was Sunday afternoon, and I was still in bed. But what she said then shocked me.

"That's OK. From now on, you don't have to go to church anymore. I am turning you over to God." I was shocked at Aunt Nellie's reply. I didn't quite know what that meant.

"Thank you so much," I said and went back to sleep until it was time to get up and go out for the evening.

But now I found myself wondering if this was happening to me because I had behaved the way I had? I found myself asking if He was even listening to my prayer? I didn't know, but one thing I had learned from all those years of attending church was that I needed to pray and have faith that God was going to answer my prayer. And when I called Aunt Nellie and told her about what had happened, she reaffirmed that thought. So I kept praying, "God. Please don't let him die!" I just sat there on the couch, repeating, "God. Please don't let him die!" It is hard to describe my feelings. But I felt dirty. I got up and took a shower, but it didn't make me feel any better.

The thought came to me to contact the hospital. I had overheard the men on the emergency truck say they were taking him to the Children's Hospital. I was able to get the number for the hospital and called. I explained to them what had happened and that I wanted to know the child's condition. They put me on hold for about three minutes and came back with another number if I got dropped when they transferred me. They were transferring me to a desk near the operating room. The person I talked to knew of the case I was inquiring about. She told me that the little boy was in surgery and in a coma, so they just didn't know if he was going to make it or not. They advised me to call back later. In my discussion with the person on the phone, I learned more about how it had happened that the little boy was alone on the street. I learned that the child lived about a half block from where I hit him in the street. He had awakened early in the morning before his parents woke up, opened the door, and walked down the street. From witnesses who observed him standing there as they waited for the light to change, they wondered why he was alone, but nobody said anything. The little boy didn't wait for the light to change, he just stepped out into the traffic in front of my car.

Linda came home from work. When she arrived, I went into more detail of what had happened. She tried to assure me that it would be OK. I continued to call throughout the night, but there had been no change in his condition. Later, I tried to get some sleep, but I found myself getting up, sitting on the couch, and praying that prayer, "God, please don't let him die!"

At about five in the morning, I called and spoke to a person near the operating room. By now, the child had been taken to a room. They transferred the call to the desk in that area. Then a person came on the phone and said, "Can you hear the screaming in the background? That's him. It means he is hurting, but he will be OK." I said, "Thank you God, for not letting him die."

I know, you probably are thinking that this experience motivated me to go back to church and follow Jesus. But it didn't. When I found out this child would live and be OK, I immediately relapsed into my hectic lifestyle with the major focus being on work. I put that completely behind me because I loved the work I was doing. It was so much fun that it was as if I wasn't working at all.

Creating Parents and Citizens for Quality Education

Time was flying by. It seemed like it was just yesterday when I took Nigel over to Gain's Barbershop to get his first haircut. Now he was entering high school this year. School had just started and a couple of times already, Nigel had brought home a notice from the school stating that his behavior was not up to par. That was not the exact wording, but that's what it meant. So I had to sign the notice to show that he had told me about it. But the night before, he gave me a notice stating that he had been suspended for two days for violating school policy. I asked Nigel what he had done in violation of the school's policy. He told me something that didn't make any sense concerning him and three other kids playing some game during lunch. So I assumed he was not telling me the complete truth. I needed to go to school to find out what was really going on.

The next morning, rather than leaving for work early, I took Nigel to school to speak to the principal to get the full story. We sat down with the principal, and he explained to me that Nigel and two other boys were playing a game called "doggy pile." One kid was pushed down, and two or three others then fell on that kid and formed a pile. I listened to what he said, and it was exactly what Nigel had told me.

"Was he in class when he did this?" I asked.

"No. They were at lunch," the principal said.

"Let me get this straight," I said. "Are you saying that Nigel and two of his friends were playing during their lunch break, a game that the school hasn't identified as being one that can't be played at school and he was suspended for it?"

"I wouldn't put it that way exactly, but he was suspended for playing the game," he said.

"Ok, with all due respect, I would like to know where Nigel's next class is, because you are not going to expel my son for playing a game during his lunch break that is not in violation of any school policy." I got up and told Nigel to show me his next class so I could escort him there.

"Maybe I can reconsider this time," the principal said as we started to leave the room.

"OK," I replied, and Nigel left the room for his class. Meanwhile, I left the campus for work.

The following week, something happened that required me to go to Nigel's school to bring him something. It was during lunch hour when I arrived. At first, I couldn't find him. I kept walking, and I could see many African American students at the far end of the campus. So I started to walk there, and sure enough, it was the African American kids there in that corner conversing and taking their lunch. I asked, "Nigel, why are you guys all on this part of campus alone?" His response angered me. He said, "If we stay here out of the way of security, then they will not bother us." I gave him what I needed to leave with him, then I left the campus for the Bay Area. But I was thinking about what he had said all the way to work—*"If we stay over here out of the way of security, then they will not bother us."*

I realized that school officials were engaging in a Jim Crow practice of harassing African American students. But the African American students agreed to be mistreated by staying out of the way and acting in an inferior manner in response to school officials' Jim Crow practice. I decided at that point that it would stop, because I was going to stop it!

I contacted several people I knew whose children also attended the school and one of the school's African American employees. I should add at this point that the school district was then predominately White. About 50 percent were White, roughly 30 percent were Hispanic, around 15 percent Asian, and about 5 percent were African American. I held a meeting at my house and organized a group named "Parents and Citizens for Quality Education." We got on an upcoming school board agenda and announced ourselves to the public. At that meeting, I presented a six-pint plan to address the issues affecting African American students and parents' concerns.

THE - 6 - POINT PLAN

- Lack Of Academic Progress Among African American Students.

- Inequitable Suspension And Expulsion Policies.

- Hostility Towards African American Students And Parents.

- Lack Of Africans Employed In the District At All Levels.

- Lack Of Adequate Safety Policies.

- Minorities Have Negative Image Of The District.

Lester Patrick
Academic Review Committee

Lester Patrick

The school district adopted the six-point plan and, for several years, it pretty much dominated the board's activities. We had regular meetings with the district representatives and state representatives over the next several years. We brought about very positive change in the district that influenced everything from hiring African Americans to specialized math programs and the suspension and expulsion rates. I have always been a firm believer in the concept of presenting a solution when you have a complaint. And I treated this no differently. Below is a list of the six items we saw as issues and several solutions we implemented to address them.

One of the advantages of being physically located in Stockton is that we are only thirty-two miles from the capital city Sacramento. The California Department of Education is located in Sacramento. So we were able to invite and have the attendance regularly of individuals from departments that could impact the goals we were pursuing. Consequently, several of the things that we implemented in Stockton in the Lodi Unified School District were adopted by the state and implemented on a statewide basis. For example, working with the district, we were able to contract Dr. Junious Williams from Oakland to conduct a project to identify why African American students were being suspended and expelled at a much higher rate than all other students. He identified why they were being suspended by surveying teachers, administrators, students, parents, etc. He then grouped them into about twenty categories and made some recommendations on how to help teachers and administrators address their behavior towards African American students. He then met with African American students and addressed how they should respond to teachers. To make a long story short, his work helped to reduce the suspension and expulsion rates for African students. But equally important is that the State

Department of Education uses the same categories today as reasons students are suspended and expelled from school. Additionally, no school districts in California were monitoring students' academic progress who were in danger of failing before we implemented it. This was another project that Parents and Citizens for Quality Education started. It was introduced to other districts within the state by state employees who attended our meetings.

We had many accomplishments that influenced the progress of African American students in the district over the years. But the reality is that our work influenced all other students as well. This was true even though our focus was on African American students. I will not discuss each accomplishment of Parents and Citizens For Quality Education individually, but I am listing several of them below:

Making Math Fun

To meet African American students' educational needs in the Lodi Unified School District, I proposed converting a mobile unit to a traveling technology classroom. This unit was equipped with twenty workstations and rotated between twenty-three schools in the district to support low-income stu-  dents. Below is a picture of that unit. The unit was also equipped with a satellite dish, overhead projector, and all other classroom amenities. Two Lodi Unified employees supported the unit. One employee was a teacher and the other a technical person. We named the unit the "Urban Technology Vehicle."

Accomplishments

A. Lack of academic progress

1. Organized the Academic Review Committee of Lodi Unified District

    One of the major accomplishments of Parents & Citizens for Quality Education is the development of the Academic Review Committee. The Academic Review Committee was designed to monitor the academic status of African Americans within the Lodi Unified School District. Although initially proposed specifically to address the academic deficiencies of African Americans, all students within the district have benefited from the work of he Academic Review Committee.

    The Academic Review Committee consists of parents, community members, school district administrators, a school board member, and ad hoc participants.

2. Started an academic progress monitoring program for African American students.
    - Implemented a monitoring and tracking program aimed at tracking the academic status of AA students in threat of receiving D's and F's.
        - Success rates varies from year to year
    - Implemented afternoon tutorial programs.
        - Minimum participation
    - Encouraged the redesigned of the GATES acceptance criteria to include more African Americans and other children of colors.
        - Went from 1% AA to the current 7%
    - District initially authorized two positions to monitor the program.

3. Proposed a program that would indoctrinate teachers to the need to be more sensitive of the needs of children of color (Different and Wonderful). This course was taught throughout the district to staff and administrators.

4. Proposed afternoon tutoring programs, and afternoon transportation program for students needing transportation. The program benefited all students.

5. Recommended the implementation of the literacy program in LUSD.

6. Recommended, developed and proposed the concept of a technology academy at Bear Creek High. The program has been implemented and is very successful.

7. Recommended, developed and proposed the Making Math Fun Program. (Joint effort with ARC)

8. Proposed and implemented the Making Math Fun Program

This effort represented one segment of a program I developed and named "The Making Math Fun Project." The children who used the UTV loved it. It made them feel like doing math and other subjects in the UTV was fun rather than learning. We saw improved math scores of those students who regularly took advantage of using the Urban Technology Vehicle.

The Algebra Project—Bob Moses Civil Rights Leader

Another component of the "Making Math Fun Project" was a program called "The Algebra Project." We adopted this project from Mr. Bob Moses, who developed The Algebra Project. He created this project after several years of teaching math in an African country. While teaching there, he noticed that children started to take Algebra at a much lower grade than typically in the United States. He taught there for seven years.

Consequently, he returned to the United States in 1976 and did graduate work in the philosophy of mathematics. He taught high school math in the public high school in Cambridge, Massachusetts. But learning from his daughter that the school at that time was not teaching algebra is what motivated him to start teaching there.

Mr. Moses received a MacArthur Fellowship in 1982. He used the award to create The Algebra Project, placing priority on improving minority education in math. He placed special emphasis on his daughter's school and classroom in Cambridge, Massachusetts.

The Algebra Project has been expanding since 1982 across the country with an outstanding track record for assisting minority students with improving math scores. Traditionally, society doesn't see the need for African American students to take and excel in math. Through The Algebra Project, Mr. Moses attempts to change that attitude by focusing on the most math deficient students and preparing them for college-level math. He has done a lot of research and development that has been incorporated into The Algebra Project. The program has received prestigious awards from the Fletcher Foundation and from the National Science Foundation.

When we contacted the office of The Algebra Project, they sent a representative to Lodi to present to the staff at the Lodi Unified School District. From that meeting, the school board authorized four of us to travel to Jackson, Mississippi to observe the program firsthand by visiting a school in Jackson where the program had made a significant difference in African American students' math scores. We also met with Mr. Moses who gave us a very good description of what had motivated him in the first place to develop The Algebra Project. We were very impressed and could not wait to get back and get the program started in the Lodi Unified School District. We started the program initially at the Delta Sierra Middle School. A couple of The Algebra Project representatives came to Stockton to instruct teachers on the project's concepts, and through demonstrations, taught them how to teach algebra to students.

I should also point out that Mr. Moses is the same Bob Moses, the civil rights activist. He is known for his work as a Student Nonviolent Coordinating Committee (SNCC) leader on voter education and registration in Mississippi during the Civil Rights Movement. He is also the co-founder of the Mississippi Freedom Democratic Party. He started working with civil rights activists in 1960 when he became the field secretary for the Student Nonviolent Coordinating Committee (SNCC). He became the co-director of the Council of Federated Organizations (COFO), an umbrella organization for the major civil rights groups working in Mississippi. He was the main organizer of the COFO's Freedom Summer Project. This project was designed to achieve widespread voter registration of Blacks in Mississippi and end racial disenfranchisement. This project attracted hundreds of young White students from the North to assist with the voter registration drive. African American voters had been shut out of the political process in Mississippi since 1890. On June 21, James Chaney who was African American, and was locally from Mississippi, was reported missing. And Andrew Goodman, and Michael Schwerner, two White men from New York, were also reported missing. They had been sent on a mission together to investigate a church burning in Philadelphia, Mississippi. Their bodies were found six weeks later buried in an earthen dam. Bob Moses pulled the volunteers together to make them aware of what they were up against. They also emphasize that they could leave if they desired to without any condemnation from anybody. All of the volunteers decided to stay.

Mr. Bob Moses had put the same commitment he displayed during the civil rights movement into developing The Algebra Project. His passion for the project was very apparent from our conversation with him. And we were excited about its potential to assist us in improving the math scores of African American students. We implemented the program at Delta Sierra Middle School.

Associate Professor of Telecommunications

I was on travel in Washington, D.C., attending a meeting. I got a call from my manager. He asked me if I had seen the email he sent out. I had not seen the email, so he continued to tell me what it said. The email was notifying his staff that he was leaving the organization for another job. He was even moving away from the Bay Area.

My manager was also an associate professor at Skyline College in San Bruno. He taught a telecommunication class. "I would like for you to replace me as an associate professor at Skyline when I leave," he said. "I have already talked to the dean of the school about you, so all you have to do is to say yes."

"Yes. I would love to, but I don't have any teaching experience," I said.

"If your answer is yes, then I will set up a meeting for the dean to come to San Mateo next week so he can meet you."

"OK. I will see you when I get back," I replied. I got off the phone with him thinking, can I do this? What makes him think I can? I don't have any experience, nor do I have a teaching credential. But he said he had already talked to the dean of the school, so I will wait until I get back and see how it goes.

I finished up my work in Washington and returned home in time to enjoy my weekend with Linda and the children. When I got to work on Monday, my manager told me that the dean of the school would be there at lunch, so make sure I was available.

He was there at lunch, and my manager introduced us. We met in the Network Control Center. I remember him saying something like, "Gary says you are proficient on all the technology in this center."

"I guess you could say that," I replied.

"My primary reason for being here today is to have you sign this application for a teaching credential," the dean said. I signed the document. He then told me that he would be taking it up to Sacramento that afternoon to walk it through and that I could come over to his office at the college the next day to pick up the credential. I said, "OK. I will see you then tomorrow." I was thinking that I knew people who had been trying to get a teaching credential for years and still had not been successful in doing so. It looked like I was going to have one in less than twenty-four hours. I couldn't believe it. But I was OK with it.

The next day I went over to pick up the credential. The dean did have a credential for me to pick up. Not only was it a teaching credential, but it was a lifetime credential. Wow, how could this be happening? God was looking out for me, yet again! But at this point, he wasn't getting anything back in return. Because I was not worshiping, attending church, or even pretending to be a Christian. But I was sure that it was God who had worked out so many things in my life just for me. And this was one more example. While I was there, I was also able to pick up the textbook I would be using and my schedule. It was the first week of December and I was going to start teaching in January. That meant that I had to spend the rest of December, including the holiday, preparing for next semester. So I did that, but with a big smile on my face.

January rolled around, and it was time for me to take on my role as Associate Professor of Telecommunications at Skyline College.

Weak Start Unapologetic Present

Skyline at the time was one of the few schools that had a hands-on lab. I taught on Tuesdays and Thursdays. So I would leave work at San Mateo and travel over to the college about ten miles away. I covered the lectures on Tuesdays and conducted laboratory on Thursdays. It worked out very well. And I loved it.

After I had taught there for two or three years, I was into the routine of leaving work and driving directly over to the college, teaching the class, and going home. This particular day I had planned to go to Oakland to attend a technical seminar during the afternoon and then leave there and go to the college to teach. That meant that I would be coming over the Bay Bridge about five o'clock on my way to Skyline College. But something happened that day that prevented me from being able to leave work and get there.

That afternoon, as I was backing out of the parking lot at San Mateo, my car started to rock from side to side. I could see multiple waves coming towards the car as if the ground was buckling. At the same time on the radio, the announcer screamed, "This is the big one! I am watching the Bay Bridge fall!" At that same time, sirens started to ring out all over the Bay Area. If I had not gotten so busy at work and had time to make it to the technical workshop in Oakland, I would probably have been on the Bay Bridge on my way to Skyline College when the earthquake struck. God had intervened again! I really wanted to attend that workshop. Even after I knew I would be late and wouldn't get the full benefit of attending the workshop, I still tried to make it. But I just couldn't.

As I approached the street on my way to school, I could see gas station shelters and other buildings that had collapsed. There were fire engines everywhere. Then I heard an announcement over the radio that the San Mateo Bridge had also been closed due to suspected damage. I did get to college, but there was nobody there. It had already been closed due to the earthquake. I then tried to get home. I stopped to make a phone call at a phone booth to let Linda know I was OK. The line to the phone booth was very long, and it took a while before I could get to where I could make a call. The first time I finally reached the phone after standing in line, I could not get a call through. To make a long story short, it took me almost all night to get home. But I eventually made it.

Leaving the San Mateo Postal Data Center for Another Position

I had been at the San Mateo Postal Data Center for about twelve years and I had enjoyed most of my time there. But there was a new Postmaster General appointed. Consequently, he had decided that he would do a complete reorganization. This meant that all Executive Administrative Service (EAS) employees like me would be the ones most impacted. Technically, those employees who did not contact and touch mail out at a post office were the ones the reorganization affected. The Postmaster abolished all of the Executive Administrative Service positions, and a new organization was created. All positions were re-announced. We then had to reapply for our positions.

My position was re-announced but it was in Raleigh, North Carolina. So I was given an opportunity to relocate to Raleigh. I had to report to Raleigh within two weeks after I was informed that I was going to be part of the new organization. For personal reasons, I declined the offer. My children were in the middle of the school year. I was in the middle of the semester of teaching at Skyline College. It was just a very bad time to relocate. Declining the offer, which I did, meant that I would be directed to a transition center to look for another job. So that is what happened. I was transferred to a transition center to look for another job. This turned out to be a very positive experience for me. There was a crew of professional people there to work with me to help bring out my strengths and identify my weaknesses related to my job search. They gave me guidance on how to apply my strengths in searching for a new job. In just a few days, I gained tremendous confidence as it related to the process. My attitude became one that viewed this as an excellent opportunity to enhance my career. And that is exactly what happened.

Veteran Health Administration

Shortly after being in the career transition center, I applied for a position with a data center at the Department of Veterans Affairs in San Francisco. It was a senior computer specialist position. I went in for the interview and was the successful candidate. I started to work there just a few days from then. The team I was hired for covered communications for the country. I was assigned to the western region, with five of us being on the team in different parts of the country. The manager was located in Silver Spring, Maryland, and we were responsible for voice, data, and video for the regions we were assigned. I covered all the states from New Mexico to the state of Washington. This meant I was the coordinator for all services for VA facilities in any of those states. This was a great opportunity. I had no idea how many opportunities came with this position when I applied. Those things were not stated in the job announcement. Even though I did not experience a pay reduction, when I first saw the job description, I thought the job was a step down from what I had done at the Postal Data Center. But once I got on the job and learned about the applications I would be supporting, the technologies I would help implement, and all other related activities, I was very pleased with my transition. I could see that God again was looking out for me.

As I stated earlier, each team member was responsible for the support of voice communications, data communications, and video. This was where it became an advantage for me, because a couple of the other team members were not strong in all three technologies. I had experience in voice, data, and video that I picked up in the Navy and at the Postal Data Center. This was not the norm for people working in the industry, and it is even more unusual today. This meant that I got many requests to participate in projects in other team member's regions. That was great because it gave me an even greater opportunity to expand my technical knowledge and exposure. But it also meant that there was an increased requirement for frequent travel.

The Veterans Health Administration (VHA) consists of VA hospitals, clinics, and other associated facilities. Our responsibility was to provide support from the ground up for this part of the organization and, in some cases, for the Veteran's Benefits and Veterans Cemetery also. Whether we provided support for other parts of the organization other than VHA depended upon the project. One example would be the wide area network.

One huge opportunity for me to work for the VA was that it didn't even have a true wide area network. But wide-area networking experience was one of the primary requirements of the job I had applied for and hired to do. They only had some connections in place that they referred to as a wide area network. It was woefully inadequate for the applications they needed to support. This is an example of what I meant earlier when I said I first saw this job as a step down from my previous position. Because they simply didn't have a wide area network with the complexity that I was accustomed to. But I quickly saw that this was an advantage for me. Because I quickly compiled a network design and a proposal for a VA wide area network backbone. It took about a year of evaluating in a laboratory environment, but the overall concept was eventually adopted and implemented. This was the VA's first robust network with the capability to support its many applications on a national basis. I developed this

Weak Start Unapologetic Present

proposal and presented a network design for the VA's network backbone based on the training I had in network design concepts at Golden Gate University when I completed my Master's Degree in Telecommunications Management.

Additionally, after the divestiture of AT&T and the cost of digital services became more manageable, I participated and helped to implement the first private national digital backbone of any Federal agency while at the San Mateo Postal Data Center. We were able to install our private digital backbone that allowed us to implement voice, data, and video between locations locally. This is so important because there was a long-distance fee associated with all calls outside of your local calling area at that time. By installing our private digital backbone, we eliminated all long-distance calling costs. There was tremendous savings to the agency in call charges. All calls, no matter where they originated or were destined for, were a local call. This is because the call went over our private backbone. That was true for data connections and video calls as well. This design approach then was the hottest network design concept around.

I need to make a point about video services. Today, most of the public didn't know that video was being used in the workplace until only recently when Zoom video calls became a norm because of the pandemic. But we were already doing video calls twenty years ago in the workplace. I made this point to say that the opportunities were even greater with my new job to deploy this technology throughout the organization. This organization had an even greater need for the technology than the Post Office. I designed and implemented several networks to support voice, data, video, and telemedicine between hospitals within the VA. I will talk about one of these projects later.

Lester Patrick

Renegotiation of Networking Contract

The federal government then had a national contract that was called FTS2000. The federal government had negotiated this contract on behalf of all federal agencies. As the coordinator for the western region, one of my responsibilities was to serve as the contact for the FTS2000 contract. That included coordinating installations, troubleshooting, enhancements, and anything related to telecommunications services for all facilities on the West Coast. One of the primary responsibilities of the San Francisco Information Systems Center, where I was physically located, was to develop and support applications for the hospitals. This meant that, once the applications had been developed or modified, they had to be transmitted to all the hospitals throughout the country. Of course that depended upon the applications. But generally speaking, that was the case. That meant that they might have developed an application and then transferred it to the Salt Lake City Hospital. I have seen times when a transmission was started at about three o'clock in the afternoon and when we returned the next morning the application was still being transferred. That was one major drawback of the network in place when I arrived. But the other drawback was cost.

I was attending an FTS2000 meeting one week in Washington, D.C. and was given a copy of the service contract. On my way back, I was reading it and came across something I could not believe. That was the cost per packet that all agencies were being charged. I took out my calculator and made some quick calculations. I was astonished at the results I was seeing. The federal government—and in particular the VA—was being ripped off by two of the largest carriers in the nation. I will not name them. They would know who they were at the time. But I could not just make accusations. I had to prove it, and it had to be accurate such that nobody would be able to dispute it. Remember, I was doing an excellent job for the organization, but I am still an African American man. And the Jim Crow attitude was still very prevalent, whereby a black man was expected to stay in his place. And generally speaking, his place was not to accuse the biggest two network providers in the country of ripping off the federal government by millions each year.

I developed a test plan that consisted of installing devices that integrated voice, video, and data over the same physical facility. I talked about this concept a couple of pages ago. The proposal to install the equipment and test the concept in this environment was completed and approved by my senior managers in Washington, D.C. and Silver Springs, Maryland. I conducted the project for about eight months. The first six months consisted of testing and monitoring different concepts. The last two months were used for collecting and analyzing data, drawing conclusions, formally documenting the process, developing a cost analysis, and making recommendations. The final report caused a major controversy, both internally and with the two networking providers. The report was arranged such that it addressed two primary categories. The first category was cost and the second category focused on the technical concept being recommended.

As for the cost, I was able to show and prove that it was costing on the average $450 to transfer a file according to the per packet cost. This meant that for a programmer at the San Francisco Information Systems Center to transfer a file across the city to the San Francisco Hospital, it cost $450. If that same file was being sent to Washington DC to a VA hospital, the cost was also $450 because the file was the same size and contained the same number of packets. Finally, the comparison I made that caught everybody's attention was, in the report, I compared an airline ticket across the country, which cost about $300 at that time. I pointed out that it cost less to put the tapes containing the file on an airplane and send it across the country than it did to transmit it over VA's network at the rate we were being charged. At first, I got some very mild pushback. But there were no legitimate disputes. As a result of my findings, both networking companies agreed to renegotiate the VA contract for a more reasonable cost. Keep in mind that these were ten-year contracts, so they had the potential to make hundreds of millions of dollars from the VA alone by overcharging.

The second part of my findings was all technical in nature. Unfortunately there was nobody in the organization who could adequately evaluate my findings. The VA established a contract with a team from Carnegie Mellon to evaluate what I had submitted. I thought they gave a reasonable evaluation but they didn't endorse or oppose what I was recommending. We ended up implementing a version of what I had recommended being implemented as VA's national backbone.

A Second Fire!

During this portion of my career, I had to do a lot of traveling. One Sunday, I left for Washington, D.C. around noon. I was there in plenty of time to get settled, get some dinner, and prepare for my meeting the next day. Usually, after I had done those things, I would call home to make sure everything was going OK. I was just about to call home when my phone rang. It was Linda speaking in a very frantic voice as she said, "You are not going to believe this, but we had another fire!"

She was correct. I couldn't believe it. I asked what had happened. She proceeded to tell me that when she came home from taking the children to dinner, she found the front door nailed up with a notice from the fire department on it. When she walked around to the back she saw major burn damage. Several things had been burned; including the covering over the patio, the patio furniture, and a portion of the roof. The trees lining the back perimeter of the back yard had also been burned. When she talked to the fire department, she learned that some neighborhood kids had built a treehouse in one of the trees lining the back of our house. They had built a treehouse on a branch that extended far enough outside of our yard that they were able to build it without us knowing they had done so. It appears they were smoking in the treehouse that day, and accidentally started a fire. So it ended up burning up our backyard and part of the roof. Needless to say, getting that report from Linda made for a very long night. But there was nothing I could do from Washington, D.C. I had a presentation to do the following day, so after doing my presentation and staying for the first day of the meeting, I returned home.

When I returned home and talked to the insurance agent, he was puzzled about how I could have two fires within a few years. He pointed out to me that most people never have a fire in their lifetime. I had experienced two fires in a few years. But the reality is, neither one of them was our fault. On the positive side, we did not have to move out of the house this time. Because of the time of the year it was, they were able to replace the roof in less than three weeks completely, and make all the other repairs in a reasonable time frame. But still, we had had two fires within a few years. I am not sure what was going on through our minds at the time, but we started to look for another house shortly afterward.

PART V

Going Back to Church

Linda had been actively attending church the whole while we had been in Stockton, but I had not. She had been trying to convince me to go with her, but I refused because I didn't think I needed to be part of a church. Her concern was about me setting a good example for the children. I always read the Bible. Most nights, I fell asleep while reading the Bible. I had been doing that for a very long time. And I even watched certain TV evangelists routinely every Sunday, but still, I didn't go to church.

Linda started to attend a new church, and she invited me because she thought I might like it. I accompanied her and the children a few times, but that church was not for me. There were about ten people in the entire church. And it just didn't motivate me to want to be part of it. But I did encourage Linda to continue to attend and take the children, until one Sunday, the church just closed down. The Sunday before it closed, the pastor announced that his wife didn't want to be part of the church any longer. I thought that was a pretty interesting position for the pastor's wife to take. Outside of God, she would know more about him than anybody. Then a couple of weeks from then, Linda came home and announced that the church was closing down. By this time, I did want to be part of a church I could feel comfortable in. So we started to visit churches across the city.

One Saturday, while the family was enjoying a holiday outing, we ran into Marilyn Gayles. She was very excited about her new church on "C" Street and invited us to come for a visit. The next day we did visit Progressive Missionary Baptist Church on "C" Street. The pastor was a man by the name of Rev. Maurice Harris. We attended a few times and decided to join. Just for the record, I never joined my wife's previous church. Some things about that church didn't sit right with me.

This time, we joined the church on "C" street and also started to attend Sunday school. After a few months, I developed a strong desire to be in church every Sunday morning, unlike how I had previously felt. If I didn't go, I felt like something was missing. On occasions, I remember having to travel back east for business travel and making sure my flight was scheduled at a time that would allow me to attend church first.

The church then had about four hundred members but was growing rapidly. I met with Pastor Harris to discuss with him my desire to establish a video ministry. I was looking for some way to contribute to the church. He agreed to the idea. So I started to video record his sermons. Recording the sermons, attending Sunday school and church gave me a sense of doing something that God was calling me to do.

About a year-and-a-half after I joined, a church disruption resulted in Pastor Harris stepping down. The senior leaders of the church sought a replacement. As a result, several preachers came during a period to deliver the sermons. Eventually, Rev. Glenn Shields from Sacramento became the pastor.

Disagreement with a Senior Leader about Scripture

For a very long time before returning to church, I had been reading the Bible. To be clear, I was not studying the Bible because my reading was not consistently focused on any one subject or principle. Nor did I usually have any specific goal in mind as I read. But I had been raised in the church since I was about five years old when I started to live with Aunt Nellie and

Weak Start Unapologetic Present

Uncle Winser. I am not sure where I stood as far as my soul was concerned. I am not sure if I was saved at the time I joined church.

Today I find myself asking the questions, was I saved then? Did I initially join church because it was the tradition for children at Good Hope Freewill Baptist to join church early? Or did I join because I was able to observe the positive responses from the adults of the church, when young people joined church? All I know is that, when I left for college, I also left the church. But when I joined church the second time as an adult, I had a powerful desire to be part of a church. Looking back I do have to believe that God had placed his seal in me from the very beginning. I understand today, after years of study and from first-hand experience when God places his seal in us, it is permanent. How much and at what rate we experience growth in Him is largely dependant upon us. In my case, I had the urge to join the church when I was about seven years old. But after being very active in the church during my teenage years, I abandoned the church as soon as I left for college. But even though I was not in church for a very long time and was not making any attempt to live the life of a Christian, I always had a feeling inside that made me know that I was wrong. The influence of the seal God placed in me so early in my life was always with me. And I know today that I could not get away from that. When God places His seal in us, we become His. We may not always live as if we are His, but we are. At some point, we come to our senses, and the urge to serve Him dominates everything. Even though we may not fully understand the desire to, we reach a point whereby we have to surrender. I will talk more about that later in the book.

I had practically been out of the church at this stage in my life, all of my adult life. Again, I had not attended church since

I was in college. But now, I was back and was serious about it. I had a family, I was happy at work—for the most part—and I was doing work in the community, but still, I had a strong desire to be part of a church. I should also add that Linda was not the only person in my life who had been encouraging me to go back to church. My aunt Nellie had been urging me to find a good church for years because the two of us talked over the phone about scripture all the time.

Most of my adult life, I had read the Bible regularly. I even conducted a bible study with the family often. But I didn't attend church. The bible study usually took place after they had already attended church. So you probably can imagine their enthusiasm about participating in bible study on Sunday afternoon after they had been in church most of the day. When things out of the ordinary would happen to me, or when unusual occurrences would occur in the world that I didn't understand, I would search the Bible for answers. That was something I learned from living under Aunt Nellie's influence. But still, I had not been part of an organized Bible study. On the other hand, Linda had been attending BSF International for several years. And usually, I was just about as anxious about upcoming and new lessons as she was. Because as soon as she finished a lesson, I would take it, read it, and make an attempt to understand what I had read. She would always say, "I wish there was a men's class in Stockton so that I could keep up with my lessons."

The new pastor, like the previous one, was a good teacher of the Word. I like that style of receiving the Word. I am not complaining about the excessive screaming and dramatization styles. Those styles meet the needs of some. But they just don't appeal to me. I like to hear the Word taught in a manner that I can clearly understand what is being said. I liked that of the new pastor and still do.

Weak Start Unapologetic Present

One Sunday, there was a sermon taught or preached that left me with major questions. That wasn't so unusual. I never understand everything there is to know about any sermon. But this was different. When I say I had major questions, I simply didn't see in the scriptures support for what was being taught and the conclusions drawn. But that wasn't the first time I had heard a sermon over the years that I didn't quite see absolute scripture to support, nor will it probably not be the last time. And I know I am not a theologian, but I can read the Bible.

Additionally, I firmly believe that if we seek an understanding of God's Word, then the Holy Spirit will teach us what we need to know. It was not the first time that I had heard a sermon that I didn't entirely agree. And I am not saying for one moment that is a bad thing. Because if one never hears anything in a sermon that doesn't convict him, then I think that introduces another set of issues too involved to address here. I have always believed that God has not made his Word so complicated that we can't understand it. It was written and given to us for our understanding. Sure, there are some concepts God has said is only for Him to know, but that is not true of most of His Word. If that were true, He wouldn't expect us to follow it and be obedient to it. One of the first things Jesus did when he ascended into heaven was to send us the Holy Spirit to teach us. And he said before ascending into heaven that when the Holy Spirit would come into the World, he would guide us into the truth. He would not speak on his own, but he would speak what Jesus told him only. The Holy Spirit will clarify what the Bible says so that if we are saved and sincere about our inquiries, the Holy Spirit will give us some insight. Put another way, the Holy Spirit will provide us with what we need to know for that time. The actual learning process about any given spiritual concept is gradual. Now with that said, the Holy Spirit does not nullify the role of preachers and other senior leaders whom God has called to teach his Word. Because those who God has given the gift of teaching and preaching have insight that God gives them to pass on to others. But I think we have been given a perfect example in Acts in the Bereans. Scripture tells us that they believed the Word, but they examined the scripture every day to be sure that what Paul was teaching was true. Even though we have people who God has called to preach to and teach us, as Christians, it is still our responsibility to search the Bible to validate that what we are taught is true. Unfortunately, sometimes when we explore the Bible for the truth about sermons, the Holy Spirit may not lead us to draw the same conclusions. Please don't ask me to explain why that sometimes happens, because I don't know. I just know from experience that sometimes that is the case. I also know that God has also given us instructions on how to deal with such situations. In Romans 14, God has given us specific instructions on how to agree to disagree when we have differences in opinions and interpretations about scripture. Paul tells us in verses 5-6 and 10 that we are to keep in mind that each of us will answer to the Lord for our opinions and how we treat each other. The bottom line is that we should not lose any sleep over it unless it is about Salvation. There is no room for disagreement over the concept of Salvation. Everything else we learn at God's pace, and our sincerity in seeking Him. So when I disagreed with a senior leader in the church over a sermon, it was not my intent for it to be viewed as personal. But one whereby I was looking for real clarification and an opportunity to express my understanding of what I believe the Word was saying and for it to be received with seriousness.

It was the response that I saw coming from some members of the church that shocked me. Somehow the word got out that I disagreed with a sermon. Like any other environment where

Weak Start Unapologetic Present

there may not be mutual agreement on an issue, when it is repeated by third parties the account of the situation tends to change. Consequently, some senior members of the church were not pleased with me, and developed an attitude towards me. That attitude was directed towards me for a short while and vanished as strangely as it had appeared. For a moment, I want to re-emphasize that I was still at that point, a person who had grown up in the church, left the church but was now returning after a very long absence. So I was a little rusty. I found myself asking, "Is this the way the church operates today?" It was a very wretched and inauspicious experience for us as members of the body of Christ. But we couldn't see at the time the blessing that was in it for us. I should also make it clear now that the subject of the disagreement was utterly immaterial. But what is important is how God used this situation to grow me closer to Him. The scripture tells us that God sometimes uses struggles or trials to grow us up or to bring us closer to Him. This is what we were experiencing during this period. It had very little to do with my disagreement about a sermon. It was a combination of things that combined to grow us closer to God. For example, most members who were discussing this had no idea of what they were gossiping. But it is human nature for us sometimes to respond that way. Our commitment to God and our level of faith were questioned by some people when this occurred. But we all know that God doesn't give any of us the authority to judge. But I have to confess that I am also guilty of judging those who judged me when this situation was occurring. And I had to repent for it. The bottom line is this. There are a lot of reasons that God allows us to experience trials. But we have to realize when we are undergoing trials that it is God working in our lives. Because I had been studying the Bible for a long time when this trial at the church occurred, I understood what was happening. It wasn't always something that was at the forefront of my mind, but it did become undeniable that what was going on was from God. And more importantly, it was not about the dispute over scripture as it had started. But God was preparing me to be useful for His cause.

Over time, I began to recognize the blessing that God had chosen for us. God doesn't always bless us in the manner or way we would have chosen had we been in charge. We are clearly not the ones in charge, when we have surrendered our lives to Him. Being a person who would always go to the Bible for answers caused me to treat this situation no differently. Remember that I went to the Bible for answers even during that period of my life when I was not attempting to follow Christ. So the Bible is where I gained the confirmation I needed to address my concerns. Who was right or wrong concerning the scripture in question is not the most important point being made here. Of course there is always a right or a wrong position to take. But what is extremely important is how I arrived at the conclusion I did and the revelation that it was God's plan for me and my growth. That's what was important!

As a federal worker all of my adult life, it had always been commonplace for me to have "loose or use leave" at the end of the year. Consequently, I would always reach a point around the holiday period between Thanksgiving and New Year's when I would have a lot of annual leave to use. So when this was happening, I took advantage of the time that I had and simply took all day for weeks just studying this subject in the Bible. I took annual leave to do this. I would get up at six in the morning, start my day studying the Bible with that subject in mind and all other related scripture. I would only interrupt my studying long enough to go jogging, take a shower, and sometimes have a bite to eat before going back to my study. Most days, I didn't even eat. Linda would return home from work, and I would still be studying. After dinner, I would continue studying until it was time to go to bed. I repeated this cycle for about six weeks. That was about the amount of leave that I would lose if I had not used it. But a fascinating thing happened.

Pretty soon in my study, I was not studying the subject I first set out to research in-depth, and that I had disagreed with a senior leader about. The Holy Spirit was guiding me to study areas that ministered to me about my relationship with God. I found myself praying more. But even more, I found myself sincerely praying for the welfare of those people who had at one time stopped speaking to us at church. It was apparent that the Holy Spirit was bringing me through a learning process that would prepare me to be useful to God. I found myself memorizing scripture that I had no idea what motivated me to memorize that specific scripture. And in most cases, I would not understand why, until I needed the scripture later in my life.

I will end my discussion about this situation by mentioning a mother in our church by the name of Mother Bessie Crosby. Mother Crosby was my Sunday school teacher and, I might add, an exceptional one. God had blessed Mother Crosby not just with the gift of teaching His Word but also we the gift of compassion. I was in her Sunday school class for years. I often commented on subjects—as a baby Christian—I know now weren't quite right. But she always gently censored me while lifting me up with the encouragement that I needed to keep the light lit. She reminded me a lot of Aunt Nellie when I would call her over the phone and talk to her about issues and questions I had about the Word and specific applications of it. Mother Crosby was very aware of the disagreement on scripture that had taken place between a senior leader in the church and me. On several occasions, she addressed the subject by emphasizing that nobody's acceptance or nonacceptance of that belief would get them into Heaven or send them to Hell. This difference with a senior leader in the church, which I found myself involved with, resulted in me developing an uncontrollable love to study God's Word like I would never have predicted. This experience marked the beginning of the framework that formed my attitude of having joy during trials. Not happiness, but joy that comes from God. There is a difference. It prepared me to recongnize the beginning levels of preserverance in faith, while at the same time developing some understanding of wisdom that developed from the trial I was experiencing. I learned to humble myself before God and to always expect a blessing, no matter how dismal the situation might appear to be. It brought me face to face with the reality that I really needed to comprehend that the trials I was experiencing was not about the people involved. But it was spiritual warfare and I needed to not fall for the delusion. Lastly it taught me that above all, I must always in those type situations and others that I had to place my faith in God and God only. This experience in a nutshell increased my faith in God and resulted in me placing greater reliance upon His Word as I dealt with the trial. The growth has continued and I expect it to continue until I die. I talk about some examples of that later. This was only the beginning of the many blessings I can attribute to this one incident I was involved with at church. And just think, it started with me viewing it as a negative, but was always a blessing from God.

Veteran Information System Networks-Telemedicine Networks

One of the things I loved about my job with the Veterans Health Administration was that I got the opportunity to conduct live "bake-offs" in a laboratory environment of numerous vendor's technical solutions of the most current and cutting-edge technology at the time. The normal process consisted of me developing a Request for Information (RFI) and having it published in the *Commerce Business Daily* for potential vendors to respond to. After receiving and evaluating the responses to the RFI's,

I would then select the ones who met the requirements based on a "requirements matrix" included in the RIF. Next, I would notify those who would be participating in the evaluation process of their selection. I would send them a copy of the contract that the Office of General Counsel had drawn up to protect both parties' interests. There were times when certain the vendor's legal department would not agree to the details and would

ATM INTEROPERABILITY TEST LAB

request modifications. Sometimes that was possible, and other times it was not. That had the potential of significantly slowing down the process, but since the general counsel's office was located in the same building in San Francisco that I was, the delay was not that significant. In any event, that was a critical stage of the process because vendors were allowing us to test some versions of their software running on their most recent equipment that may not have been yet released to the general public.

Once all these detailed steps were followed, schedules were set up so that evaluations could begin based upon the test plan that I had included in the original RFI. So all vendors who were selected to participate knew up front what to expect. Only the vendor whose solution was being evaluated at the time was allowed to attend and observe. And the vendor was only allowed to be present at certain intervals of the evaluation. This is because, in many cases, the evaluations went on for sixty days and sometimes even longer. But there were always critical parts of the test plan that vendors wanted to be sure to have their technical people on-site to ensure that their solutions performed as they had responded to the RFI. The evaluations usually included several vendors' networking equipment and was integrated with VA's current network configuration to determine the expected performance using any given vendor's networking equipment. I followed the same process for the evaluations of Wide Area Network (WAN) Local Area Networking (LAN) or Metropolitan Area Networking (MAN) solutions.

Several network evaluation projects I conducted were designed to test the capability of supporting integrated voice, data, and video. During this period, voice and data used different transmission facilities even if they resided on the same network. There was a voice network to support voice phone calls

Weak Start Unapologetic Present

and a separate network to support data and video calls. This approach was deployed simply because of the technology that existed up to this point. After the divestiture of AT&T, customers were able to purchase and install their own private digital backbones. And equipment that would allow them to integrate the three services. It became a reality integrating these three different types of traffic over the same transmission facilities.

The diagram shows a project that resulted in the design of an Intra-VISN network to support telemedicine and other services between locations in Texas, which include; Ft. Worth, Bonham, Dallas, San Antonio, Temple, Austin, Waco, Corpus Christi, Loreda, McAllen, Kerrville, and Victoria.

The diagram below is demonstrating that concept for the Palo-Alto-Livermore Metropolitan Area (MAN) Network.

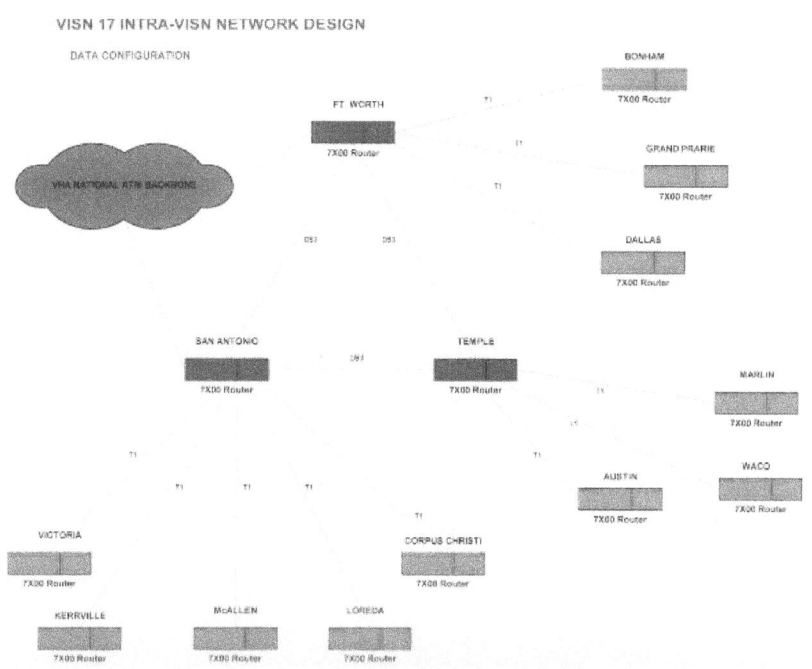

The objectives here were to test the capability of the vendor's equipment to support integrated voice, data, and video over the same transmission facilities. This proposal was also

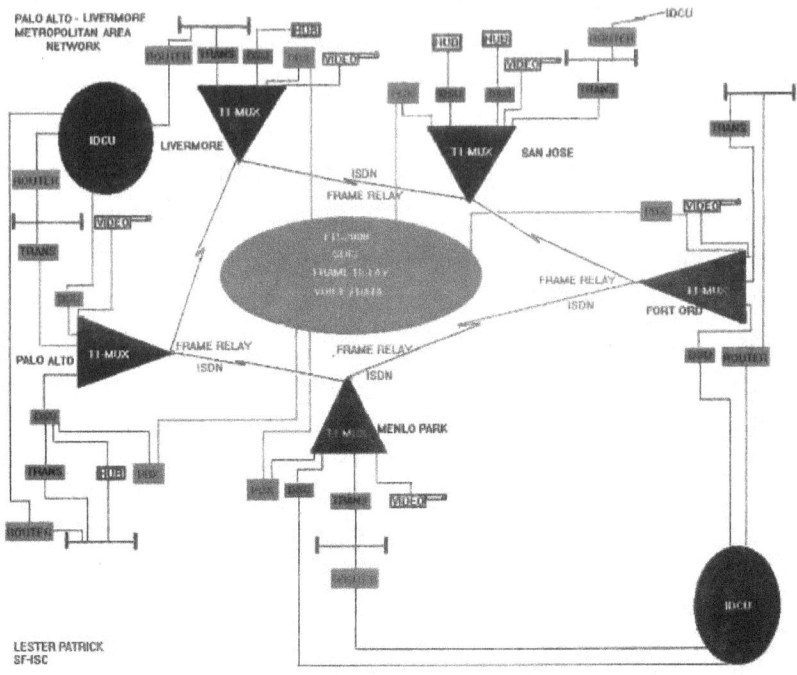

demonstrating a Metropolitan Area Network to interconnect major Veteran Administration hospitals between Livermore, Palo Alto, Menlo Park, Fort Ord, and San Jose. This network configuration was also designed to demonstrate the capability to support telemedicine over the network.

The above design evolved from the following network topology that included Hines, Illinois, Washington, D.C., Salt Lake City, Birmingham, Ala., Albany, N.Y., and San Francisco.

The VISN15 telemedicine network design connects Wichita, Topeka, Leavenworth, and Kansas City.

Based upon the evaluation project, I designed and recommended several Veteran Information System Networks (VISN)

Weak Start Unapologetic Present

across the country to support applications such as telemedicine, distance learning, web traffic, video conferencing, voice communications, and a host of other applications. These are just two examples of projects I worked with while working as a senior communications specialist for the Department of Veterans Affairs.

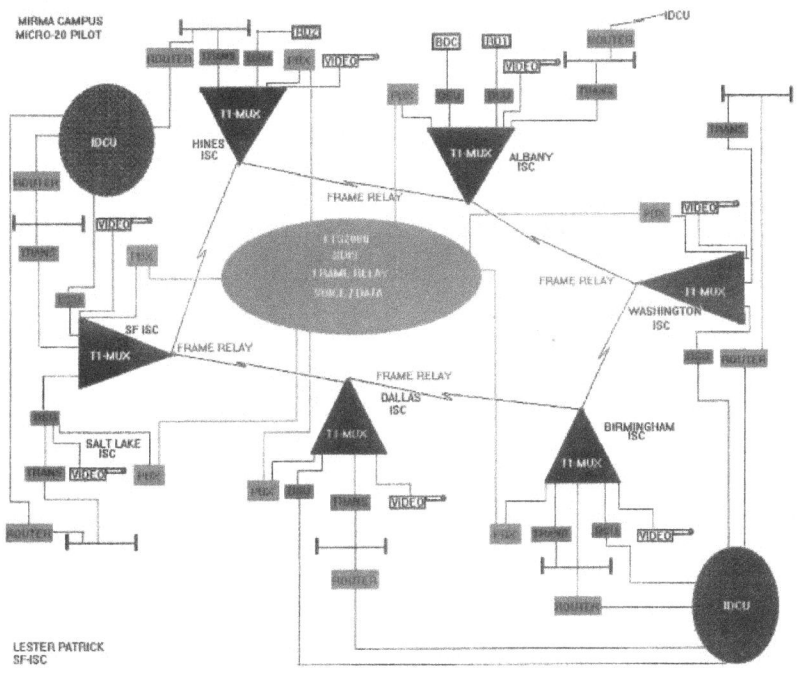

Working as a communications specialist was a gratifying career. One of the other things I loved to do was to present at the Information Technology Conference (ITC) in Austin, Texas every summer at the Austin Convention Center. This required a lot of preparation. But it was worth the effort for the part of the organization I was involved with. It allowed me to make information resource managers, who worked at hospitals, aware of projects we were currently doing regionally and nationally. The diagram on the following page is a cover page for a session I conducted on Metropolitan Area Networking at the ITC in Austin, Texas.

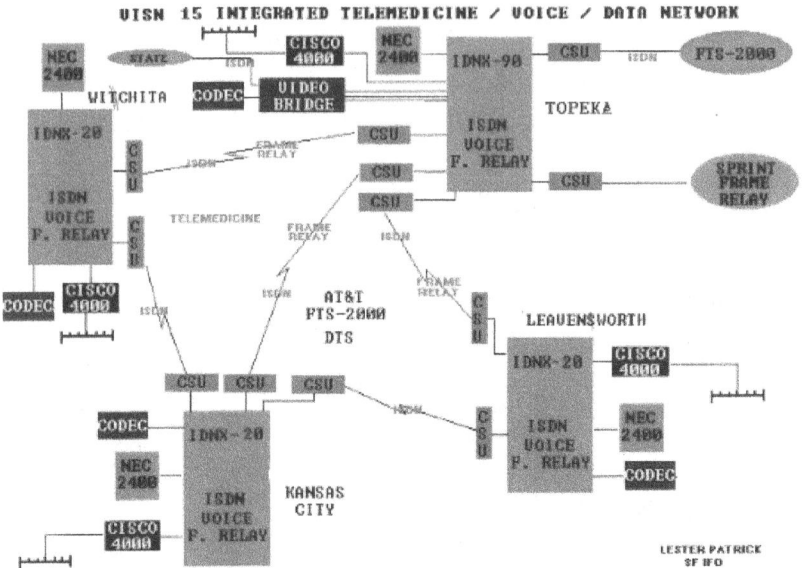

Finally, in the networking industry, one of the most essential networking aspects that have to be verified is interoperability. The reason for this is because, even though all vendors will say their equipment and software meet international standards (ISO), there were sometimes minor deficiencies. If this is a major issue for your organization, then the only way to ensure proper interoperability is to test it in the laboratory. The above diagram represents a very long and detailed interoperability test between multiple vendors' equipment to validate interoperability. I conducted the tests in reference to specific Wide Area Network technology.

During this time frame, the VA implemented an off-campus

METROPOLITAN AREA NETWORKING

ITC 95
LESTER PATRICK
SF ISC

project management program with George Washington University. University professors taught the program at five locations nationwide. The training sites included; San Francisco, Salt Lake City, Silver Spring, Chicago, and Bay Pines, Florida. To complete the program, any participants had to travel to those locations to take any given class. It took between twelve and eighteen months to complete the entire program. George Washington University awarded me a master's certification in project management upon completion. The program also prepared me to take the project management test for receiving the PMP certification. Later, while still in the VA, I also completed my Cisco Certified Network Associate (CCNA) and my Cisco Certified Network Professional (CCNP) certifications. I was extremely proud of these two accomplishments because these were certifications I had to spend a lot of personal time preparing. Also, the failure rate for the CCNP is very high, but I scored a perfect score.

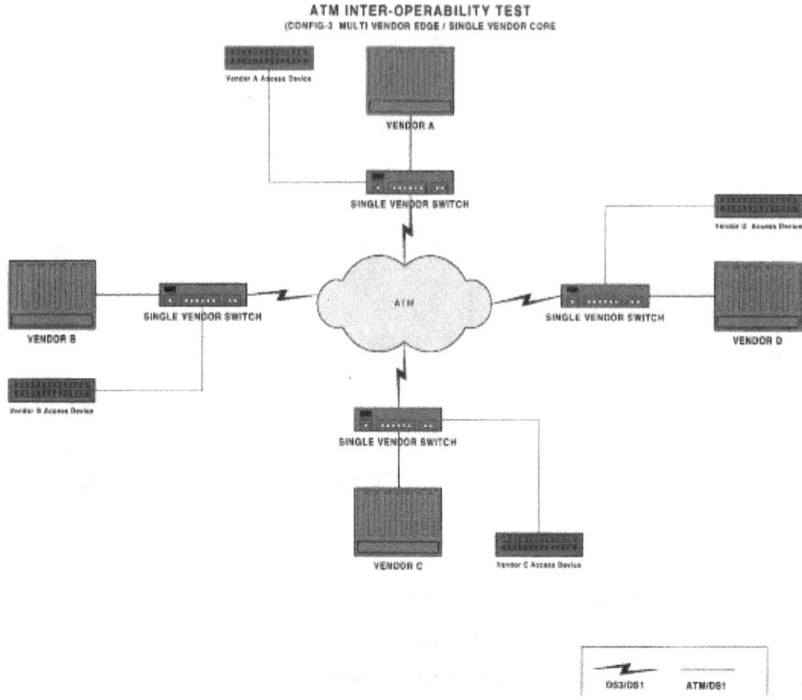

Spiritual Awakening—My Wife's Carjacking

By now, after having had the experience at church that put me on the path to try to serve God, I was doing everything I knew to do and understood that I needed to do to serve God. I was trying my best to be a good father, husband, employee, and Christian. But things were still not perfect.

My son Nigel had graduated from high school. He had a very slow start in high school, which I pointed out earlier in the book. But by the time he was a senior, he had turned things around. He was very good in art and had won several art contests in the local area. In his senior year, as part of the advanced program, he was required to send fifty pieces of his art to Ohio to be evaluated by a panel of artists. When he got his results, he had received a perfect score. At the time, there had been no perfect scores on any AP Art program in San Joaquin County. We were incredibly proud of his progress.

That fall, he traveled to St. Augustine's College in Raleigh, North Carolina to attend college. He was in his junior year when one night I got a phone call from him. He started the conversation by telling me that he had something he wanted to say to me. I said, "OK." He went on to tell me that his girlfriend was pregnant and they were expecting a baby in April. It was then March. I was shocked. I know my initial response to him was not the best. But my response to him was, "Are you crazy! Do you not know that it will take money to support a baby? Money that you don't have! You do know that you are not married?" His response was, "I know, dad. I might have to quit school and go to work." Then he proceeded to tell me that his girlfriend was on the line, too. We hung up the phone and I told Linda. We started to investigate to find out what we could do to help.

So in May, I became a grandfather of a little girl. Her name is Kayla. From the time she was two weeks old, we started to keep her for periods of time and tried to be the best grandparents we knew how to be. My son came home that summer and decided that he would  not go back to Saint Augustine's College. He applied and was accepted at Sacramento State. On the day he was to report, just minutes before we were to leave, I went into his bedroom to remind him it was time to go. It was then when he informed me that he didn't want to go. He relayed to me that he had decided that he wanted to work with his hands. I don't know what that meant, but he ended up joining the Army. About three years later, my son became a father again. Our new granddaughter's name was Leilani. Above is a picture of my son, his daughter Kayla, and my wife Linda...

Right after boot camp, he was sent to Iraq to fight in the war. He was among the first troops to enter Iraq. Needless to say, this was a challenging experience for my wife and me. I had always been able to do what I considered as protecting my son. Now, in reality, I could never protect him. It was always God who was doing the protecting. But I remember when he was a sophomore at Saint Augustine's College, there was a severe hurricane approaching North Carolina that was expected to hit Raleigh. I flew into Washington, D.C, a couple of days before the storm. I then drove to North Carolina, checked into a hotel, and picked up my son from the dorm so he would be safe. I know that sounds extreme, but that is what I meant when I said I had always tried to protect him. Now he was in Iraq, and I would go for weeks at a time without me even hearing from him.

I could not protect him in Iraq. I couldn't even fool myself into thinking that I was protecting him. I had to rely solely upon God to protect him. One night as I watched the late news giving an account of the war, the phone rang. It was from Nigel. He explained that he had been standing guard on a tower for over two weeks and could not call home. It was then that it became so clear to me that it was entirely out of my control. I had to place all my faith in God to keep him safe. This was a major growth experience for me in faith. And I could understand it because I had been so persistently studying the Word. It was then that I started to realize why I had the uncontrollable desire to study the Word. Other things would happen that would further reveal God's involvement in my study of His Word.

Several months had passed, and we had gotten used to simply relying fully and completely upon God to bring our son home safely from the war. One day, as I was coming from work driving from the Bay Area, I got a call from Linda. I was just approaching the Altamont Pass, so the signal was beginning to weaken. I answered, and she was crying and screamed,

"Our son is...!" Then the call dropped. I didn't know what her last words were. I tried to reach her but was unable to. I pulled over as soon as I could and said a quick prayer. I asked God to be with us, whatever the situation was. I got back on the freeway, trying to take my mind off the words I heard Linda scream. Soon I was home, but she was not there. I continued trying to reach her but was unable to. So I simply had to wait. When she came home, she was so excited. I told her I couldn't make out her message. Her response was, "I said our son is back in the United States! He is in Texas!" Then she went on to tell me that he would be calling us later. So we needed to arrange to go and see him immediately! I was relieved, and I thanked God. But I had just experienced more growth towards God. Because even during that period that I didn't know what my wife's message had been, I still had faith that God would do what was best.

But with these things happening, I still struggled with placing all of my faith all the time in God. Because some other things were happening in our lives that I could not explain, and that didn't seem congruent with God's way. So at times, I found myself still questioning God in ways I shouldn't have done. So one day, I just got fed up while I was praying and mustered the nerve to say, "God, I really want to know. I know I am not worthy, but I have to know for myself that you are real." I didn't want to continue spending the rest of my life sometimes relying upon God and then other times wondering if this really was God or not. When I knew that God was involved in situations in my life, I felt good about it, but I wasn't consistent in that belief. And I just didn't want to continue that way. I was in my bedroom at the time praying. I had committed to God that I would not allow any days to pass when I didn't give my undivided attention to Him during some part of my day. So I posed the question.

And He answered.

I will not be able to explain His response in a way that any reader of this will be able to follow. So I will not spend any time attempting to do so. All I can say is that for me, instantly, I felt a presence that overwhelmed me. That is the best way I can explain it. But I understood that it was God. And it took away any questions that I had about whether He is real. I was left still not knowing the answer to a lot of other questions. But the one

Weak Start Unapologetic Present

thing I will never have to wonder about again is whether God is real. He is real! Trust me!

But God didn't stop there. A few weeks later, I worked on a project that needed to be delivered to Sacramento and time-stamped by four o'clock that afternoon. I also had to make an appointment in Stockton at a business that closed at five O'clock. I planned to complete the project, print a hard copy by about 1:30 p.m., and then drive it over to Sacramento and hand-deliver it to the dropbox where I could be sure it would be time stamped by four o'clock. That would give me plenty of time to get back to Stockton through traffic and make my appointment. I was finished with the project by around 1:00 p.m., but when I went to print it, for some crazy reason, I could not. It was a huge document, and I just could not get it to print for a period of time. Finally, I was able to get it to print. But by then, I only had just enough time to jump into my car, get to Sacramento if I was to speed and get back to Stockton for my appointment.

I jumped in my car and started to back out of the driveway into the street. I got a powerful urge to pray. My thought was that I have to make sure I pray on my way to Sacramento. But as I backed out of the driveway, I couldn't continue. The urge was overwhelming. So I drove back into the driveway and parked the car. I then went to my bedroom, got on my knees to pray. As I was walking up to my bedroom, I could only think of my son living in Atlanta at the time. I could only feel that he needed prayer right then, at that moment. So I started to pray for him. But as I began to pray for him, my words were, "God, please protect my wife." I didn't pay any attention then to the fact that I was praying for Linda. So when I finished praying for her, I proceeded to pray for my son. Then I rushed out, jumped into my car, and hurriedly drove to Sacramento to make the delivery that I needed to.

Lester Patrick

I was not only able to reach my destination in time, but I was also able to drive back to Stockton and make my appointment there. After making my appointment, I returned home. Linda had not come home from work at 5:30. Shortly after six o'clock, I got a call from a number that I didn't recognize. Unlike most other times, I answered the call. It was Linda calling from another person's phone. She was at a check-cashing facility in Southwest Stockton. She had been carjacked as she attempted to get into her car earlier. Linda worked at the library. She left the library and walked to her car. When she bent over to put her purse in the car, a robber put a gun in her stomach and ordered her to get in.

The two robbers first directed her to drive to the ATM, where she withdrew cash. But there was a limit on the daily amount she could withdraw. In her attempt to cooperate, she agreed to go inside the bank to cash a pay role check they found in her purse. They didn't trust that, so they directed her to drive across town to a check-cashing bank. One robber escorted her inside the bank and held a gun to her side. The other robber stayed outside in the car with the engine running to be ready for a quick getaway.

While standing in line, she faked a heart attack and fell to the floor. All attention was then on her. The carjacker ran, got into her car, and they took off. She then got up and explained to the teller what was happening. At that time, the police were called. That's when she called me, and I went to pick her up. It took weeks before she was comfortable going out alone.

But with God's help, we got through it. Once again, God was showing me that he was real. It was He who had given me the uncontrollable urge to go back into the house and pray. When I started to pray for my son, it was the Holy Spirit that only allowed me to utter prayers for my wife. It was God continuing to answer my prayer to show me that He is real! And I was very thankful for God, giving me the courage to ask the question!

Almost all the times I had ever gone on business travel, I always drove myself to the airport and parked my car there while I was out of town. The reason being that if I had the opportunity to leave early from my trip, then it wouldn't interfere with Linda's schedule in picking me up. She could be at work or it could be in the middle of the night. I needed to travel out of town, but for some reason, I asked Linda to drive me to the airport. As I expected, I did get the opportunity to leave early.

I contacted Linda, and she met me at the airport. When I got in the car she said, "I have something to tell you but I need to say it before we leave." She then proceeded to inform me that my father, Uncle Winser, had died. She had waited until I returned from traveling because she didn't want to tell me while I was out of town. That was a very dark time in my life. Uncle Winser was born in 1914, so I know that he couldn't be with us forever, but it was still a shock when she told me.

I had to teach school that night at Delta College. I only had enough time to get home, pick up my school material, and get to class. I felt terrible, but it was simply too late to get a substitute. I struggled through the night and made arrangements for us the following day to travel to North Carolina for the funeral. But it didn't stop there.

The following month, Linda's grandmother, Miss Ethel, died. Even though Miss Ethel was Linda's grandmother, she had raised her. Linda thought of her as being her mother. We all were very grieved by the passing of both Uncle Winser and Miss Ethel during the same summer, just weeks apart.

Lester Patrick

Joining Bible Study Fellowship International (BSF)

For years now, I had been enthusiastically studying the Bible, but with no specific purpose other than the desire to know God's Word. There are a couple of minor exceptions. Each week, in Sunday school, Mother Crosby and Sister Cynthia Childress, co-teacher always assigned the questions at the end of the chapter to individual students. Usually, the questions guided the discussion of the lesson. You were expected to have done your research and give a thorough explanation of your answer when it was time to discuss the question you were assigned. It was OK sometimes to include your opinion as long as you could support it through the scripture it was based on. It was like you were doing a mini report on that subject to answer your assigned question. Participating in that class did allow for some level of focus on specific concepts and Biblical events. But for the most part, even though my study over the last several years had been consistent, it had not been focused. The other exception would be the exposure I got from reading Linda's Bible Study Fellowship International (BSF) lessons over the last several years, after she had finished with them.

About thirteen years ago, Linda came home from her BSF class and told me that there would be a men's BSF class starting this year. She gave me the contact information for me to follow up to get the specifics. I did that, and I learned that the program's overview would be held at the Progressive Community Church that next Monday evening. I made arrangements to be there. I was surprised to see that there were only four people there. The BSF teaching leader, the BSF administrator, a progressive deacon, and myself. John presented details about the program and emphasized the upcoming start date. The sessions would be held every Monday night at 6:50 p.m. at the Quail Lakes Baptist Church. I was very excited about it.

Weak Start Unapologetic Present

I attended the first session at Quail Lakes. I believe there must have been somewhere around ninety to one hundred men present. About 85 percent of them were White, and the rest were a mixture of the general population. There might have been ten African American men there. And that might be a stretch. The teaching leader and the admin staff explained how the class would be conducted and assigned us to our groups. We then followed our group leaders to our designated rooms, where we became more familiar with other group members through introductions. The group leader also talked more about how the sessions would be conducted, the BSF guidelines, and what would be expected of group members. After about forty-five minutes, we returned to the room where we had first gathered in and sang two hymns and had a short prayer. Then, John Vaughn, the teaching leader, gave an introductory lecture. We were then dismissed but received our next week's lessons as we exited the church.

The lessons were designed to be done daily. There were fifteen questions with the questions being distributed over five days, and a sixth-day summary question that addresses more or less the application of what you got from the lesson and how you were able to apply it. Over the years, BSF has been evolving to be more open and application-based. I think the change has been good. Because just learning the Word for the sake of learning the Word only scratches the surface of what God has in store for us through studying His Word. Every Monday night the questions were discussed inside our groups. The advantage here was undeniable. We got the opportunity to hear the Holy Spirit's answers to other people during the week that also blessed each of us individually. There was only a minimal amount of space allocated to each question, so answers needed to be very succinct.

Lester Patrick

Additionally, not everybody could comment on every single question. But most importantly, group members could not talk in class unless they had written their answers down on their papers. This was extremely important to me because it is very common in some bible studies for some participants to dominate the discussion even if they haven't taken the time to prepare for the lesson. The way BSF is designed prohibits that from happening. That was one of the primary things I loved about it. Additionally, the overall structure of methodically addressing the subject for discussion greatly impressed me.

After my first session, my thought was that this is going to be a real commitment. It is not just answering a question on Sunday in Sunday school that you have had all week to prepare for. This was not just reading the Bible daily or reading the notes for Linda's lessons after she has finished with her lessons. This was going to be serious, and you have to make a real decision as to whether you are willing to put in the necessary time required. I started to think about the fact that I commuted, and that my job was very demanding, and other things. I found myself listening to some of those thoughts coming to my mind about the study. But after about three or four classes, I was approached about considering being a group leader. My initial opinion was that I was not ready. John Vaughn, the teaching leader, asked me if I would consider coming in early before class to discuss the possibility of becoming a group leader.

I went home that night, and I told Linda. She said, "You are not ready for that."

"I know," I said. "I will meet with him next week and let him know." The next week I met John before class. We met outside in the churchyard to discuss my being a leader. I told him that I had thought about it and I didn't think I was ready. His response surprised me. He said, "None of us are." Then he explained to

Weak Start Unapologetic Present

me that he had been meeting for around five years every week to pray with five or six other men for God to send a men's BSF class to Stockton. And God had answered their prayers.

We were living it right then. But they had also asked God to send group leaders to lead the groups. Then he said, "God has sent you. That is the reason I have approached you." But he went on to say that if you were ready, then God would not be able to use you. I thought about it, and I agreed to do it. When I got home, I told Linda about my decision. She knew I had done what I felt the Holy Spirit was guiding me to do.

I started my training the following Saturday morning by meeting with the other group leaders and administrators at 6:30 a.m. We prayed together and for each other. We discussed the lessons using the same format we would facilitate our groups on Monday night. This was part of the weekly training. But we also had other specific training each week for group leaders. As group leaders, we were assigned between fifteen and eighteen men. We were expected to shepherd these men by making weekly contact with them to pray with them if they needed prayer, discuss issues with them when necessary, or direct them to scripture to address situations. So a good deal of the training on Saturday morning does involve training for shepherding. BSF Men's Group consists predominantly of White men. In the men's group in Stockton at the time I became a group leader, there was only one other African American man in leadership. That is still basically the case today.

Almost all of my work experience has been in environments whereby I was, in most cases the only African American or one of maybe two. But due to the field I was in, it was expected to be that way, so I got very accustomed to it. In the United States, church worship is segregated. There are some minor exceptions, but overall the American church is segregated. So

Lester Patrick

obviously, joining BSF in leadership was a new experience for me. As far as BSF is concerned, even though it is not a church but a Bible study, we are still worshiping God together. And we are worshiping God together as predominately Black and White Christians. When we come in on Saturday morning and get on our knees and pray together and for each other, we are not thinking about whether we are Black or White unless something in our prayers reflects that. The point I am making is that, never in my wildest imagination would anybody have convinced me that I would for the last thirteen years been meeting with a group of about twenty White mostly conservative Christians for Bible study. I mean not just meeting, but looking forward to it every Saturday morning for the last thirteen years. Only God could pull that off! It was not very long after I agreed to become a group leader when I understood that God had called me to this ministry. BSF, like all other elements of our society, doesn't operate in a vacuum. Its members are exposed and influenced by what goes on around them. So it is not perfect.

The escalation of social unrest in this country over the last three or four years is undeniable. Consequently, I have had some concerns about the silence on this issue by BSF leadership and the leaders of most Christian churches in the country. There has been social unrest like we haven't seen since the sixties. Racism and police brutality still persist, as they have since the early period of Jim Crow.

I think BSF is in a position to have a significant influence on what is going on nationally. I say that knowing BSF is not a church. But BSF consists of a group of 250,000 people who are Christians. So taking a visible and unambiguous stand on specific social issues is one thing that God has called Christians to do. It doesn't matter whether it is viewed as political or not. That is not the important thing here. Some of the things we

Weak Start Unapologetic Present

classify as being political are just pure and simple sin. By BSF and any other Christian church not publicly denouncing hatred, injustice, and racism is to send the false message to the World that it endorses these horrible sins that directly opposes Jesus' teachings on love. But lets' be clear, this responsibility doesn't begin and end with BSF. The leaders of all Christian organizations should publicly denounce, racism, and injustice in accordance with the teachings of scripture. According to Paul we are all part of the same body of Christ. Therefore what negatively impacts Black and Brown Christians also negatively impacts White Christians. The negative impact is not always obvious to all. But if we are part of the body of Christ, then we are all spiritually impacted when a large group of Chrisitnans are misstreated. Additionally, not speaking out on behalf of Christians is a sin according to scripture.

Until recently I was greatly concerned that the absence of BSF making a public announcement against racism could be viewed as support of some of the oppressive and racist comments that are presently happening in the country. Consequently, earlier I wrote to the executive officer of BSF outlining scriptural reasons why BSF's responsibility is to publicly speak out against the sin we are seeing dominating our country today.

I am very pleased to report that the Executive Officer has recently recorded a video denouncing racism. I cannot say nor is it my intent to insinuate that my email influenced this action. Because we are dealing with Christians here, I do feel very confident that there were also other emails and phone calls from concerned BSF members. Additionally, last week, as I was wrapping up this book, I got an email from the executive officer that was sent to BSF Group leaders denouncing the behavior of Christians not being able to get along. Her comments were very much related to the way Christians are treating the election and politics. She recommended a blog post by Dr. Darrell Bock from the Dallas Theological Seminary entitled, "Testing Ourselves in Challenging Times." That commentary was very timely and gives me great encouragement that BSF leadership has a desire to play a role in influencing how Christians deal with this very serious race problem our society is faced with today. Overall, being in BSF has been a tremendous blessing for me. I have grown in my faith beyond what I ever could have imagined. Thank God for BSF International!

PART VI

Community Work and Advocacy

I have been involved with community work and advocacy all of my adult life. Linda and I first got involved in community work when we were in the Philippines. I learned then that God uses us wherever we are to make a difference for his people. My community work has always been based upon my understanding that God expects us to be a blessing to those who, for whatever reason, cannot bless themselves. I know a lot of church people would disagree with me, and that is OK. My experience is that church people's general belief is that community work has to be done through the church. I could not disagree more. Because if that were the case, then a lot of things simply would not get done. That is not to criticize the church, but just to point out that there are so many needs that church members simply don't see as the church's responsibility. It doesn't matter whether the community work we do is being done through our fraternities, sororities, nonprofits, or on an individual basis as long as we know we are doing it for God. How we approach a community issue is what is important. If we ask for God's direction and blessing on whatever it is we are doing, He will bless it whether we do it in conjunction with the church or any other organization. I can attest to that. It is not just because the Bible tells us in scripture, but also because of how I have seen God's involvement in the things I have done in the community.

I will highlight several projects I have been involved with in the community through advocacy and as a community volunteer. I will also highlight some of the issues I have felt compelled to speak out against because it is our responsibility as Christians to speak out against oppression. This is true even at times when it is not popular to do so. I emphasize that point because there are those of us who will only speak out against an issue after they have taken a very close and hard look at how the general public is responding before they will respond. Then they might speak out. The point made here is straightforward. We should never only speak out when it is safe to. And secondly, many times when we oppose oppression, we might be the only ones doing so. That has been the story of my life, in almost all cases, when I have consistently spoken out against those things that I know are wrong. Generally speaking, the general public views people who speak out consistently as being the bad guys. This is true even amongst those who will eventually get the nerves to speak out on the same issue once they see it is safe for them to speak out. But I guess the real point that needs to be made is that when God calls us all to speak out against oppression, He also prepares us to withstand the criticism that usually fosters growth. That has been my experience.

I have been involved with too many projects of this type over the years to include them all here. And it would take too much time to describe the ones I am choosing to include, if I didn't post a picture to assist me in my description of these events. For that reason, I will use several images to cut down on the amount of descriptive writing. We know that a picture is worth a thousand words. So I am going to give just a brief description of a few images of some of the activities I have been involved with over the years. Some of the pictures below are actually articles that I wrote about the situation at the time.

I mentioned earlier that when you speak out against racism and hatred, people usually don't view you in a positive light. This is true for both African Americans and White people. Black people, in many cases, are embarrassed by the fact that they are very likely to be discriminated against in many of the situations they find themselves. That is not an easy thing to deal with when it is constantly in your face. It has never been a secret, but many Black people have taken the false attitude that if he would just shut up about it, then the racism will just go away and nobody will notice. But it will not just go away any more so than the coronavirus will just go away if we ignore it. It always has to be addressed.

Then there are some members of the White community who would like for you to shut up about it because it just might make them aware of their negative behavior that contributes to the problem. It also can have the impact of reminding some members of the White community of the unpleasant reality that the problem really is still with us despite their attempts to behave as if it isn't. So on both sides we have people who like to see the racial discrimination we have in our society just go away. But it will not until we all do something to make it just go away. And that is not difficult to do.

Most people would be shocked to know how far some will oppose those who speak out against oppression and racism. About the time I organized Parents and Citizens for Quality Education, school superintendents across the state of California developed a statewide "enemies list" of parent groups who they considered disruptive and posing a threat to school districts. I was recorded as one of the enemies on the list. I learned about being on the enemies list from a news reporter from *Los Angeles Times* who called requesting an interview with me about it. I was placed on the "enemies list" because of my insistence on publicly naming administrators at board meetings. He called to ask if I was aware that my efforts and the efforts of another group in southern California had inspired a state bill to be passed giving parents the right to publicly name administrators at the school board meeting. I did not know at the time that the assembly had passed a bill to address it. Prior to this bill being passed, parents could not name administrators at school board meetings who were the subjects of their complaints. Nor could parents discuss with the school board or the superintendent anything specific to an administrator in privacy because it was considered a personnel issue. So parents were caught in a catch 22.

But my approach was to consistently go to the school board and publicly name school administrators. I consistently did this against the warnings of the president of the school board. At the same time I was engaging in this activity, another parent's group in southern California was also doing the same thing. Eventually, some state legislators paid attention. They then drafted and passed a bill to give parents the right to name school administrators at school board meetings publicly. During the interview, I learned about the statewide "enemies list" and that my name appeared on the list. A copy of one of the articles can be seen below.

There is always an exception. I will comment once more on how people sometimes respond when you speak out against racism and discrimination. I had been speaking out against district policies that were impacting students at a particular high school. In all instances, the assistant principal opposed me each time I spoke out. She aggressively defended and upheld the district's unfair policies. After several years, the assistant principal retired. Shortly after her retirement, I was shocked to receive a handwritten letter from her thanking me for speaking out on behalf of the students and instigating positive change in the district. The point being made here is that sometimes people respond the way they do because it's their official responsibility.

Weak Start Unapologetic Present

We can't be deterred by people's responses or opinions relative to our actions of speaking out against oppression.

Below is an article that was published by *Los Angeles Times* concerning opposition that I led and another parent group in southern California participated in that resulted in legislation giving parents the right to announce administrator's names at school board meetings.

Lester Patrick

Institutionalized racism is alive and well in all aspects of our society. On the following page is an article I wrote relative to that to remind everybody of that fact.

Weak Start Unapologetic Present

The second article below came about due to an outright racist incident at the Lodi Unified School. Not very many people would deny that this incident was pure racism. But some did. I will not go into the details because of the sensitivity to the targeted African American student. In this case, an African American student at a local school in the district found his locker defaced with the letters "KKK" and a swastika." The newspaper article below describes a meeting between the Academic Review Committee, which I chaired and included the superintendent and his staff and public members. One of the things that I had requested at a previous meeting was a hate crime policy. At the time of this meeting, the district had not finalized the policy. One of the other things that the committee had requested was diversity training for teachers. At the time of the meeting, diversity training had started. In general, teachers welcomed the training and wanted to see more. The meeting ended with a commitment to continue the diversity training and finalize and implement the hate crime policy. Both of these recommendations were eventually implemented throughout the district.

> **Don't ignore signs of 'institutionalized racism'**
>
> An outside consulting firm evaluated the environment in the Lodi Unified School District the past three years and, through focus groups and other techniques, "racial predictability" was identified as a trend.
>
> In other words, one can look at a given class in elementary school and predict what ethnic groups will fail and succeed.
>
> In situations where such predictability is shown, the underlying reason is institutionalized racism.
>
> So when district Superintendent Bill Huyett drafted a staff memo hinting at the presence of institutionalized racism, he was right on target.
>
> Many times an individual might exhibit behavior that has a negative impact on others without being aware of it.
>
> Whose fault is it? That isn't important anymore. What's important is that each time a black or Latino student is unsuccessful in any school in America, it brings each middle-class American closer to a lower standard of living.
>
> We're in a very serious situation that gets worse with each failing student.
>
> We must stop bickering, identify innovative ways of making each student a success and remember it's no longer a black or Latino problem, but an American problem.
>
> If we don't, we'll all lose.
>
> Lester Patrick
> *Stockton*

Prior to this meeting, there had been a couple of other public gatherings. This meeting, like the others, were also attended by representatives from the California Department of Education. I have emphasized this earlier in the book. Several of the recommendations that Parents and Citizens for Quality Education proposed and implemented in Lodi Unified School were also later implemented at other districts throughout the state. This is partly because the department of education was very aware from the beginning of the resolutions we were proposing and the potential impact on the problems we had identified.

I made it very clear at this meeting that things were not moving as quickly as they should. It has been my experience that usually when it comes to resolving issues related to race, those in authority general hold the attitude is that it takes time. The point that I made then and still believe is that it doesn't. All it takes is the commitment to do what is right and proper. That's it.

Believe it or not, the next article on the following two pages describes a debate between a group of White parents and me from Lodi, who had endorsed a practice of segregation within the district. I should add that they enjoyed the support of the school board. The Lodi Unified School District had approved, by a narrow vote, to build a new school in north Stockton and satisfy their request.

They intended to prevent students in north Stockton from attending a predominantly White school. The school of controversy was a school for gifted children. Several children chosen to attend the school were not gifted at all. I asked to see some data relative to the selection process and support data they used to decide who was selected to attend the school. I remember that there were students whose math scores were in a percentile, in some cases, less than some of the minority students who had been denied admission to the school.

This group of parents attempted to label me as being a racist, because I spoke out against segregation. Just to emphasize, this took place in Lodi, CA around 2003 and not the southern United States. There is nothing more Jim Crow than this behavior, whether it happened in Lodi or Mississippi. This event proves that the Jim Crow attitude is not just confined to a specific section of the country. But it doesn't stop here. There are plenty more examples. I will only have space to cite some of them here that I have spoken in opposition to while advocating for African American students and their parents' rights.

Several of these parents continued to support this attitude

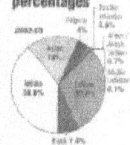

that many African American parents viewed as a segregationist attitude, even after the general public was aware of their goals. It was then very similar to what we see today coming from the White House. Their belief was simply that their children should not have to interact with general education students. Many of the children being denied the opportunity to attend this school were minority students. Additionally, I was at the time a board member of the Bond Oversight Committee. Its responsibilities were to monitor the disbursement of the funds approved by the voters to build the new schools in the district. And secondly, to keep the public aware of the kinds of things that were happening then that would impact this school and other new schools being built.

Weak Start Unapologetic Present

I have learned that one of the most effective methods of advocating for justice is through the newspaper. Throughout my life, I have taken that opportunity to use the local newspapers to voice my views and opposition against policies that negatively impact people of color and on the general public. I have taken the liberty to post three examples of my advocacy through the opinion page here.

I wrote the following opinion in response to the behavior of White parents and school district officials' attempts to support a segregated approach to educating students.

All recommendations I have ever made ended up benefiting all students in the district. This has been the case even if the proposal was initially designed to improve African American students' conditions. The interesting thing about advocating for African American students is that most Whites see this as a racist act. They don't see the all-White school board who don't advocate for African American students as racist acts. Isn't that interesting?

At this meeting, I presented a six-point plan that included: mandatory biweekly status reports for students in danger of failing, a quarterly review of suspension and expulsion rates, an aggressive recruitment policy for African American teachers and staff, expansion of the community liaison program, and others.

THE - 6 - POINT PLAN

- Lack Of Academic Progress Among African American Students.

- Inequitable Suspension And Expulsion Policies.

- Hostility Towards African American Students And Parents.

- Lack Of Africans Employed In the District At All Levels.

- Lack Of Adequate Safety Policies.

- Minorities Have Negative Image Of The District.

Lester Patrick
Academic Review Committee

The Lodi Unified School District adopted the plan. As a result of the board adopting this six-point plan, several programs and projects evolved that, over time, had a positive impact on the success of African American students and the school district in general. Below is a bullet format copy of the issues that initiated the six-point plan. There was also a "six-point resolution" and an executive summary distributed to interested parties. The article on the following page describes the public introduction of the plan. It includes both the issues identified and the recommended solutions for each. We worked with the school district, community, and the California Department of Education to implement this plan.

I should also add that other school districts across the state also adopted some of the resolutions we implemented in the Lodi Unified School District.

Weak Start Unapologetic Present

Sometimes, advocating for African Americans can mean

[Newspaper clipping: "Race relations focus of meeting — LUSD parents propose solutions" by Toni Merilnos-Mete, News-Sentinel staff writer. Continued article titled "Race" with bulleted list of proposed solutions including mandatory biweekly status reports, incentive programs, hiring of ethnically diverse hearing officers, quarterly review of expulsions and suspensions of African American students, cultural sensitivity and conflict resolution training, formal reprimands for employees who willingly ignore hate crime, training for staff on gang clothing/symbols/activity, more aggressive recruitment of African Americans for teaching, expansion of the community liaison concept.]

confronting ourselves in ways that cause us to take time and think about what we are doing and how it is impacting us and those around us. The article below is exactly what I was attempting to do. I was trying to cause African Americans in the local area to focus on the problems we have and make some attempt to address them ourselves. This is not to say that we don't welcome and value non-African Americans' support, but to emphasize that, ultimately, we must claim responsibility for ourselves. What could be more fitting for a Black History Month celebration? And I am still challenging my Black brothers and sisters to step up to the challenge! Put your gloves on and let's fight against those ills that are preventing us from moving forward.

Lester Patrick

This next article is a description of a meeting in Stockton to

make the Federal Department of Education aware of the concerns that African American parents in San Joaquin County were having concerning their school-age children. The meeting was organized by the NAACP's local branch and allowed us to make complaints to the agency to support a formal complaint against the school districts in the area. My comments were relative to the Lodi Unified School District and represented many African American parents whose students attend school in their district.

NAACP hosts meeting
Parents say they face discrimination in area's schools

By Dogen Hannah
Record Staff Writer

Parents of Stockton schoolchildren turned out for an NAACP meeting Wednesday night to tell a U.S. Department of Education official they have far-ranging concerns about the administration of the city's public schools.

About 50 people attended the meeting called by officials with the Stockton chapter of the National Association for the Advancement of Colored People. Area NAACP leaders said the town-hall meeting was a chance for parents and others to lodge their complaints on the record and present a petition signed by more than 500 people requesting a federal or state investigation of Stockton Unified School District.

U.S. Department of Education Office for Civil Rights Division Director Charles Love was on hand to receive the petition and listen to the complaints.

NAACP officials said that parents have been complaining to district administrators for years about what parents see as discriminatory treatment of African-American students and employees. The meeting was called this week because some people believe that Franklin High School's principal, an African-American, has been unfairly treated by district officials who are investigating his con-

"We're not seen ... by teachers as capable of performing. And that's a problem."
— Lester Patrick,
Stockton parent, left

duct.

"The community has kind of said: 'Enough is enough.' And we really need to address what is going on," said LaJuana Bivens, communications and publicity chair for the chapter.

In an interview earlier Wednesday, Stockton Unified Superintendent Gary McHenry strongly denied that race was a factor in district officials' decision to place Principal Ola Murchison on paid administrative leave while officials investigate allegations that

Franklin staffers doctored school records so a student could retain an $84,000 scholarship to play college football.

Some parents and district staffers have questioned why Murchison is on administrative leave while Stagg High School Principal Richard Yescas was allowed to remain on the job as officials looked into allegations involving his conduct. Yescas has admitted to

Please see NAACP, B2

Peer Mentoring Program

In 2006, I developed and implemented an African American male peer mentoring program. I created an extensive list of subjects that have been used to mentor the boys in the program. I enjoyed the overwhelming support of my Alpha brothers from Nu Beta Lambda Chapter of Alpha Phi Alpha from the very beginning. I do need to give special thanks to the following brothers; Judge Bill Murray, Brother Johnnie Ford, Dr. Ashlyn Brown, Brother Ben Reddish, Brother Al Brown, Reverend Brother Curtis Kimbro, Brother Rawlin Davis, Brother Roland Davis, Brother Todd Summers, Brother Michael Merriweather, Brother Exodie Roe, Brother Doug Martin, and Brother Greg Brezensky. I extend my special thanks to brothers Judge Murray and Ben Reddish. They have been there for the mentoring program at times when it was very difficult for them, due to their schedules. On behalf of the young men you have mentored over the years, thank you brothers.

We also had participation from Congressman Jerry McNerney, Mayor Ann Johnston, Mayor Michael Tubbs, Dr. Daryl Camp, Dr. Irvin Jefferson, Mr. John Ivy, Randy Malandro, Family Resource and Referral.

My very special thanks goes to Barbara Shadrick, Dr. Camp, and Dr. Irene Outlaw. Barbara was my primary contact at the schools and was vital to the success of the program at all stages. She was the community liaison, but she went far beyond what her duties called for to address the needs of these boys. Dr. Outlaw was the first elementary principal to embrace the program. She also opened up her school to support the Algebra Project. I will not name the principals at the other elementary schools because they have changed several times over the years.

Community Peer Mentoring Program

- Why do we do this?
    - To supplement parents and the school system in their efforts to develop disciplined academically successful students.
    - To provide insight to young men on a broad range of subjects
    - To inspire commitment and motivation.
    - To nurture the building of positive character.
- Who is it who does this?
    - community members
- How does the program benefit students?

We initially adopted the program as a fraternity project. But over the years, it evolved to become a community program. I designed it as a peer mentoring model.

Consequently, on Tuesdays, my Alpha brothers or other adults mentored high school students on a given subject. And then, on the following Thursday, these same boys traveled to two elementary schools to deliver the message to elementary students. The article below was written about one of our orientation meetings at the beginning of the school year. But preceding the articles are two pages that give a bullet description and a list of the program's goals and several of the subjects we covered. Due to the pandemic, the program is not operational now.

I organized the mentoring program to allow for one-on-one

Community Peer Mentoring Program

Mentoring Topics
- Introduction to mentoring.
- Orientation
- Developmental asset survey.
- Responding to people in authority.
- Some characteristics of a real man.
- Steps to becoming a model citizen.
- Making the best of your time.
- Overcoming the fear of public speaking.
- Being on your best behavior in class.
- Forming study groups.
  - Benefits and advantages of study groups.
- Standing on the shoulders of others.
- Racism is not an excuse.
- Setting goals and objectives.

Mentoring Topics
- Coping with stress.
- Skills in planning your life.
- Making your ideals known through good writing skills.
- Job interview skills.
- Dealing with difficult people.
- Health and nutrition for young men.
- Career opportunities in the information industry.
  - Career workshop
- The proper way to treat girls.
- Two field trips.
- Foot ball / basket ball / fun and play day.
- Closing session.

group mentoring sessions and a format that gives them exposure to things outside of their community. One such event is shown in the picture below. I took them to the state capital, where they were invited to sit on the chamber floor and observe state legislators debating. I required each boy to wear a tie but provided most of the ties and collected them after the event. They looked impressive to everybody at the capital. And they also received several compliments. It is not legible enough to make out, but the marquee in the background is welcoming us to the capital.

Assembly Member Cathleen Galgiani and her staff met with the students. She is shown in the center of the picture above. The chief of staff also greeted them from the office of the speaker of the Assembly. But equally impressive as the picture was the conversation on the bus on the way back to Stockton. They were discussing and debating gun control and foster care services. These were two of the sessions they sat in on and listened to. Obviously, they were paying attention; I was very proud of them. This is what I was trying to cause to happen for them.

A positive influence

Bear Creek's Tyson Walton, left, and Dwayne Lee, both 13 listen to Lester Patrick, director of a peer mentoring program conducted by Alpha Phi Alpha's Nu Beta Lambda Chapter in Stockton. This was an orientation meeting between mentors and students from Bear Creek High and Delta Sierra Middle School, where the meeting was held.

Students join mentoring program to help younger peers

By Keith Reid
Record Staff Writer

STOCKTON - Bear Creek High senior Siaosi Haleufia wants to be a positive influence on his younger classmates, especially those who may struggle with some of the same social etiquette nuances that he once did. Things like public speaking, dealing with difficult people, how to treat girls and coping with stress are some examples, he said.

For these reasons, Haleufia, 17, has joined the Alpha Phi Alpha, Nu Beta Lambda Stockton chapter's peer mentoring program. Haleufia and other Bear Creek boys receive mentoring from fraternity members on how to be successful in life, and in turn, the high schoolers deliver the same messages to Delta Sierra Middle School students.

Lodi Unified community relations director Irvin Jefferson said the program, now in its second year, is one that reaches out to boys in all walks of life. Some come from families without a father in the home and are in need of a man's guidance. Some are students who have been in trouble at school. Others still are students who have simply chosen to be involved.

In all, more than 100 Bear Creek and Delta Sierra students have joined the program.

"It's going to help us in college and in our careers," Haleufia said.

The peer mentoring program is led by Lester Patrick, a Stockton resident who is also president of the Lodi Unified academic review committee. Patrick said the program's goal is to "develop discipline and inspire commitment" for students who could be potentially persuaded by less positive influences.

"The fraternity is worldwide, and we just want to broaden these young men's potential in a variety of topics," Patrick said, noting that Martin Luther King Jr., former U.S. Supreme Court Justice Thurgood Marshall, former San Francisco Mayor Willie Brown and six active members of Congress are among the most famous members of the traditionally black fraternity.

"It's no longer exclusive. Other ethnic groups are allowed in the fraternity, too," Patrick added.

At an orientation for Delta Sierra students on Thursday, Patrick broke the students into small groups, each with a mentor. A "get to know you conversation" was an icebreaker.

In the coming weeks, the process begins. Fraternity mentors will meet with Bear Creek students weekly, and the following day, the high schoolers will meet with the middle schoolers to mentor them.

"A lot in life is making good first impressions," said Bear Creek freshman Artell Merritt, 14. "That's why I'm here. I want to be seen in the right way." Contact reporter Keith Reid at (209) 367-7428 or kreid@recordnet.com.

Most young boys love sports. And most young boys enjoy interacting with sports figures. Michael Merriweather, a former NFL player and a member of Nu Beta Lambda, has always mentored the boys. The picture below shows him on one of those occasions playing a game with  them. So, they all can say they have played a football game with a Pro Bowl linebacker. They have always enjoyed sporting events, as you might imagine. We have also had other sports figures to come and mentor them. Merriweather recommended one of them.

The Urban Technology Vehicle

Community work not only involves advocating to bring about improved change, but it should also include recommending solutions and planning to implement the solutions necessary to address the issues. I have tried to use that concept throughout my entire life of community work. The picture below describes one such project. As the Academic Review Committee chairman, I recommended that we implement a "Making Math Fun" project. I designed this project to address the lack of interest that the African American students had in math, reading, and other subjects.

I recommended that we purchase a mobile unit and convert it into a traveling technology center. The unit was equipped with twenty computer workstations, a pull-down screen for teaching, a full-time teacher, a technical person, and a satellite dish. It traveled between nineteen schools throughout Stockton and Lodi neighborhoods, providing computer services to students who didn't have those services in their homes.

Additionally, we teamed up with the school and the city to implement a summer school program for those students in the local communities who couldn't get to summer school. We did pre- and post-testing of the students who took summer school in the Urban Technology Vehicle (UTV), and those who attended summer school in a traditional classroom setting. The students who attended summer school in the UTV far outperformed those in the conventional classroom setting. The reason was straightforward. We had made it to appear as fun to them

Lester Patrick

rather than work. They enjoyed it! They loved it, and couldn't wait to experience it daily!

The picture below shows that.

Maicoe Xiong, 10, works on a project Monday at Ansel Adams Elementary School in the Urban Technology Vehicle, a motor home full of Apple laptop computer stations. The Lodi Unified School District, the city of Stockton and the Alpha Phi Alpha and Nu Beta Lamda fraternities came together to fund the vehicle, which will be used by 19 Lodi Unified schools during the school year.

Tech center a group effort
Stockton, Lodi Unified and fraternities fund lab on wheels

By Keith Reid
Record Staff Writer

STOCKTON — Nine-year-old Evelin Sanson has a new favorite computer program: Apple's iPhoto.

Before last week, the Westwood Elementary School fifth-grader had never used iPhoto, and she admits that she is not the most skilled digital photographer at her school.

"I just like taking pictures from the Internet and doing my picture project," she said.

Evelin has a chance to learn iPhoto because her summer school class has had daily access to the Lodi Unified School District's mobile computer lab, known as the Urban Technology Vehicle. It is a 40-foot motor home that has been fitted with 30 laptop computer stations.

The $350,000 vehicle is paid for and operated in a joint effort by the city of Stockton, Lodi Unified, the Alpha Phi Alpha Fraternity and the Nu Beta Lambda Stockton chapter, said Lester Patrick, Lodi Unified's academic review committee chairman.

"This is the type of thing that can happen when groups come together and collaborate," Patrick said. He added that he would like to see a mobile lab with services that extend even deeper into communities by traveling into Stockton neighborhoods where more people can have access.

During the school year, the vehicle moves around to 19 Lodi Unified schools. All of them are classified as Title I, meaning that a high percentage of students attending the school also qualify for the free or reduced-price lunch program.

This summer, the Urban Technology Vehicle is being transported between the district's two summer school program sites at Oakwood Elementary and Ansel Adams Elementary schools in north Stockton, where students are using a program called Riverdeep, which tests their English, language arts and math skills.

On one work station, 9-year-old Jordan Young did a word puzzle to work on spelling. At another station, Jonathan Min, 7, read a fairy tale that he will be tested on later.

"Each student logs in, and the content is individualized to them based on their skill level, which is calculated by assessment tests," said summer school technology teacher Robert Seymour.

"At the end of this pilot run with Riverdeep, these students will be tested to see how they responded to working with the program."

Along with the academic program, some students like Evelin are using iPhoto for a project. There is otherwise no time for play in the lab.

"We don't have any video games here," said 10-year-old Ismael Carrillo. "It's still fun, though."

Lodi Unified community relations coordinator Irvin Jefferson said the mobile computer lab is not intended to replace computer labs at elementary schools, but a supplemental option for students that need extra help keeping up with their studies.

Contact reporter Keith Reid at (209) 367-7428 or kreid@recordnet.com.

Serving on Bond Oversight Committees

One of the most effective ways of advocating for the community's resources to support those in need is by serving on local boards. For example, in the Lodi Unified School District, I served on both the Measures K and L Bond Oversight Committees. I served as both the chairman and as a committee member.

In 2002, voters passed a $109.3-million school bond. At the time, this was the first school bond successfully passed in twenty-eight years. The funds were used to help build a new high school, a middle school, and four elementary schools. Two elementary schools were built in Lodi and two in Stockton. And the funds also provided for renovations at twenty-two other schools throughout the district. To complete these projects, the district was also able to supplement these funds by tapping into state construction funds.

As a board member, I was responsible for keeping the public informed of projects sponsored by the bonds, reviewing expenditures, developing an annual report, presenting the annual report to the Board of Education, and monitoring the projects' progress. To monitor the expenditures of funds, it became necessary to make site visits to observe the projects' progress. This was an important task when Ronald McNair High School, Christie McAuliffe Elementary, and the other elementary schools were built. As a committee member, I also helped monitor the expenditures for projects at Bear Creek High School. Some of the projects included building the football and track field, the new auditorium, cafeteria, the exercise room, and some smaller but important projects. Because these schools were new, each had to be named. My wife Linda, who was on the naming committee, submitted a recommendation to name it the Ronald McNair High School. It was accepted and approved by the school board.

Site visits were essential because only by visually observing the work could we assess whether it had been done. The site visits also presented an opportunity for the committee to visually inspect the general building of the school. Once we took a site visit to Ronald McNair High School as it was being built, I noticed the flooring buckling as I walked into the building. I brought this to the attention of the project manager of the facilities department. The entire flooring on the first floor had to be replaced. I could cite other examples of situations like that. But the point that I am making here is that when you sit on the boards, you are able to ensure that the funds are being spent as the voters have approved them. If they are not, then as a committee member, you can make the public aware.

Each year there was an independent audit by an independent auditor. The audit used a performance-based method, which allowed the committee to get a professional and external look at the financial transactions. With this audit, we could also validate that all funds were being expensed towards projects that could only be funded by funds from these two measures.

While I was on the committee, I had an opportunity to advocate for Delta Sierra Middle School to get a complete makeover, inside and out. This project greatly improved the community's appearance and positively influenced the attitudes of students and staff. But if I had not been on the committee, I could not have helped this to happen. All I could have done would have been to complain about how the school looked and its negative impact on the image of the local community. These are just a couple of reasons why it is so important to be engaged at this level on boards that can impact and change the community.

The citizens bond oversight committees I have described above were responsible for monitoring funds for a K-12 school district. But I also currently serve on another bond oversight committee for San Joaquin Delta College. The responsibilities are the same, but the projects are different. Because here, we are talking about the distribution of funds to support a college campus with about 20,000 students. The projects are very big, but again, all the tasks are the same as those for the K-12 school bonds committee, so I will not go into the details concerning this committee's responsibilities.

Board of Directors for Family Resource and Referral Center

I am blessed to have been part of this organization for ten years, serving as a director on the board of directors for the Family Resource and Referral Center. There are many service organizations within San Joaquin County, but none are more service-oriented than Family Resource and Referral. At the core of this organization's mission is connecting parents to quality childcare, which meets their needs, and providing child care assistance to parents attending school or working. It distributes about $50 million into roughly thirteen counties throughout California. The overwhelming majority of that is distributed here in the local community of San Joaquin County.

Family Resource and Referral Center was organized forty years ago by Joan Richards. Since that time, it has expanded its services extensively and geographically to include multiple counties throughout the state. Its mission is:

> "Family Resource & Referral Center strengthens
> the lives of children, families, and communities."

This organization provides a broad range of services to the community relative to families and children's support. It serves as a referral agency to those in need of childcare services, parenting, nutrition, and childcare safety. It also administers childcare and nutritional resources and conducts workshops in effective practices of child-rearing, childcare, and child safety.

The agency was founded on the principle that children and families are vital to the success of high quality of life in San Joaquin. The staff demonstrates this principle daily as they interact personally with families and their children.

The Center's staff reflects its belief system as it:

- Promotes community awareness concerning the needs of children and families
- Participates in building community coalitions to develop solutions for those needs
- Works with parents, care providers, business and community leaders to promote quality services for children and their families
- Provides childcare referrals to all parents in San Joaquin County
- Administers childcare and nutritional resources, conducts workshops on effective practices of child-rearing, childcare, and child safety
- Provides advocacy, information, training and direct services to enhance childcare, child development, and family well-being in San Joaquin County.

Family Resource and Referral Center provides programs and services for both parents and their children. Below is a list of those programs and services:

- Health and safety training
- Increasing quality of care
- Education and training for childcare providers and parents
- Instructional materials and resources for childcare providers and parents
- Education, training, and intervention services for providers of children with special needs.

To give an idea of its impact on the community, I will cite some statistics impacting some of the programs and services in a recent year. Over 10,758 telephone calls were received by 2-1-1 staff from individuals looking for information and/or assistance with all kinds of life events, including the following most requested needs:

- Low-cost home rental listings
- Rent payment assistance
- Food pantries
- Homeless shelters
- Comprehensive information and referrals
- An additional 13,440 requests were received via website users at 211sj.org
- 1,834 childcare referrals were made so parents could work or attend school while their children were learning
- 4,091 families and 6,794 children received financial assistance with childcare costs through the Subsidized Child Care program
- 838 children received free Ages & Stages Questionnaire screenings for early identification of childhood developmental concerns
- 24 childcare providers participated in the First 5 Raising Quality! IMPACT
- 84 families received Parents as Teachers services through our First 5 Home Visitation Initiative program. The program served high-need children ages 0-3 from diverse populations living in five specific SJC zip codes. Raising a Reader book bags were also provided to these families to develop literacy and promote the shared book experience.
- 11,281 youth were served by FRRC's Teen IMPACT Center and their Teen Leadership Council
- 77 children received services in licensed, high-quality family childcare homes through our Early Head Start-Child

Care Partnership (EHS-CCP) with Stanislaus County which provides early, continuous, intensive, and comprehensive child development and family support services to infants and toddlers and their families
- 1,640 parents received HSA-contracted case management services to help clients become self-sufficient. Parents received assistance with work-related activities and supportive services, including transportation reimbursement, childcare referrals, welfare-to-work planning, and work activities.
- The Child and Adult Care Food Program provided services and recruitment in FRRC's primary service area of San Joaquin County, as well as in the following counties: Amador, Butte, Calaveras, Los Angeles, Orange, Placer, Riverside, Sacramento, San Bernardino, Stanislaus, and Yolo
- $6,648,368.56 in reimbursement payments were made to 907 childcare providers for meals and snacks served to 8,899 children in both Northern and Southern California
- Agency staff conducted 2,981 monitoring visits to childcare sites, as well as provided technical assistance, mandated annual program training, and resources and nutrition education materials from numerous sources to all participants

As a board member, I am proud to say that the above lists of accomplishments represent several of the services provided during one recent year at Family Resource & Referral Center.

One of the most effective services Family Resource & Referral Center provides for teens is the operation of the Podesto Teen Impact Center. I have developed a summer networking program that consists of six, two, and half-hour workshops that I implemented at the teen impact center. Teens who attended were extremely interested and attentive to all the labs and the lecture as well. The labs were designed in a way that resulted in them having designed a working network once they had completed the program. Additionally, the software they used allowed them to transfer and observe traffic over the network they had designed.

Below is a copy of the flyer that announced the program.

Introduction to Basic Networking Concepts

When: 6.28.2017, 6.30.2017, 7.6.2017, 7.10.2017

Time: 1:30 to 4:00

Successfully complete this program and receive a free Galaxy Nook Tablet!!!!!!!!!!!

You will become familiar with industry standard network software used to design and model networks

Becoming familiar with network types and topologies

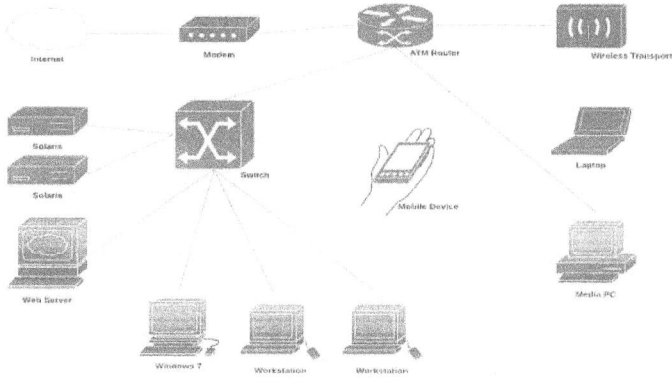

Learn the seven layers of the OSI network model and the networking activities at each layer

Compare the seven layer OSI network model with the TCP/IP model

Trace and observe how network packets move over the Internet from your PC, to its destination and back, through both landline and wireless networks

Participate in 3 Labs that teach you basic design and configuration concepts

Understand the proper cables, network hardware devices, etc. that make up a network

Where: **Teen Impact Center, 725 N Eldorado St.**

Sponsored By Family Resource and Referral Center!!!!!!!!!!!

PART VII

Retirement

After retiring in 2015, I made myself available for other board positions. I am proud and privileged to serve on the boards of the Housing Authority of San Joaquin County, the Hunger Task Force of San Joaquin County, and the Strong Communities Committee of the City of Stockton. I was appointed to each of these positions after I retired. I will talk a little about my role serving with these organizations below, and how these organizations impact the citizens of these communities.

When I retired, I had forty-two years of federal service. At the time, I just planned to attend guitar classes, do volunteer work in the community, and go home as often as possible to visit Aunt Nellie. Unfortunately, I only got the opportunity to visit her once after I retired. Just six months after I retired on June 7, 2015, Aunt Nellie passed away. She was eighty-five years old. For a while it was as if somebody had stuck a spear through my heart. For a long time I lived with a feeling of emptiness in my heart. But like all other things that we have to adjust to, eventually I was able to move on.

Commissioner of the Housing Authority of San Joaquin

I have served as a commissioner of the Housing Authority of San Joaquin County since 2016. I mentioned earlier in the book about the advantage of serving at the board level in the community. That concept could not be more obvious than serving on this board because it involves a lot more than monitoring the organization's expenditures. But there are direct impacts on the local community.

The housing authority currently has a staff of about ninety-two employees. It distributes roughly $50 million annually into the local community. We shelter approximately 19,000 people in San Joaquin County and provide rental assistance and affordable housing for over 6,000 households countywide.

We own and/or manage:

- 1,012 public housing units
- 81 market rate units
- 30 year-round farm worker units
- 285 seasonal agricultural migrants housing units
- 5,080 housing choice voucher

We also serve our residents with employment and educational opportunities, referrals, utility assistance and recreational opportunities for youth who live in the developments. I will highlight some of the specifics of these below.

As one of the commissioners of this board, our collective responsibilities include the following:

1. Ensuring the federal and state funds are managed without waste, fraud, or mismanagement
2. Understanding the needs of low-income persons of the community as it relates to housing in order to provide safe, decent, and sanitary housing
3. Ensuring that independent audits are performed on an annual basis
4. Also ensuring through the executive officer that all board established policies are followed by staff
5. Ensuring that the Agency has depository agreements with all financial institutions we do business with
6. Assuring that the EO is not paid more than what employees are compensated under the Federal Executive Level IV Schedule base wages

Since I have been a member of this board, we have approved and monitored the implementation of several projects. I will name just a few of them here.

1. Victory Gardens – a 49-unit affordable supportive housing development for the homeless veteran. Units will be subsidized with housing choice program vouchers through the HUD-VASH program.
2. Turnpike Commons – a 9-unit housing development for the homeless in Stockton. Will be completed in 2021.
3. Charter School – The Housing Authority of San Joaquin County is in the process of implementing a charter school at Conway Homes and Sierra Vista.
4. Sonora Square Apartments – a 19-unit housing project for individuals and families experiencing homelessness and mental illness.

5. Sierra Vista 1 – replacement of 63 aged and deteriorating public housing units with 115 modern, energy-efficient affordable housing units.
6. Sierra Vista 2 – this phase replaces 57, old units with 100 modern, energy-efficient affordable housing units.

These projects were completed using a combination of capital contribution, Low-Income Housing Tax Credit (LIHTC), city of Stockton Home funds, and permanent financing. Additionally, we are currently in the process of pursuing other public housing opportunities. The Conway project is shown below.

Conway unveiling
possible glimpse of future

As a commissioner, I have recommended to the Board of Commissioners for approval proposals designed to improve public housing residents' living conditions. A brief description of several of them follows:

A. Family Self Sufficiency/Program Jobs Plus Program

Early on as a member of the Board of Commissioners, I presented to the board as a discussion and action item a proposal to apply for funding for the Family Self Sufficiency Program and the Jobs Plus Program. Having the conscientious executive officer we have, when I presented the proposal, he had already applied for one of the programs but had not been a successful applicant. Since that time, we have been granted funds to implement these programs at the Housing Authority of San Joaquin County. Tenants are benefiting greatly from both of the programs.

B. Internet Security Program

There are many needs within the housing authorities other than housing needs but needs that simply mirror the general population's needs. One of those needs includes being knowledgeable about cybersecurity and how to protect yourself and household against attacks. Public housing residents don't have legal funds to fight a case of identity theft, internet bullying, and other related attacks.

I developed a plan to conduct several hands-on workshops at the housing authorities to educate tenants about things they can do to protect themselves against cyberattacks.

I presented this proposal and curriculum first to the Board of Commissioners and then to the Resident Committee at the public housing facility, who expressed excitement about receiving the workshops. I presented the proposal to them in 2019 and plan to implement it in 2020. But due to the pandemic, I have not been able to do so. But as soon as it is over I will.

Internet Security Workshop

Background1. The digital divide is very present amongst residents of public housing. Multiple programs have been introduced at the local, state, and federal levels to address the problem. Some progress has been made, but like any technology implemented to improve the quality of life, there also comes unwanted outcomes. In this case, the undesirable result is increased vulnerability to cyberattacks and identity theft.

2. This workshop focuses on presenting the housing authority with a tool kit that can be used to assist residents in protecting themselves against such attacks. The focus will be placed on Android phones, Windows-based connected computers, the wireless access point, and other networking components.

Learning Objectives

1. To assist the housing authority with the background to expand services to tenants by making them aware of potential threats that arise when connecting phones and computers to the internet and how to address them
2. To provide the attendee a step-by-step procedure to make connected devices owned by tenants more secure and assist them in becoming more Internet security literate
3. To aid the tenant in reducing the risk of cyberattacks and identity theft when engaging in activities such as electronic rental payments, email, K-12 online homework assignments, web browsing, online adult training, etc.
4. To assist in making internet-connected computers owned and supported by the housing authority more secure for those tenants who use housing authority computers and connected devices.

C. Food Insecurity Awareness

Food insecurity is a problem across America. Roughly 13 percent of the general population experience food insecurity. The people we support in the housing authorities are just one subset of the country's food insecure population, San Joaquin County, and California. But the food insecurity problem affecting residents of housing authorities across the country has virtually gone untouched. I believe that a primary reason has been that housing authorities have viewed themselves strictly as being housing providers and that their responsibility stops there.

I believe we have a responsibility to address the needs of the whole person where possible. For that reason, I initiated an effort to educate the national housing authority officials in every state on the food insecurity problem that impacts housing authority residents. In addressing this problem of lack of awareness of this issue, I have opened people's eyes here in this county and other parts of the country and those having interaction with housing authority residents.

As a member of the National Association of Housing Authorities, I was given the opportunity this year to conduct a Food Insecurity Round Table Discussion at a national conference of housing officials. The organization's name is NAHRO and stands for the National Association of Housing and Redevelopment Officials. There are about 18,000 members, and the majority of members are public housing employees or commissioners. The committee included a Ph. D. from a major university and a manager from one of the country's largest and busiest food banks. It went very well and increased the awareness of people first-hand of the problem. One would think that people supporting public housing residents would be aware of the food insecurity problem they face. But the reality is that food insecurity is one of the problems that cannot always be visually

Weak Start Unapologetic Present

identified. I have had the same discussion with commissioners of San Joaquin County. Awareness is only the first step.

In consulting with counterparts in other parts of the country and other sources, I have identified some next steps to help eliminate the problem. Much research validates the link between food insecurity and poor health, poor school performance, and behavior problems in children and adults. Addressing food insecurity in housing authorities will have a major impact on our local economy here in San Joaquin County, California, and across the country.

For residents to be prepared to take advantage of opportunities that can help them improve their lives to the point that they will be able to move out of public housing, this problem will need to be addressed.

Below is an excerpt from the introductory page from the roundtable discussion I facilitated at the national NAHRO conference. It shows the panelists and the objectives of the discussion.

Panelists

Melanie McGuire
Chief Program Officer for
San Antonio Food Bank

Kathy Kray, Ph.D.
Director of Research and Administration,
Baylor University's Texas Hunger Initiative

Lester Patrick, M.S.,
Commissioner,
Housing Authority of
San Joaquin County

The Hunger Task Force of San Joaquin

I have been a member of the Hunger Task Force of San Joaquin County since I retired in 2015. Since that time, I have served as the legislative advocate for the organization. My role has been to keep the committee aware of state and federal legislation affecting food insecurity. And to encourage elected officials to support food insecurity bills that will impact hunger in San Joaquin County, whether state or federal.

Performing in this role has allowed me to meet along with other members with both Congressman McNerney and Congressman Harder to discuss food insecurity and what can be done to address it. I have also continued my lobbying for food insecurity annually in Washington, D.C, lobbying multiple congress members and senators. I had the opportunity to speak before the agricultural subcommittee concerning the farm bill's passage when it was up for review in Congress. Additionally, I have served

Keep up opposition to 2018 Farm Bill

Congress recently voted on the Farm Bill of 2018. It failed. But this was a positive outcome, because if the bill was approved in its current form, millions of people nationwide and thousands in California would lose access to nutritional food.

The Farm Bill is the supplemental food program for millions of low-wage workers, children, people with disabilities, and seniors. It contains programs such as the Supplemental Nutrition Assistance Program and CalFresh, which provide food assistance for low-income people.

According to the Department of Education, 63 percent of all school-age children in San Joaquin County are eligible for free or reduced price school meals. About 25 percent of all households in the city of Stockton have an annual income of less than $25,000.

SNAP is among the nation's most important anti-hunger programs, assisting 45 million low-income Americans in achieving a relatively adequate daily diet.

In May, Congress failed to pass the Farm Bill, but they will try again.

Please contact your congressional representative and request that they oppose the Farm Bill of 2018.

Lester Patrick, legislative advocate, Hunger Task Force of San Joaquin County as the vice-chairman of the Hunger Task Force of San Joaquin County for the last two years.

As I pointed out earlier in the book, one of the most effective means of advocating for any issue is through the newspaper. Consequently, as the legislative advocate for the Hunger Task Force of San Joaquin County, one of the things I have done to fight food insecurity is, I have submitted letters to the Stockton Record to educate the public on food insecurity.

Two of those articles are enclosed here.

By Lester Patrick/Special to the Record
Posted Dec. 18, 2019 at 4:15 p.m. (Updated Dec. 18, 2019)

Strong Communities Committee

One of the committees I have been appointed to since retiring is the Strong Communities Committee.

In November of 2016, the citizens of Stockton approved a one-quarter cent sales tax during the general election. It was call Measure M on the ballot. It went into effect April 1, 2017. Strong Communities was approved as a special tax that is dedicated to the City of Stockton recreation and library programs, services, and facilities.

The funds are restricted and are kept in a separate fund. These funds can only be used for City of Stockton recreation and library programs and services. It is estimated to generate $9 million per year. It will be in effect for sixteen years.

- Funding is being used in the following ways:
- Safe places for after-school programs for children and teens by extending the number of days and hours that community centers and libraries are open
- Homework help centers and Science Technology Engineering and Math (STEM) education
- Storytimes, literacy, cultural and sports programs, classes, and facilities
- Preservation and expansion of the existing library and recreation programs
- Re-opening and upgrading of facilities, services, and collections
- Extension of services to under-served areas of the city

Lester Patrick

Council hears pitch for north Stockton library

By Wes Bowers
Record Staff Writer

STOCKTON — Community members raised concerns about the state of libraries during a Stockton City Council special meeting to approve the 2018-19 budget Tuesday evening, asking for a branch in the north part of the city and additional funds for services.

Lester Patrick, a member of the Strong Communities Committee, asked the council to consider putting a city library somewhere in north Stockton, citing the children in that area have limited access to existing branches in neighboring areas.

"We passed Measure M to address this issue for children throughout Stockton, and as you know, the city is in the beginning stages of implementing this program," he said. "However, many members of the community would like to see something done immediately, on an interim basis, until a permanent long-term solution can be implemented."

Measure M was passed in 2016, and created a one-quarter-cent sales tax dedicated to the city's recreation and library services. The measure helped the city reopen the Fair Oaks Library in east Stockton last year, after a seven-year closure.

Patrick recommended the City Council make funding available in the 2019 budget for some sort of library service, even it means a library room at a community center or a bookmobile.

Vice Mayor Elbert Holman agreed a library is needed in the northern area of the city, particularly northwest Stockton near Trinity Parkway.

As a special, dedicated sales tax, Strong Communities proceeds are subject to an annual audit conducted by an independent firm of certified accountants. The yearly independent audit includes financial activity and complies with the Strong Communities (Measure M) ballot language and the Advisory Committee's charter and bylaws.

One of the responsibilities of the committee is to review and approve the annual independent audit. Since being on the committee, we have supported the audits for 2017, 2018, and 2019. And we have reviewed and approved the annual reports for FY 2016/2017 and FY 2017/2018.

Measure M was adopted to implement the increase in sales tax and establishes the requirement for a citizens' advisory committee. It requires the committee to meet at least annually and make recommendations regarding expenditures to the City Council. Unfortunately, we have not functioned efficiently as a committee for making recommendations to the City Council.

In keeping with the requirements of Measure M, I have gone to the City Council to recommend that funds be allocated to North West Stockton to build a library. There is a great need for a library

Weak Start Unapologetic Present

in that part of the city. Additionally, I have recommended that abandoned buildings be refurbished for the purpose of satisfying library needs in that part of the city. Above is a description of my presentation to the council.

Below are several accomplishments completed with Measure M funds this year. Each project has been monitored by the Strong Communities Committee for its adherence to the guidelines for the distribution of Measure M funds.

ACCOMPLISHMENTS IN 2018-19

Restore Services:
- Expanded hours at libraries and community centers
- Hired or promoted six full-time and additional part-time staff to support expanded hours and programming
- Extended pool hours for "Family Nights"

Priority for Programs and Projects with High Community Benefit:

- Library users gained access to streaming films through the Kanopy platform
- Hosted nineteen "Ultra Friday Nights" with extended evening hours
- ecTrac became available for online bill payment and other features
- Increased participation in the Summer Reading program with 62,204 books read

Improve Assets Whenever Possible:

- Troke Library children's area was remodeled
- Completed re-seeding project at Stockton Soccer Complex

- Conducted assessments and completed modifications to improve safety at facilities
- Holiday Park swimming pool brought up to code to be operational for community in summer of 2020
- Submitted application for Proposition 68 Grant to renovate McKinley Park

Focus on Underserved Areas:

- Micro libraries were opened in Rue and Stribley Community Centers
- Free wifi in all community centers
- Partnered with YMCA for Jump Into Summer Healthy Kids Day with over 1,000 in attendance

Leverage Partnerships:

- Partnered with Stockton Unified School District to host Family Literacy Camp for ESL families at Seifert Community Center
- With University of the Pacific's Beyond Our Gates, offered LENA Start program which promotes the building of early literacy skills in infants and toddlers (0-32 months)
- With the San Francisco Junior Giants, offered Hit, Pitch, and Run program for community youth
- With four nearby library systems and with funding from the California State Library, presented English Conversation Club and Bilingual Storytimes to community members through the use of Zoom app
- Provided free meals (lunch, snacks, dinner) with support from Stockton Unified School District
- 22,050 books were read in the first Winter Reading program for children ages 6-12 made possible with support from the Stockton Heat

- Partnered with Stockton Police Department to have Sentinels and Cadets at Oak Park and Sousa Pools to build trust and relationships within the community

Epilogue

Writing this book has been an enjoyable experience for me. It has allowed me to revisit areas of my life that I haven't thought about for decades. During the process, I learned that even though I have recorded fond memories, accomplishments, experiences, and tragedies as part of this process, they still don't fully express my life's totality. One blessing that I experienced as I wrote this book is that I had to be very selective in deciding what I would include in the book. When I first thought about writing this documentary of my life, I thought about compiling a scrapbook with brief descriptions of a group of pictures. That idea quickly vanished as I started developing an outline of what I would include in the book. Then I attempted to limit myself to between 100 and 150 pages. That idea quickly became a very distant idea after briefly touching upon my childhood and passing a hundred pages. At that point, I decided I needed to settle down and write what came to my heart to share in this book and not let the length of the book be the driving catalyst. I couldn't ignore the book's size, so once I got to over 300 pages, I decided that I would try to limit it to the 400-page range.

I am emphasizing this to make this point. There is so much about my life that is not contained in this book that I already have plans to write a second book to focus on specific parts of my life because I simply could not put everything in this book. I am not looking to write a book with everything about my life, but I would like to share many of those experiences I have had over my seventy years that might help my offspring and in the process somebody else. I mean I have made mistakes, had successes, and experienced tragedies. I have experienced tragedies so profoundly that I didn't think it would be a good idea to include them in the book. I will need to do much more thinking about relaying the stories behind them so that they might bless somebody. I am not sure that a book is the best vehicle to use to help others in that area. I will need to do more serious thinking about that. Other areas where I had to be extremely limited in what I could share are my advocacy and community volunteering work. I was equally limiting when it came to my career and family life. There is another book in each of those areas.

For example, as I pointed out in the book already, I have forty-two years of experience working in technology. To be more specific, my experience has been in networking. I have always been concerned about the lack of African Americans working in the technical fields. I gave a brief description of my work background in technology and some exciting work experiences. I selected to share the specific areas that I did, hoping that I might influence some children through their parents to consider careers in technology. I have, in the past, developed an Introduction to Networking Workshop for teenagers. I have implemented this project at a city level to teens and at a junior high level to primarily African American students. As I was writing this book, suddenly the idea came to me to write a textbook specific to young people about networking basics. At least two other images also flooded my mind about other books I should write. Once this one is published, I definitely will be taking on those projects.

This book discusses how I had such a weak start in my early life but was always able to rebound and overcome struggles that could have caused me to simply give up at an early age. And about when I was at crossroads and could have taken the wrong turn but didn't. In most cases, I took the right turn. But when I didn't, I was able to recover from it. I did not give up, but so many children today do. It is especially true of African American boys. I have had the misfortune of observing this when coming in contact with some of them during the mentoring sessions I have conducted. It is a very heartbreaking experience. But it doesn't have to be that way. This is where African American men fall short in contributing to helping stabilize these young boys' lives. When we think of mentoring African American males, we usually think of formal processes to guide younger males. Some of that visual image of the mentoring process is true, and not every African American man is prepared to do that. I understand. But the thing that we overlook so often is the impact that an African American adult male's presence can have on young African American males. We can make sure that more of us make ourselves physically available to young African American males. It can make a huge difference in their lives.

I had to start making decisions at a very early age about my welfare. It started with who I would live with. I know now that God gave me the vision to select my aunt Nellie and uncle Winser. This was one of the crossroads I just referred to. It started very early for me. Had I made any other decision, there is no doubt my life would have been much different. That was a weak start. At such an early age, I was placed in a situation whereby I had to make a major decision about where I was going to live. The underlying blessing at that early stage of my life was that I did have a choice to make. A couple of other family members were willing to step up and give me a home. So many children today don't have that option available to them. Even though being in that situation was not the norm, I was still fortunate.

Because my mother and father were not married, I was labeled an illegitimate child. I was illegitimate! I was not a legitimate person. I was not authorized by law to exist. I was not in accordance with the standards and rules of the time. These were society's definitions of me when I was born to unmarried parents. And also the definition of others born under similar circumstances. I was also born during Jim Crow, was African American and not equal to Whites in the eyes of Whites and the law. Nor was I thought of by African Americans as equal to those whose parents were married. Nobody said that to me, but I sometimes heard other children referred to as being illegitimate. When I was old enough to understand what that meant, I understood that I was also an illegitimate child.

But I had an additional issue. That issue was that I simply didn't care about doing my school work for the first five years of school. I didn't see any connection between going to school and life other than merely being something I had to do. I do mean I had to do, because I didn't miss one day from school in my entire first through twelfth grade. So Aunt Nellie knew the connection, but I didn't. When you combine these elements—a child without a home, an illegitimate child, low school performance, an African American male, the impact of Jim Crow—you quickly get the picture of a young person with many reasons to give up and just say, forget it. As I wrote this book, I tried to write it in a way that would make these different elements very clear to the reader, because they didn't all just go away. Each was something that I had to deal with and was influenced by throughout my life. Each of them having varying impacts at certain stages of my life but still present. The stories I shared centered around these elements and can encourage and teach some children that it is not up to society as to how they turn out. You don't

Weak Start Unapologetic Present

have to settle for somebody else's vision for you, only the image you decide on and adapt for yourself.

In my case, there is one very important element I left out from the above comments. With all the negative elements that were part of my early life, there was one enormous positive that outweighed everything. That positive was a strong father and mother figure. Even though Aunt Nellie and Uncle Winser were not my biological parents, they could not have been better parents. So despite all the negative elements I have named and lived with, I had an extremely happy childhood and was a very happy youth. I was raised by two encouraging parents who loved me, and it always overshadowed any negatives. It was natural for me to receive encouragement from other family members, the church, the school, and the adults in the community. In several of these areas today, our society falls short in providing that kind of support for all children, and we can see the result of its lack.

Even though I had a weak start in the early part of my life, being surrounded by positive people motivated me not to accept what society's expectations would have been for me. Society didn't expect me to go to college, but my parents, cousins, and teachers did. That level of expectation made my very weak start, one in which I only had to stay focused on what I knew was possible. I could not fully comprehend what my teachers meant when they said we would one day sit in the same classroom as White students and compete against them. When I graduated from high school in 1968, that transition had not occurred, but a few years later, when the high schools were integrated, their dreams materialized. They based their hopes on Brown vs. the Board of Education that was passed in 1954. That decision by the U.S. Supreme Court eliminated segregation. But still not a lot changed in the South. Most things still continued to be segregated. I should point out that the South was not the only place where segregation was practiced. It was also very prevalent in other parts of the United States, whether the North, West, or the East. It was still very much part of the American experience for African Americans.

But nevertheless for my teachers and parents, Brown vs. The Department of Education marked an extremely significant milestone. With its ruling, it opened the door to numerous challenges to segregation. Some of them I discussed in this book. Even though we have seen civil rights laws passed since that time, we still have a long way to go to obtain justice for all in America.

When I left North Carolina A&T, I had no idea that the time I spent there was the end of the civil rights era. We placed faith in the laws and little attention to our responsibilities to ensure that the laws were followed. I believe it is each of our obligation to be an advocate in any way we can. Because if we don't advocate for our own freedom, we should not expect others to do it for us. That doesn't mean that we should not welcome others' support, but we should not sit back and wait for others to lead the way. There are many reasons why we shouldn't, but as African American, we must face the fact that we are still dealing with some of the same attitudes as before. We must speak out against it under all circumstances.

I know some African Americans will not agree with this premise. I discussed in the book examples of internalized oppression. Many of us suffer from that condition today. It is real, and we need to address it as a group of people. Sure, I understand that this behavior represents some people's response to Jim Crow and being oppressed themselves. But the time is up to ignore it and just excuse African Americans for supporting policies that hurt other African Americans. That is insanity. I am not a politician, so I can state it as it is. We have to call these people out. We cannot criticize White people who support policies that hurt Black and Brown people without including Black people in the discussion who support these same policies. Don't get me wrong. I believe everybody has the right to support whichever political party they desire. But to me, anybody who supports policies that aim to hinder my ability to vote is not a supporter, whether they are Black or White. I say that for several reasons. Their support of these policies sometimes encourages White people to embrace them also. It makes sense if you are White to believe that if you see African Americans opposing their own rights and the rights of other Black people to vote, then, maybe, you would think that you are not wrong in doing so either. Or if I am White and I see African Americans supporting the elimination of a health care program that will disproportionately affect African American citizens, then maybe I am not wrong, if I also oppose it as a White person. It all makes sense to me. But what doesn't make sense is for both Black and White citizens who know better and who support fundamental common human rights for all to challenge White citizens but not African Americans who support the same wicked policies. We, as a society, need to be more proactive in addressing this.

My career in technology started in the Navy. I pointed out some examples of my experience with Jim Crow while I was in the Navy. I also discussed one specific example that led to a very long fight with the Navy to defend myself against false accusations. But this book involves a journey through Jim Crow and the Information Age. So I talked about the technology with which I worked in the Navy. I tried to bring out the level of excitement derived from working in that technical environment. I hope this will influence those in positions of influence over African American children to encourage them to seek careers in a technical field. Hopefully, some of my offspring will be affected by this and will pursue technical careers. It is critical for more African Americans to be involved in the technology industry. There is too much for me to go into here, but many racial biases are designed into some technologies of today. Without African Americans being involved in the technology industry, it will get worse.

My career in technology continued over thirty years after leaving the Navy. It was a gratifying experience. The Jim Crow influence was still present. But for the most part, I learned to manage it successfully. Like everything else in life, you have to have a plan when you experience it. You cannot wait until you come face to face with it and then respond because your response will be an emotional one more times than not. But if you have a plan, you simply follow it, just like you would any other project.

During my time in the technology industry, I was able to get exposure to everything from designing networks to troubleshooting networks. Additionally, I obtained two master's degrees and two professional certifications. For several years I concurrently taught networking classes as a college professor at two different colleges. Teaching the technology at the college level was almost as enjoyable as working directly with technology. I was doing this work at the peak of the information technology boom. It was a fascinating time that I tried to bring out in the book. I am sharing these comments because this is what I meant partly at the beginning of the book when I said I was born and raised during the Jim Crow era but had been able to overcome its impact. None of the experiences I have cited in this book were without the influence of Jim Crow. That is very important to understand. I was always faced with a choice. Do I give in to it, fight it, face it, or ignore it? I choose to do some of all the above except give in to it.

I shared some of my experiences advocating and volunteering in the community. I believe that all people should find something in the community that they can influence using the skills and talents God has given them. That is the reason He gave us the talents, after all. So why not use the talents He gives us to help others. I have had several discussions with church people whose belief is that the church should only be concerned with other Christians and people who attend church. I hate to disappoint anybody, but they are wrong about that. God expects us to help those who need help, whether they are part of the church or not. And let's keep in mind that most people are not part of the church.

As an African American, I have had to live with Jim Crow attitudes wherever I was. The interesting thing is that I went through phases as to how I would deal with it or what I would allow to influence me. I have learned that African Americans must have the willpower to resist the temptation to resort to hate. We have so many reasons and opportunities to do so. For me, I had to learn and relearn the lesson before I got it. But I do know people who have become victims by giving in to hatred. This is an area where White people can learn a lot from Black people. Due to our experience in America, we have had to learn to deal with racism without resorting to hatred ourselves. That is not an easy thing to do, but to be successful as an African American in the United States, it is a necessary skill we must learn. This is what I mean when I say many African Americans my age have overcome Jim Crow. We have learned to manage it without the hatred that can destroy us if we give in to it. It is a vital survival skill that White people can learn from Black people, and will become more important for White people to master as the demographics in America changes. It could prevent so many White Christians from seeking alternative ways to deal with the changing demographic , and give them confidence to understand that inclusion and respect will result in a better America for everybody. That is probably the most significant point I can make concerning Jim Crow. Its impact on society doesn't just hurt Black people, but White people as well.

I started writing this book around the end of March. We were several weeks into the pandemic. My biological mother, Christine Worsham, was one of the first victims of the coronavirus. She lived in Raleigh, North Carolina in a senior citizen's facility. It was especially stressful because of not even being able to travel to the funeral. Later in May, with the murder of George Floyd and Breonna Taylor, it became difficult to focus on the book. These were two more killings in a long list of Black citizens unjustifiably killed by the police that got national media attention. This book looked at the impact of Jim Crow activity in my life going back to when I was a child. Police were killing and abusing Black people since we were brought to the United States. Like any sane individual, whether Christian or non-Christian, I oppose the innocent killing of Black people. Now, that is not to say that I oppose the police. But I do oppose the police killing of innocent Black people. There have been no real efforts to stop the innocent killings. I can also add Willie Grimes to this long list. Some students at North Carolina A&T said Willie Grimes was shot and killed in 1968 by the Greensboro police. To this day, nobody has been held responsible for his death. For whatever it is worth, the Willie Grimes case should be reopened and resolved.

When does this stop? I believe it stops when we Christians seriously consider and believe what God's Word says about us being in a spiritual war. Wouldn't it be something to see

Christians exhibiting the same level of disgust with social injustice as we saw during the summer when Americans of all races took to the streets to protest injustice? What would happen if we saw Christians place the same level of commitment in following Jesus's command to "love thy neighbor as thyself," as the current commitment to fight any change that causes us to look ourselves in the mirror and admit that we are a significant part of the problem? Imagine if we Christians genuinely believed that God has made us the salt of the earth and start to behave as if we do. I believe that is when it will end. But for now, we are some ways away from that time.

As I wrap this project up, I can hear in the background from the television the sound of news commentators discussing how the 2020 presidential election will end and why. Some comments I agree with, but others I don't. This election is indeed an active demonstration and revelation of America's heart. It is my prayer that after this election, we will have revealed a heart that God approves of.

Just to reemphasize, based upon what I have learned from studying God's Word, He has called each of us to speak out against oppression. For that reason and some others, I am unapologetic for having spoken out all of my life wherever I was against oppressions, hatred, and racism. Lastly, I am unapologetic for being a Christian, and will always seek ways to help bring about positive change wherever I am. And I will continue to do so with God's blessing until I die.

Meanwhile, may God bless those who read this book. And may He bless America with an abundance of leaders with caring hearts.

Lester Patrick
Author

Acknowledgements

I would like to take this opportunity to thank everybody who has played a role in supporting me in my career, community work, encouragement, and spiritual growth. These people have had a major positive impact on my life in at least one of these areas. Some have gone beyond what is normal to offer their support. And I will always be grateful.

Ms. Barbara Shadrick	Mr. Gary Wayman
Dr. Irene Outlaw	Mr. Bob Simons
Dr. Mamie Dalington	Mr. Ben Reddish
Dr. Daryl Camp	Mr. John Vaughn
Dr. Irvin Jefferson	Dr. Odie Douglas
Mr. John Ivy	Mr. Al Brown
Ms. Dorthy Maxson	Mother Bessie Crosby
BSF Group Leaders	Pastor Glenn Shields
Robinson Union teachers	Occeletta & Bill Briggs
Mrs. Jacqueline Cannon	Mr. James Finney
Mr. Randy Malandro	Sister Cynthia Childress
Mr. Leroy Edmonds	Mr. Larson
Mr. Pierre Kirby	Judge Bill Murray
Family Resource and Referral Center	Mr. Percy Barrows

Bibliography

1. Ballotpedia. "Article VI, North Carolina Constitution." Accessed https://ballotpedia.org/Article_VI,_North_Carolina_Constitution.
2. Berry, Mary. "Reckless Eyeballing." The Matt Ingram Case and the Denial of African American Sexual Freedom.
3. Bowers, Wes. "Council hears pitch for north Stockton Library." June 8, 2018, The Stockton Record, http://www.recordnet.com
4. Carolina Times, May 31, 1969. "Browse Issue-The Carolina times. (Durham, N.C.) edition 1," May 31, 1969. http://newspapers.digitalnc.org/lccn/sn83045120/1969-05-31/ed-1/.
5. Christian Today. "Bishop Says Family, Society Under Threat from Government Legislation." February 14, 2007. https://www.christiantoday.com/article/bishop.says.family.society.under.threat.from.government.legislation/9547.htm.
6. City of Stockton. "Strong Communities." Accessed http://www.stocktongov.com/government/departments/manager/pubStrongCom.html.
7. David, E.J.R. "Internalized Oppression The Psychology of Marginalized Groups." 2014.
8. Davis, Ronald. "Racial Etiquette: The Racial Customs and Rules of Racial Behavior in Jim Crow America." Jim Crow History, accessed http://www.jimcrowhistory.org/resources/narratives/Theme-Etiquette.htm
9. Davis, Ronald. "Slavery in America: Historical Overview." April 16, 2008. http://www.slaveryinamerica.org/histor.

10. Family Resource & Referral Center. "About Us." Accessed http://www.frrcsj.org/Common/AboutUs.html.

11. Ferris State University. "What Was Jim Crow." Accessed https://www.ferris.edu/jimcrow/what.htm.

12. Finney, John. "Senate Unit Finds U.S. Has Secret Base In Morocco for Navy Communications." *New York Times*, July 28, 1970. https://www.nytimes.com/1970/07/28/archives/senate-unit-finds-us-has-secret-base-in-morocco-for-navy.html.

13. Gonzalas, Neil." District's diversity debated." The Stockton Record, http://www.recordnet.com

14. Hannah, Dogen. "NAACP hosts meeting. Parents say they face discrimination in area's schools." The Stockton Record, Sept. 17, 1998, http://www.recordnet.com.

15. History.com editors. "Dred Scott v. Sandford." History, November 4, 2019. https://www.history.com/topics/black-history/dred-scott-case.

16. Housing Authority of San Joaquin County. "2019 Annual Report." https://www.hacsj.org/

17. History.com editors. "Plessy vs. Ferguson." History, October 29, 2009. https://www.history.com/topics/black-history/plessy-v-ferguson.

18. King, Colbert, "Trump's rules of etiquette are straight out of the Jim Crow playbook." *Washington Post*, November 10, 2018. https://www.washingtonpost.com/blogs/post-partisan/wp/2018/11/10/trumps-rules-of-etiquette-are-straight-out-of-the-jim-crow-playbook/.

19. Leslie, Laura. "Remnant of Jim Crow era remains in N.C. Constitution." WRAL Capitol Bureau, February 7, 2019.

20. Measure M Bond Oversight Committee. "Annual Report." San Joaquin Delta College, accessed https://deltacollege.edu/sites/default/files/sjdc_004_coc17-18_annualreport_final.pdf.

21. Merlinos-Mata,Toni. "Race relations focus of meeting." The News-Sentinel", http://www.lodi news.com

22. NCpedia. "Black Codes, 1866." Accessed http://www.ncpedia.org/anchor/black-codes-1866.

23. Newkirk II, Vann. "The Battle for North Carolina," *Atlantic Daily*, October 27, 2016. https://www.theatlantic.com/politics/archive/2016/10/the-battle-for-north-carolina/501257/.

24. North Carolina Advisory Committee. "North Carolina State Advisory Committee to the United States Commission on Civil Rights (Report)." U.S. Commission on Civil Rights, 1970. https://www.usccr.gov/pubs/sac.php.

25. North Carolina Agricultural and Technical State University. "Rankings, Recognitions & Prominent Alumni." Accessed https://www.ncat.edu/about/rankings-and-recognition/index.php.

26. Open Computing Facility. "Legality of Slavery in America." Associated Students of the University of California, accessed https://www.ocf.berkeley.edu/~arihuang/academic/abg/slavery/legal.html

27. Oto,Clifford. "Conway unveiling possible glimpse of future." The Stockton Record, Feb. 9, 2016. http://www.rerecordnet.com.

28. Prados, John. "The John Walker Spy Ring and The U.S. Navy's Biggest Betrayal." USNI News, September 2, 2014. https://news.usni.org/2014/09/02/john-walker-spy-ring-u-s-navys-biggest-betrayal.

29. Pilgrim, David. "What Was Jim Crow." Ferris State University, September 2000. https://www.ferris.edu/jimcrow/what.htm.

30. Reid, Keith. "A positive influence." The Stockton Record, October 26, 2008. http://www.recordnet.com.

31. Reid, Keith. "Students get lesson on success" The Stockton Record, May 7, 2010. http://www.reccordnet.com

32. Reid, Keith. "Tech center a group effort." The Stockton Record, June 22, 2007. http://www.recordnet.com.

33. Swaminathan, Aarthi. "Educational Redlining." Student Borrower Protection Center, February 8, 2020. https://protectborrowers.org/wp-content/uploads/2020/02/Education-Redlining-Report.pdf.

34. United States Government Printing Office. "Radioman 3&2." United States Navy, 1972.

35. Walbert, David. "Black Codes 1866." Accessed http://www.davidwalbert.com/pdf/learnnc/black-codes-1866.

36. Wikipedia. "Bob Moses (Activist)." Wikimedia Foundation, last modified September 23, 2020. https://en.wikipedia.org/wiki/Bob_Moses_(activist).

37. Wikipedia. "History of Slavery in North Carolina." Wikimedia Foundation, last modified October 13, 2020. https://en.wikipedia.org/wiki/History_of_slavery_in_North_Carolina.

38. Wikipedia. "Jim Crow Laws." Wikimedia Foundation, last modified October 30, 2020. https://en.wikipedia.org/wiki/Jim_Crow_laws.

39. "Woolworth's Lunch Counter Photo, Feb 1, 1960, Greensboro Uprising Photos." May 1969. Greensboro News and Record / Winston Salem Journal.

40. Yoshimo, Kimi. "Opinions split on progress of race relations." The Stockton Record, http://www.recordnet.com

Appendix

LODI NEWS-SENTINEL

SATURDAY, SEPTEMBER 27, 2003

Chet Diestel
Opinion Page Editor
368-7035 ext 258
E-mail: chetd@lodinews.com

Opinion

E-mail to send letters to the editor: letters@lodinews.com
www.lodinews.com/opinion

LUSD's segregation policy must end

Lester Patrick

On Aug. 13, the Lodi Unified School District Board of Trustees made a decision that casts a very strong and negative message throughout the community — that the district supports segregation so long as the segregation primarily benefits middle and upper middle class Caucasians and their children.

That event will undoubtedly come to be viewed as one of the darkest days in this community's history. It's sad enough that the board would support segregation, but even worse, that when shown how destructive this decision has become, it's too insensitive to the community's needs to correct their mistake.

Acting upon a request from professional middle and upper middle class Caucasian parents, the board — against the recommendation of its own superintendent and staff — approved a plan that keeps in place a school for students identified as gifted that, by design, operates in complete isolation from all other schools in the district.

The board's decision to support the request of the parents of Elkhorn Elementary School will cost a minimum of $1.1 million more than the district's proposal. It's bad enough that the board approved such a request, but even worse, that it raised in favor of these parents given the reasons they used to support their position.

Parents pleading not to have Elkhorn expanded to deal with much-needed population growth proclaimed that their children needed to be isolated from average children because interaction with average children would hinder their academic development. This is the same reason that parents and organized hate groups used in the South in the early days of the Civil Rights Movement to oppose the integration of the public school system. School segregation was wrong then and it's wrong today.

Although Elkhorn parents contend that students need to be separated from a regular school setting and average students in order to maintain the high test scores on the SATs achieved by students at Elkhorn and another all day gifted program operated school, the facts don't support their argument. A comparison of average SAT 9 scores for the reading portion of the tests taken by gifted students attending Thirwood Elementary and Elkhorn shows Thirwood students averaged reading test scores of 83.88 while Elkhorn students averaged 85.0.

The students at Thirwood attend a program for gifted students in a regular school setting and are taught by regular teachers not specifically trained to teach only gifted students. There is only a 1.6 percent difference between the average reading scores of the two schools. This clearly proves that it's not necessary for Elkhorn students to attend a school isolated from a regular school setting and average students.

When the board took a stand to support segregation it sent a signal to parents and teachers that it's OK to support segregation and to discriminate against people of color in this community. This is one reason that parents are rising to the occasion. Since the board's decision parents from Beckman Elementary School are opposing a district decision to have minority and economically disadvantaged students from Heritage Elementary School attend their neighborhood school. Like the Elkhorn parents, they have as an alternative plan for the board or phasing the students elsewhere — anywhere else, that is except with their children.

My hard-earned tax dollars are being spent to support a private school for over-achieving, upper middle class children while under-achieving and average student's needs go unmet.

The demographics of this community have changed. It has the potential of becoming one of the most diverse communities in the country. There is much positive potential that will result from this rich diversity. Thus the board's action was not in the best interest of this community nor its citizens.

As such, LUSD board members must begin to understand that legalized school segregation has been over for 40 years and it's time they abide by the law. They must step up to the plate and take the responsibility of passing school policies that reflect the diverse population the district serves. If they cannot serve all of God's children in this community, then they must resign and allow people who have the interest of all the children serve.

We, the people of this community, must stand up against segregation to ensure that this community remains a pleasant place to live for people of all ethnic backgrounds. I urge you to contact your state representatives, the Department of Education, local officials, school board members, and other LUSD officials to express your disapproval for segregation within the Lodi Unified School District.

Lester Patrick is co-chair of the district's Academic Review Committee, which monitors and seeks to improve the academic standing of under-achieving students and is a member of the Measure K Oversight Committee. His child attends Bear Creek High School.

Lester Patrick

For African-Americans, it's a half-empty cup

The month of February marked the 78th annual celebration of "Black History Month" in the United States. Initially, this celebration began in 1926 and was called "Negro History Week." Whether or "Negro History Week" or "Black History Week", Dr. Carter Woodson, the celebration's founder, made significant improvements to the mostly negative image at the time of African-Americans in the world when he highlighted their worldly contributions to history by initiating "Black History Week."

Since that time we have celebrated contributions of African-Americans dating back to the dawn of civilization up to the present.

Like other African-Americans, I love to celebrate "Black History Month," but every year after the celebration is over I find myself asking the same question: Has this month-long celebration helped to improve the African American situation in this society?

Don't get me wrong; I am not suggesting that we stop celebrating "Black History Month," but I am suggesting that we become more mature in our celebration by focusing more on what we as African Americans need to do more of to help make things better for our African-American brothers and sisters who are not exactly living the American dream.

When some of us look at our situation and the things around us that affect these situations, we see a cup half-full. Others see a cup half-empty. I think it is a good idea to always have a positive outlook on life, but it is never a good idea to ignore problems such as teenage pregnancy; illiteracy; disproportionate incarceration of African-American males; and the list goes on.

As a very concerned African-American male, my view is that our cup is half-empty, and we must do something about it or the half-full cup will eventually erode.

If you were to take a half-full cup of water and sit it aside for a time period, you will find that it will start to evaporate. If you leave it alone long enough the half-full cup of water will eventually become empty. So it is with the African-American population.

Over the years we have made lots of progress, but in recent years much of that progress as a group of people has started to erode or has increased only minimally when compared to others.

For example, according to statistics from the U.S. Census Bureau the percent of increase of households with a median income over $100,000 increased by 10.2 percent for whites between 1972 and 2001, but for the same time period that increase for African-American households was only 5 percent.

Census Bureau statistics also show that African Americans made up 31 percent of all people living below the poverty line in 1975 compared to 9.7 percent of whites, and in 2001 African Americans living below the poverty line was about 25 percent while only 9.9 percent for whites and 10 percent for Hispanics. This is an improvement going from 31 percent to 25 percent, but that is still almost 1 of every 4 African Americans living in poverty. That is still bad.

I could go on all day with the statistics but I think you get the point. As African-Americans we must start to focus more attention on that part of the cup that is half-empty.

I challenge all middle-class (and wealthy), professional and blue-collar African-Americans in this community to identify one problem affecting African-Americans living in poverty, adopt that problem, and make a commitment to work towards changing it within 10 years.

Lets make an assessment in 5 years to see how much that half-empty cup has increased.

Lester Patrick of Stockton is co-chair of the Lodi Unified School District's Academic Review Committee, which monitors and seeks to improve academic standing of underachieving students, and is a member of the Measure K Oversight Committee.

District's diversity debated

By Neil Gonzales
Record Staff Writer

A decision involving a program for gifted and talented students. Proposed changes to campus attendance boundaries. A discrimination lawsuit filed by Latino parents.

Such recent events have sparked an emotional debate over diversity, educational access and fair treatment of minority students in the Lodi Unified School District.

The debate comes as Lodi Unified continues to grow ethnically and in overall student population. It also comes as the 28,400-student district is pushing forward into a new era of school construction, funded by the $199.4 million bond measure approved last year by voters.

Some parents feel that the district needs to do a better job of accommodating all children in the educational system and are wary of what they perceive as resistance at certain schools to include particular groups of students.

"The demographics of this community have changed," district parent Lester Patrick said. "There is much positive potential that will result from this rich diversity."

Lodi Unified Superintendent Bill Huyett said he believes that issues of multiculturalism lately have reached the forefront of people's discussions partly because the district is undergoing plenty of changes with new schools opening up and the need to rearrange attendance boundaries.

"We have growth issues," Huyett said, "and that's part of the equation."

But the district has long made efforts to encourage diversity, such as finding ways to include more minorities in the Gifted and Talented Education program and hiring more people of color as teachers, he said.

"I don't think [the latest set of concerns over diversity] is that unusual, to be honest with you," Huyett said. "That's part of our agenda all the time. It's really important ... to talk about diversity and have it a part of what we live and learn in schools."

> "People try to make it a race issue because it's sexy. I don't think Elkhorn had anything to do with ethnicity."
> — **Linda Lofthus,** parent

Signs of segregation?

Still, Patrick — who is black — sees he sees forms of segregation taking root in Lodi Unified.

FORUM
Continued from B1

The forum began with presentations and ended after participants gathered in small groups to share and brainstorm on transportation, environmental and housing issues.

Roundup: Baccam, who works at Head Start, said one of the biggest problems of the county faces is the lack of affordable housing for low-, moderate- and medium-income people.

"There aren't enough vouchers, it's still not affordable," she said. "And even with vouchers, many people are poorly educated about credit, how to buy a house and how to save for a down payment.

"If you've never had a family member purchase a home, where do you start?" she asked. "Who is your role model?"

Mary McDonough of the Federal Highway Administration Research Center in Chicago spoke about the ways government agencies can better solicit input from communities to reach better solutions on how to spend tax dollars.

"It's about being fair to people," she said. "Fairness is where prospects go, who gets the money and who gets the priority."

And she said she thinks such events as Saturday's forum are excellent ways for bureaucrats to reconnect with the people for whom they are working.

"It helps when the agencies take the citizens' concerns seriously," she said. "The citizens also have to take responsibility for holding the agency accountable for its decisions."

■ To reach reporter Linus Hughes-Kuchnuki, phone (209) 546-8297 or e-mail lkirch@recordnet.com

DIVERSITY
Continued from B1

One such case, he argues, involves a narrow approval in August by the district board to spend $23.5 million more to build a new campus in north Stockton instead of expanding nearby Elkhorn Elementary, which houses GATE.

The fiscal consequence alone bothers Patrick, who is also a member of a citizens committee monitoring district spending on bond-funded projects.

But he viewed the board's action as catering to a group of Elkhorn parents, who expressed concerns about a plan to bring in hundreds of general-education students to the campus of about 250 gifted and talented youngsters.

"The (Elkhorn) parents don't want average kids with their (GATE) kids," Patrick charged. "That is absolute segregation."

He also pointed out that black and other minority students are underrepresented in GATE.

Administrators are well-aware of that underrepresentation, said John Coakley, the district's GATE coordinator.

Districtwide, GATE serves about 1,400 third- to 12th-graders.

About 3 percent of GATE students are black and 10 percent are Latino, according to Coakley.

Those percentages don't match up to districtwide figures. Blacks make up about 7 percent of Lodi Unified's student population, and Latinos represent about 36 percent.

In contrast, whites account for more than 60 percent of GATE children while comprising about 49 percent of the total student body, Coakley said.

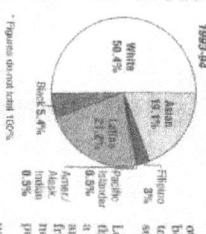

Lodi Unified racial percentages

2002-03: White 38.9%, Asian 15%, Filipino 4%, Pacific Islander 0.5%, Amer/Alask Indian 0.7%, Multi unknown 6.1%, Black 5.4%, Latino 30.4%

1993-94: White 56.4%, Asian 10.1%, Filipino 3%, Pacific Islander 0.5%, Amer/Alask Indian 0.5%, Black 5.6%, Latino 21.7%

Source: California Dept. of Education
Figures do not total 100%

"People try to make it a race issue because it's sexy," Loftus said. "I don't think Elkhorn had anything to do with ethnicity."

Rather, Loftus saw the board's choice of having another school site instead of adding on to Elkhorn as a way to address the surging residential development in north Stockton, she said.

Other parents maintain that GATE children need to be challenged in an accelerated learning environment so they don't lose interest in school and can continue to progress.

Attendance boundaries

For Patrick, the controversy over revising attendance areas because of new schools also touches on issues of race and socioeconomics.

He criticized parents from Lodi Borchardt Elementary for their public reluctance to accept a district plan to redraw boundaries and transfer some students from low-income, minority neighborhoods to the new campus in Lodi.

"Basically, the parents are using all kinds of reasons to not have (the other) kids in that school," Patrick said.

But Borchardt parents say their concerns are legitimate and have no connection to a student's ethnicity or economic background.

"We are concerned about overcrowding," Borchardt parent Bill Crabtree said. "Parents are also concerned about having everyone's needs met."

Crabtree noted that students from other schools with federal Title I services — which target underprivileged children — would not have those same programs at Borchardt.

Title I schools have a high percentage of students receiving free or discounted lunches.

Equal treatment

Elsewhere in Lodi Unified, other minority parents are calling for the district to be more equitable.

Earlier in the month, Latino parents from Lawrence Elementary filed a discrimination lawsuit against the district. Filed in federal court, the suit alleges that the district unfairly punishes Spanish-speaking students and discourages bilingual education.

About the same time, parents from Bear Creek High School complained of a cultural bias against blacks in the aftermath of a large fight on campus.

Bear Creek High parent Diana Murry has expressed concern about how the district metes out student punishment, saying a disproportionately large percent of minority students seem to be disciplined.

District data appear to bear that out. Although black students account for about 7 percent of the district's enrollment, they represented 20 percent of suspensions and 20 percent of expulsions for the past school year.

Ongoing efforts

Administrators are mindful of those statistics and strive to close the gaps, Huyett said. "We are constantly vigilant about that."

With all students, he said, administrators make sure expectations about behavior are clear. The district also intervenes early on with children who may be at risk for trouble, he said.

Teachers receive training on working with different cultures, he said. "We're training teachers how to motivate students and treat them with equal attention."

The district also is continuing to recruit minorities for teaching and administrative positions, Huyett said, although he acknowledged that the staffing still doesn't reflect the student body.

"We're still making progress," he said.

About 16 percent of district teachers and administrators are minorities, according to state Department of Education figures.

But the district does have about 1,100 teachers qualified to work with English learners — 70 of those instructors speak Spanish, officials said. The district employs about 1,500 teachers in all.

The district also is working with minority parent groups such as the Academic Review Committee, co-chaired by Patrick.

The committee was formed several years ago to explore strategies to improve achievement among black, Latino and other minority students, Patrick said. The group also tackles issues of teacher recruitment and discipline as they relate to minorities.

Such efforts are as needed now as in the past, Patrick said. "It's a continuing thing."

■ To reach reporter Neil Gonzales, phone (209) 367-7428 or e-mail ngonzales@recordnet.com

ANOTHER VIEW

Food insecurity causes unhappy holiday

By Lester Patrick
Special to The Record

One of the most memorable activities for many people during the holiday season is sitting down for a meal with family and friends at Thanksgiving, Christmas and New Year's. We look forward to very hearty and satisfying meals consisting of our favorite dishes. This is the season we have all agreed it is OK to overeat, overindulge.

Unfortunately, too many people across Stockton, San Joaquin County, the state and the nation will not share in that experience in the same way. The reason some will not is due to "food insecurity." The United States Department of Agriculture defines a "food secure" household as being one in which there is access by all people at all times to enough food for an active healthy life.

A "food insecure" household is characterized by the existence of household-level economics and social conditions resulting in limited or uncertain access to adequate food. Simply put, there is not enough money in these households to purchase enough food for all members of the family to eat at all times.

About 11 percent of all Americans live in "food insecure" households. This equates to a little over 14 million households and affects more than 37 million people nationwide. Here in San Joaquin County 13 percent of the population, or 95,260 people, suffer from "food-insecurity." Across the state "food insecurity" affects about 12 percent of the population.

The United States Department of Agriculture has identified a list of characteristics that are true of the national food insecure population. One characteristic involves annual household income. If a household has an annual income less than 185 percent of the federal poverty line, that household is more than likely to be "food insecure." The national federal poverty line for 2018 was $25,465, so 185 percent of the federal poverty line for 2018 was $47,110.00. Senior citizens and children are disproportionately represented in this income range.

A 2017 study conducted by a nonpartisan network of pediatricians and researchers to identify the cost of "food insecurity" in the state of Massachusetts showed a direct link between cost, long-term "food insecurity" and seven chronic diseases. The list included Type 2 diabetes, obesity, chronic pulmonary disease, rheumatology diseases and several other medical conditions.

This study suggests that if we reduce "food insecurity" we will realize a corresponding reduction in medical costs.

For several years, the most successful effort in the fight against "food insecurity" has been through a federal program called the Supplemental Nutrition Assistance Program, or SNAP. Today, about 43 million people receive SNAP benefits. In recent months, the USDA has proposed a new rule that would cut more than 1.7 million households from receiving SNAP benefits with more than 600,000 of those being senior households over 60. If the new rule goes into effect, it will impact more than 230,000 low income households in California. Other rules that would cut SNAP also have been proposed. In all cases, children and seniors are most affected.

I urge all residents of San Joaquin County to take a stand against "food insecurity" by contacting your representatives in Congress during this holiday season to request that they oppose any rule by the USDA to cut SNAP benefits.

Lester Patrick is a legislative advocate with the Hunger Task Force for San Joaquin County.

Lester Patrick

LODI UNIFIED
Opinions split on progress of race relations

By Kimi Yoshino
Record Staff Writer

LODI — A community task force working to improve race relations in Lodi Unified School District told trustees Tuesday that the district is making progress, but one parent on the task force blasted the board for insensitivity and its lack of a district hate-crime policy.

Lester Patrick, a representative of Parents and Citizens for Quality Education, praised the district for an anti-prejudice program it is using but took issue with the lack of a hate-crime policy six months after "KKK" was written on a student's locker at Henderson School.

"Here we are sitting here, six months later, and we still have not done anything about it," Patrick said.

"I don't think that there's any excuse that it would not be written," he said. "No disrespect to the board, but it's been six months. Some things take time. This is not one of them."

Superintendent Del Alberti said administrators are reviewing policies in other districts. He also said the board has adopted a policy on racial climate that will lay the groundwork for a hate-crimes policy.

"Progress has been made, and we will work to find common ground on the issues still remaining," Alberti said.

Patrick said he hopes the work continues.

"I think we have the framework in place that can impact the community positively, ... but it's going to take a lot of work," Patrick said. "I do believe that if we continue and keep the commitment, I don't see why we can't see positive results."

In January, a 13-year-old African-

> "No disrespect to the board, but it's been six months. Some things take time. This is not one of them."
> — Lester Patrick,
> representative,
> Parents and Citizens
> for Quality Education

American student's locker was defaced with the letters "KKK" and a swastika, but it took the district three days to completely remove the graffiti.

The district was criticized for its insensitivity and since then has been meeting with a community task force to improve race relations.

Among other changes, the district created an advisory Academic Review Board to continue making recommendations and will also hire a half-time community-relations coordinator who will work directly with students at risk of failing academically.

Several teachers have gone through a diversity-training program called "Unlearning Prejudice." The district has scheduled two additional sessions because of teacher demand.

Bear Creek High School Spanish teacher Linda Weiss-Fraracci said she spoke on behalf of the teachers when she described her five-day experience with the training as thoughtful, thought-provoking and life changing.

"Please don't make this a one-shot deal — not a drop in the bucket, but more like the floodgates at the Folsom Dam," she said.

A positive influence

Bear Creek's Tyson Walton, left, and Dwayne Lee, both 13, listen to Lester Patrick, director of a peer mentoring program conducted by Alpha Phi Alpha's Nu Beta Lambda Chapter in Stockton. This was an orientation meeting between mentors and students from Bear Creek High and Delta Sierra Middle School, where the meeting was held.

Students join mentoring program to help younger peers

By Keith Reid
Record Staff Writer

STOCKTON — Bear Creek High senior Siaosi Haleufia wants to be a positive influence on his younger classmates, especially those who may struggle with some of the same social etiquette nuances that he once did.

Things like public speaking, dealing with difficult people, how to treat girls and coping with stress are some examples, he said.

For these reasons, Haleufia, 17, has joined the Alpha Phi Alpha, Nu Beta Lambda Stockton chapter's peer mentoring program. Haleufia and other Bear Creek boys receive mentoring from fraternity members on how to be successful in life, and in turn, the high schoolers deliver the same messages to Delta Sierra Middle School students.

Lodi Unified community relations director Irvin Jefferson said the program, now in its second year, is one that reaches out to boys in all walks of life. Some come from families without a father in the home and are in need of a man's guidance. Some are students who have been in trouble at school. Others still are students who have simply chosen to be involved.

In all, more than 100 Bear Creek and Delta Sierra students have joined the program.

"It's going to help us in college and in our careers," Haleufia said.

The peer mentoring program is led by Lester Patrick, a Stockton resident who is also president of the Lodi Unified academic review committee. Patrick said the program's goal is to "develop discipline and inspire commitment" for students who could be potentially persuaded by less positive influences.

"The fraternity is worldwide, and we just want to broaden these young men's potential in a variety of topics," Patrick said, noting that Martin Luther King Jr., former U.S. Supreme Court Justice Thurgood Marshall, former San Francisco Mayor Willie Brown and six active members of Congress are among the most famous members of the traditionally black fraternity.

"It's no longer exclusive. Other ethnic groups are allowed in the fraternity, too," Patrick added.

At an orientation for Delta Sierra students on Thursday, Patrick broke the students into small groups, each with a mentor. A "get to know you conversation" was an icebreaker.

In the coming weeks, the process begins. Fraternity mentors will meet with Bear Creek students weekly, and the following day, the high schoolers will meet with the middle schoolers to mentor them.

"A lot in life is making good first impressions," said Bear Creek freshman Artell Merritt, 14. "That's why I'm here. I want to be seen in the right way."

Contact reporter Keith Reid at (209) 367-7428 or kreid@recordnet.com. Visit his blog at recordnet.com/blogs.

Race relations focus of meeting

LUSD parents propose solutions

By Toni Meriños-Mata
News-Sentinel staff writer

STOCKTON — Academic review boards, quarterly critiques of exmembers, parent critiques of school boards and more minority hiring are among the solutions proposed by African American parents and community members to improve race relations and student achievement at Lodi Unified campuses.

At a special community meeting held Wednesday at Plaza Robles High School, about 40 African American parents and community members gathered to discuss the issues they say are preventing their students from being successful in school.

They described incidents where African American pupils were graded differently, had high failure rates, were automatically considered gang members if involved in a fight and more likely than white children to be expelled from school.

Parents also said they had been intimidated by school officials even to run off campuses, when they tried to get involved.

Teachers also earned a failing grade from some of the parents at the meeting who said the structure lacked the sensitivity and cultural training to teach African American students and failed to communicate with parents when there were academic problems.

"We need to leave here tonight with some commitments," said Lester Patrick, an LUSD parent and member of Parents and Citizens for Quality Education. "We are ready to move forward. Let's look at solutions."

Among the policy changes promoted by the people who attended Wednesday's meeting were:

■ Creation of academic progress

Turn to RACE, Page 10

Race

Continued from Page 1

review boards at all campuses.

■ Mandatory bi-weekly status reports for students who are failing.

■ Incentive programs for teachers who reduce their student failure rates.

■ Hiring of ethnically diverse, bearing officers to reside over expulsion cases.

■ Quarterly review of expulsions and suspensions of African American students.

■ Cultural sensitivity and conflict resolution training for staff.

■ Formal reprimands for employees who willingly ignore a hate crime.

■ Training for staff on gang clothing, symbols and activity.

■ More aggressive recruitment of African Americans for teaching

liaison concept.

■ Expansion of the community

"Somewhere along the line the district did not learn how to deal with ethnically diverse students," said Bobby Bivens, president of the local chapter of the National Association for the Advancement of Colored People. "The school district has been remiss in protecting the civil rights of African American students. I hope this (meeting) is not a facade."

The meeting was arranged by the school district after a flurry of criticism by the African American community, starting Jan. 2 with a dismal report on the number of African American employees to an incident a few days later in which racist graffiti was allowed to remain for three days on a 13-year-

old African American boy's locker at Henderson Elementary School.

Several representatives from the Stockton Unified School District Black Employees Union attended, who urged Lodi officials to draw from its experience on these issues.

After 2½ hours of discussion, the meeting ended with a promise for a smaller committee to work out details to the proposed solutions. Serving on the committee will be parents and community members Alex Godoy, Katie Peters, Lester Patrick, Dorothy Nixxon and Mattie Darlington, and LUSD officials Rich Ferrua, Claudette Berry, Bol Vlech, Lisa Boje, Sherry Leonard, Kelly Price and Pat Hill.

Another community meeting to look at the action plan's details is set for Feb. 21

www.ingramcontent.com/pod-product-compliance
Lightning Source LLC
Chambersburg PA
CBHW071233160426
43196CB00009B/1044